Looking Back in Wonder:
Diary of a Dance Critic

OTHER BOOKS BY WALTER SORELL

The Dance Has Many Faces
The Story of the Human Hand
The Dance Through the Ages
Hanya Holm: The Biography of an Artist
The Duality of Vision
The Dancer's Image: Points and Counterpoints
Facets of Comedy
The Swiss
The Other Face: The Mask in the Arts
The Mary Wigman Book
Three Women
Dance in Its Time: The Emergence of an Art

GERMAN PUBLICATIONS

Knaurs Buch vom Tanz
Europas kleiner Riese
Am Rande der Zeit. Aufzeichnungen 1972–1982
Aspekte des Tanzes
Der Tanz als Spiegel der Zeit
Mary Wigman—ein Testament

TRANSLATIONS

Erich Maria Remarque: Arch of Triumph
Wilhelm Herzog: From Dreyfus to Petain
Goethe's World, an Anthology
Hermann Hesse: The Steppenwolf
Mary Wigman: The Language of Dance
Johannes Urzidil: Prague
Georg Büchner: Woyzeck

PLAYS

Isadora Duncan: And Every Spirit a Bird
Everyman Today
Resurrection After Cocktail Time
The Flowering of the Barren Fig Tree

Looking Back in Wonder

Diary of a Dance Critic

WALTER SORELL

COLUMBIA UNIVERSITY PRESS
NEW YORK   1986

2 19882

Library of Congress Cataloging-in-Publication Data

Sorell, Walter, 1905-
Looking back in wonder.

Includes index.
1. Sorell, Walter, 1905-   2. Dance critics—
United States—Biography. I. Title.
GV1785.S64A35 1986   793.3'2'0924 [B]   85-31380
ISBN 0-231-06278-8

Columbia University Press
New York   Guildford, Surrey
Copyright ©1986 Columbia University Press
All rights reserved

Printed in the United States of America

This book is Smyth-sewn.

Book design by Ken Venezio

To Genevieve Oswald
and all those dancers and choreographers
who have made my life more meaningful

Contents

Preface

"It is a strange thing that in sea voyages where there is nothing to be seen but sky and sea," Francis Bacon wrote, "men should make diaries; but in land travel, wherein so much is to be observed, for the most part they omit it."

In my journeys through the world of dance I have recorded some of my thoughts on this art form for more than three decades, have put on paper my reactions to certain dance events or personalities, yes, have even committed myself to printing some of it in a very similar way or different fashion. I found the world of dance full of long stretches of land—to stay with Francis Bacon—in which much more happened than could be observed by two eyes which like to watch movement in general and dance in particular. In the flow of things there were barren patches and lovely landscapes and often, in the midst of sameness, an image of stupendous beauty. However, it was in the moments at sea with nothing but the sky above and the water around me that I could envision a sky full of cloud formations and a sea-like abundance of shapes in their indefinite surge and search for their own meaning. This was the time of selective seeing and of storing images in my memory.

Looking back over three decades the events seem to be endless. Of necessity, so much had been written, some under the pressure of time, some in leisurely hours helping to savor one's memory. In retrospect, some of the events appeared cruelly trivial to me. Quickly I had to turn leaves. Some stood out in my capricious eyes as having been worth my while. Some still bore the sensation of artistic adventures. Other entries simply seemed important to me, even though they were obviously written on the margin of a quickly passing time. I may be guilty of having seen certain incidents with myopic eyes or of not having been present at the flowering of certain phenomena.

The selecting and editing had to be done with the same arbitrariness with which the recording was set down. The journal of a voyage is a most personal account of what one sees, of what one wishes to see, and the way one cannot help seeing. What such a diary can do is to draw an historic picture of remembered moments and of a lifetime of accumulated thoughts and feelings. Sensations in the past had to be telescoped. Luther's legendary saying, "Here I stand. I can do no other" must be paraphrased in this context: There I stood, and even today I cannot help it.

Acknowledgments

As indicated within the text, some of the material published in this book appeared over the decades in the following magazines: *Dance Magazine, Impulse, Dance News, Dance Observer,* and *Dance Scope.* Wherever used for *Looking Back in Wonder* it was edited and partly rewritten. I wish to express my gratitude to the editors of these magazines for having invited me to write for them. Especially, my thanks go to the editors of *Dance Magazine*—the only still extant periodical of those abovementioned—for their kind cooperation.

Diary Notes:
1949–1960

1949

"Movement is the cause of all life," Leonardo da Vinci wrote in his *Notebooks*, and movement per se has always fascinated me. How people gestured, how they smiled and walked, how they stood still—it all meant to me a way of coming closer to them, of understanding what made them tick. Already in my adolescent years I could watch and absorb the expressive attitudes of people with astonishment and pleasure. Somewhat later, my interest turned to movement as an aesthetic experience. When I read from Martha Graham's lips that "movement never lies," it did not come as a revelation.

Since I have never been a dancer or a choreographer myself I have often been asked to explain what made the dance as an art form so attractive to me. The nicest thing about our life's experiences is the ambiguity of their whereabouts, the mystery of their raison d'être. It is like one's inspiration, which one should accept without questioning too much its origin or source. So much, perhaps all, in life is chance, but what we do with it becomes our destiny. There were many chances to nurture my interest in the dance, and I seemed to have said to all of them with a most audible voice: "Yes! Yes! Yes!" But no doubt there also must have been inaudible voices in me that tricked me (in the double sense of the word) to see in dancing the approximation of spiritual fulfillment, of a poetic vision or the closest realization of illusion. It was probably all this and something as simple as a passing love for a dancer.

All kinds of theatrical marvels fascinated me: marionettes, clowns and mimes; the meaningfulness of the word on stage and the dramatized dream of movement. In mentioning Théophile Gautier at this point, not the slightest suspicion should be aroused that I would dare measure myself against him as a critic. His image is evoked as a simile only. Mainly, he was supposed to review the plays of his time. It was, however, the era of the well-made play which he found papery in spirit, pedestrian in pace, and predictable with the unavoidable letter in the third or fourth act

Movement is the source and essence of life. Drawing by the author.

clearing up the lifeless concoctions of the previous acts. What a disappointing dénouement! So whenever he could he sneaked out of the plays and found in the ballet poetic excitement, a beautifully painted world of dreams.

In a way—a metaphorical way—my experience was similar. Already at the age of ten, when World War I was in its second year, I found the world a stage on which the directors from both sides fouled up the play, where the principal actors were miserable hams, moral pigs, spiritual pimps. I could not help escaping this theater of frightening reality, and from my tenth year on I sneaked out of this bloody well-made play and found myself at least twice a week in the world of make-believe. Theater is theater is theater and whatever it may have been, the enacted life of illusion became and remained a world of reality for me. How I could relive the tragedies and comedies on the stage of my world! The word (written or spoken) always seemed to have been the key with which to unravel the mysteries of life. Gradually, dance also became a central experience to me, as if the word would fail and betray me at moments of crucial desire to reach out to be the inexpressible.

With much too much reality having constantly caught up with me and fortunately also passed me by, with the tragedies of the world having surpassed all Shakespearean horror scenes, another and even more horrifying war, holocaust and exile, I found even greater solace in the silence of movement, as if only gradually the word could be restored again to its lost dignity and, with a borrowed tongue, I would be able to say again what is so inexplicable and wondrous about life. But when all is said, no expression can be louder and more articulate than silence. And in the silent language of the dance my eyes could rest, my mind could become inflamed, my entire being enraged or enthralled. It was and is like a next-of-(s)kin experience which never failed or left me.

Sometimes the past can be very much alive and close, sometimes silhouette-like remote. Yes, I saw Mary Wigman onstage, brushed the wings of Laban in Vienna; I saw Isadora Duncan in her very last days; and then in a Parisian restaurant someone pointed out to me that Isadora Duncan was passing by: to see her in reality's close-up only fortified my vague notion of her greatness that I have taken with me from that almost unreal moment. I recall having seen the sisters Wiesenthal and Rosalie Chladek in Vienna. A poet friend (whose name history defied to keep in mind) once sent me with a message to the dancer Gertrude Kraus (who later became a leading personality in Israel). This incident drew me closer to her magnetic, even though strange appearance. In her group I also met the gentle and lovable soul of

Fred Berk. While many months spent close to Gertude Kraus and her group, one of its dancers held me captive. I don't think she had, at that time of my life, to convince me the hard way of how beautiful dancing can be, particularly when one is in love. This reminds me of Matisse saying that love is the creator of all things.

I recently ran into Erwin Piscator, the great innovator of the stage in Berlin in the twenties. He was the creator of what was known as the political theater. He invited me to help his wife, the former dancer Maria Ley, to build up the dance department of his well-known theater workshop in Manhattan. It seemed to be an agreeable challenge, and I must have done right by him, by the actors, and by the dance world in New York, because the editor of *Dance Magazine* invited me to write for her publication. It so happened that Gertrude Kraus had come to visit the States, not to dance, but to see America dancing. The first feature I wrote for this magazine was on her.

Was it mere coincidence that I should begin, where I had left off in the thirties in what was a New World for me? Was John Milton right when he said: "Next Him high arbiter Chance governs all," or rather Voltaire who thought that "Chance is a word void of sense; nothing can exist without a cause." Naturally, both were right in my book. I have always believed and stated time and again that chance is everywhere in life and that we are the arbiter about what to do with our chances. Was not Voltaire right, since the cause for my getting more deeply involved with dance in my new environment went back to my love for Elfie (I could not think of a nicer cause, as there is no greater human experience than love) and, ultimately, to my love for movement per se.

For the last ten years now—I saw the Statue of Liberty for the first time in 1939—I have tried to catch each dance event as much as my meagre means permitted: the works of Doris Humphrey, Hanya Holm, Helen Tamiris and Martha Graham. The opening night of *Appalachian Spring* was a memorable event for me and so was another Graham performance during which the conductor, Louis Horst, took off his coat—the heat in that small theater on

41st Street was hardly bearable—and conducted in shirt sleeves. I still recall the strong impression *Oklahoma!* made on me, I think of *Frankie and Johnny* and of Ruth Page's overpatriotic speech at a gathering of American choreographers at the Museum of Modern Art, a speech to which George Balanchine could not help retorting with his heavy Russian accent: "I'm a Yankee, too!", thus delightfully making light of all ugly chauvinism.

As insignificant as this incident was, it tore up not-yet-healed wounds of persecution and of an adventurous flight from fear in which it took me more than a year to reach this land of refuge. Was it the land of the free? It certainly was, measured by European experiences. But I soon learned that certain hotels were "restricted" (that means not to be frequented by Jews) and I could not sit down at Schrafft's with a friend whose skin was black. I was surprised to find heated prejudices and xenophobia in a land of immigrants, and very soon it dawned upon me that I will feel apologetic for not having come to America on the Mayflower. (Am I not allowed to consider myself a human being without having been present at Cain's or Abel's Bar Mitzvah?) I realized at this early stage that my process of Americanization would of necessity be a slow and only gradual one, particularly considering the relatively small scope of the dance world and its cliquishness, which is dictated by one's common heritage, work and goals. I read John Martin's chauvinistic attacks on Balanchine in the late thirties. I thought that I would have to prove my merits to be not only tolerated, but also accepted.

These realizations did not keep me from marvelling about the burgeoning life of the dance all through the forties. My interests were somewhat tilted towards the modern dance which, as it seems to me at that point, was finding its own greatness. This caused me to be a frequent guest at the Lexington "Y." My fascination with the dance grew, and I began to meet some of the dancers personally, something one can hardly circumvent. One of the first was Pearl Lang, whom I had met in the Adirondacks early in the forties. And then in the course of the decade I became friendly with quite a few whose lives, works, and integrity I came to respect. I learned to know some of the dancers well and to live with others at a nodding distance. I learned to love most of them in spite or because of all their idiosyncrasies, the "lone wolves" as well as those "cocoon-enveloped" and "I-am-different-from-you" personalities. I thought they were the bearers of that rare joy of living that is caused and directed by movement.

1950

If I say that of all Ashton ballets *Illuminations* is closest to my heart, I do not wish to intimate that I am not appreciative of his other work; and I certainly do not feel so because it seems to be the most un-Ashton-like ballet. In *Notes on Choreography* which he wrote for my *The Dance Has Many Faces*, he said:

And consciously all through my career I have been working to make the ballet independent of literary and pictorial motives, and to make it draw from the rich fount of classical ballet; for, to my way of thinking, all ballets that are not based on the classical ballet and do not create new dancing patterns and steps within its idiom, are, as it were, only tributaries of the main stream . . . If the ballet is to survive, it must survive through its dancing qualities, just as drama must survive through the richness of the spoken word. In a Shakespearean play it is the richness of the language and the poetry that are paramount; the story is unimportant. And it is the same with all the greatest music, and dancing and ballets. In a ballet it is the dance that *must* be paramount.

Sir Frederick Ashton wrote the above about the time when he created *Illuminations*. Although the dancing in this ballet was enthralling in spots and always engaged my senses, I doubt that the dance was the paramount aspect that made a beautiful ballet convincing and, at least for me, unforgettable. What struck me as being so intrinsically great about it was its accomplishment of transfiguring the poetic symbolism of Rimbaud's lived poetry into movement. The vignettes, or tableaux dansants, became phantas-

Frederick Ashton's Illuminations *at* The New York City Ballet, *1950. Courtesy New York, Public Library Dance Collection.*

magoric experiences around a poet who was removed into a fairytale setting of lyric reality.

As Ashton remembered, he had wanted to choreograph something about Rimbaud for a long time, but never got around to doing it until Lincoln Kirstein served as inspiration, prompter, and catalyst. Perhaps it needed a poetic nature like Kirstein's to make it click. It needed an adventurous spirit to create something that is so wonderful in its within-ness and so turbulent and violent on all edges of existence. How both were to fuse under a lovely exterior full of romantic and bewitching visual surprises and to rise to a spiritual loftiness exceptional on any stage! The symbolic accents are set masterfully by a knowledgeable theaterman, so masterfully that they seem to fall with random gestures between a vulgar sideshow peopled by eccentric shapes thrown into grim happenings and passionate glimpses of a strange poet's struggle with life, glimpses of a homosexual poet whose glowing vowels were pitted against the ordinariness of life. His virulent relationship with Paul Verlaine is touched upon by innuendo only, as Rimbaud's love for the dark, mysterious Africa is shown by the appearance of a black man. First, mesmerized by a figure that Ashton calls Profane Love, apparently the devouring, destructive lust which he ultimately denies, the poet evokes the vision of Sacred Love in the spirit of a dream; she is queen in his eyes. He weds her by tearing the crown from her king's head. Crowning himself king he desires to create a new harmony among men. He still sees the wisdom of beauty born, before Profane Love, taking her revenge, has him murdered. But the ultimate dream of the poet's immortality is, at the end, fully realized.

I have wondered how I could accept the many bits of theatrical crudities couched in the mood of imaginative notions, or how I could reconcile the Grand Guignol style of shots as well as fake blood with some of the most esoteric images of danced beauty. I have no answer for it except that these two extremes seem to embrace one another onstage like Rimbaud's life experiences do with his inmost visions. Perhaps I saw Ashton stage the momentary invention of a poetic language accessible to all the senses. Rimbaud invented the colors of the vowels ("A black, E white, I red, O blue, U green"), and probably all my senses became absorbed and saw what they heard and heard the seeing lifted onto an undefinable level of hallucinatory power where the visualization of an image became the optical form of thought.

What I could experience came close to what Rimbaud expressed in his *Illuminations* when he said: "J'ai tendu des cordes de clocher à clocher; des guirlandes de fenêtre à fenêtre; des chaines d'or d'étoile à étoile, et je danse." (I have hung chords from tower to tower; garlands from window to window, golden chains from star to star, and I dance.) For Rimbaud, sounds belong to the intuition of happiness like movement and dance, like the melting of each detail into a whole. The words were sung to

Cecil Beaton's décors for Frederick Ashton's Illuminations.
Courtesy New York Public Library Dance Collection.

Benjamin Britten's haunting score in the third section of the ballet. What Rimbaud seemed to have envisioned was a superhuman dancer connecting the far with the near, the little with the great, the lost with the found, creating a coherence which ultimately was an all-embracing harmony of discords. Garlands and golden chains turn heaven and earth into a single dance floor, and the chords make us hear sounds from distance to distance. The dimensions of our illusions are as huge as the danced images insinuate. The lines of the poem live on the tension between the simple and the inexplicable. In no other *Illumination* did Rimbaud evoke this all-embracing harmony with such a paucity of means in such a perfect manner. And in no other *Illumination* did the poet envision himself as mythical dancer who in a star-born hour added the One to the All.

Perhaps it is much simpler than it seems to be: Ashton, with the help of Rimbaud, aided me in the duration of a one-act ballet to illuminate my private illusions. But this is what good ballet or any theater is here for.

1951

Anthologia meant a collection of epigrams in New Latin. The ancient Greeks took this word for the description of flower gathering. It is probably one of the nicer feelings to gather flowers for a bouquet in which each flower has its own fragrance, form and color, not only fits to all the other flowers, but also enhances the total impression through its own unique being.

I wanted to collect more than epigrams. It ought to have been a nice bouquet of essays on the dance. I had a very distinct vision of what they should look like, of how to mix their perfume. There was a structure in my mind, an edifice which the significance of each essay should have held together.

I soon found out that collecting essays for an anthology is not at all like putting a bouquet of flowers together. It is rather like staging a play. And like any producer or stage director, I had to deal with human beings and the fragrance of their idiosyncrasies, with dancers and their colorful ambitions, with living masks and playacting gestes and dire needs. I wanted everyone to be himself and to shed the strongest light on his chosen subject, the one with which he is most familiar.

Dancers, mainly modern dancers, are particularly articulate. But some, as I found out, are not articulate with the pen. Like every stage director I badly needed some name actors for this play of mine. On the other hand, I thought of some who are not as well known as others, but who also ought to have their say. It was more than discussing a theme and then picking up the script. I often had to play midwife. Finally, I was ghostwriting nine of twenty-nine essays, trying always to remain true to the spirit of the writer. After all, I had translated several books by then and knew how to catch a man's spirit, the lilt of a mind, the flair of feelings.

Thus, I gained insight into personalities which otherwise would have remained vague silhouettes or idols. In the process of doing this anthology some idols became silhouettes and some silhouettes idols for me. It often was a heartbreaking job, but, I suppose, this experience was also greatly responsible for my having lost my mind and heart more and more to these exasperating and fascinating creatures who call themselves dancers and choreographers. I played the role of psychologist, editor, and lover, almost always in a different sequence. It was a mental ordeal which I seemed to have endured to the point of loving it.

The result was called *The Dance Has Many Faces*, a title that came about through long discussions with Waldeen, an American choreographer who lives most of her life in Mexico City. It was all mad and beautiful, but I swore I would never try again to put another anthology together. I am sure I will resist any such temptation. Unique experiences should never be repeated.

1952

Bert Lahr's clowning and miming of a tatterdemalion tramp in Samuel Beckett's *Waiting for Godot* is a unique experience. With a single gesture he can create the entire tragicomedy of mankind. Every movement of his widens the meaning of his words and gives his character of a battered and bewildered human being a symbolic universality with Chaplinesque overtones. He is Everyman in disguise, waiting without hope for the great dream to dawn without really knowing why he lives or what he dreams of. Beckett wrote this play without a plot, which moves like a symphony, composed of the most ordinary words, to the heights of poetry. It was staged ingeniously like a dance without movement.

Hardly ever before have I seen a stage, almost bare and most of the time commanded by only two people, so full of life, of living experience. The play was absorbingly elusive in its meaning and movements. However, if you have eyes to see, ears to hear, and a heart to feel, it casts a strange and powerful spell over you.

It is a play about man's failure and endurance, about his frustration and dream of tomorrow. One can say it is an account of man's misery written by a cynical pessimist, or the tale of man's struggle against defeatism and his own blindness told by a poet who believes in the will of God. It is ordinary, often to the point of vulgarity, and, by the same token, sublime. It crushes all your hopes and elates you. The four characters speak literally about nothing, and yet say everything that matters in life. This elusiveness in its essence made *Waiting for Godot* look so very much like a dance to me. To make matters seem even more contradictory, the play is written in a scientifically cold, almost clinical way by an intellect running amuck, and it is nothing but feeling, completely disarming you by sneaking under your emotional skin. It is static and at the same time it is a dazzling dance of words and symbols, of gestures and allusions. And the bit of acutal dancing woven into this plotless action is just right; the marionette dance of the slave and puppet man is pathetic in its pitiless candor.

Some people may say the whole thing is a hoax. I am inclined to think that it is a rare theatrical miracle, composed of contrasts, of reality obscured, of the irrational made limpid; while emerging from nowhere and going nowhere it throws its devastating message with loud laughter into our lap.

I am grateful to my eyes which, over the years, have learned to see dance even in non-dancing.

1953

Mass media are mass media are mass media. Dance is doing marvellously well on television at the moment. It is not a question of how good this new medium will be for the dance; it will be a question of how good dance will be on this technical novelty, how it can learn to adjust to the camera's eye, how fast it can educate itself to triumph over the camera's limitations.

The dance will have to shed some of its ambitions; it probably must in time appease the demands of this medium. It may not necessarily have to go the way of all commercialism, but it will be caught by the fever of wanting to please the people in the living room, of keeping them, at every turn or jeté, from going to the refrigerator to get another beer. This fever will be a symptom of the real disease: the popularization of the art of the dance. We will not be able to avoid a close-up of our minds and feelings. The camera exploits the dancer-choreographer, it has a way of consuming his imaginative, inventive power rapidly. If he is trying to choreograph for television exclusively (as some are now doing), he will easily run out of ideas, repeat himself and others.

Perhaps later on this medium will rely on picking out the raisins from a huge cake and will, moreover, enchant its audience with keyhole views of the artist's private life and his opinion on his own craft and genius (called "interviews" or "brief biographies" to satisfy the insatiable curiosity of the public).

Nevertheless, the potential advantages are tremendous: dance consciousness will grow all over the country, dancers will have a chance to be seen where otherwise they would never have had a way of showing their artistry, and the public will be afforded the pleasure of getting acquainted with—let us say—the Balinese dancing girls with their quivering headdress and their fluttering hands. And we will believe their delicate charm is giving us an idea of life on Bali.

The other day we have seen and heard Agnes deMille explain her ballets before they were shown, a kind of documentary on the dance itself. Certainly educational, profitable. This could be the best way for dance and television in the future.

But this medium is a hydra, devouring the buds before they can flower, while corroding the artist's integrity. I can foresee it will not be easily satisfied and will demand one concession after the other from a well-intentioned crew. What price glorified publicity?

1954

François Rabelais coined the phrase of *horror vacui* in his satirical novel, *Gargantua et Pantagruel*: the horror of emptiness, a notion he deduced from the Latin *nature abhorret vacuum*.

The fear of facing a white canvas, a blank piece of paper, the mirrored walls of an empty dance studio may easily overwhelm the artist with a feeling of panic (most often without being aware of it), before the first stroke with the brush, the first sentence of the first paragraph, the first steps in the studio are done. He may immediately find himself master over such a short traumatic moment (call it stage fright), which, by the same token, may also lead to hesitation and from there to self-doubt and despair.

Moreover, there is another aspect of the *horror vacui*. Do we not sometimes betray our own talent by overwriting, by adding another coda to our symphony, by leaving no air to breathe to our design on the canvas, by overstating our dance composition? We have no one to blame for it but the hidden *horror vacui* in us.

Let us take it one step further: there is the hour of awakening. We enter the reality of another day, busy ourselves with getting ready. How lucky we are that there is no need to look into our subliminal feelings while looking ahead. Is there really no uncertainty about what we prepare to do with ourselves while brushing our teeth? Do we clearly see the chartered route of our day in front of us while we wash or shave? When we face ourselves in the mirror of each morning, is there no feeling of uncertainty or insecurity, no ambiguous thoughts or vacillating feelings which ought to be redirected, no place of the *horror vacui* to be quickly filled? The void can become a frightening, devouring beast which tests and traps us with many questions.

Then, there is our time which may not be of our liking, which at times seems irresponsible, tricky, treacherous with its empty stare and open ends into who-knows-where. We must admit that our time has more questions than answers. It has the genius of a ropedancer who trusts his megalomaniac equilibrium and sneeringly challenges the wrath of the gods with every forward step. The only thing that can save him is the illusion to walk toward certainty, toward a goal. Without this dream of reaching the other end, of being able to hold on to a tomorrow again, he must plunge into the abyss of his own emptiness.

I went to see it whenever it was done. I can't quite say what fascinated me. I was drawn both to music and choreography because they seemed far removed from everything else, they beautifully fused into something which I thought I had never experienced before. I went there each time to rediscover what rhythmic inventiveness can do to music and what visual splendor can come from an adventurous mind.

The ballet I saw was George Balanchine's *Ivesiana*. He probably brought so many new and daring images to the ballet because Charles Ives—who had died the very same year in which Balanchine's ballet was premiered—was a rather recent discovery of his. It was stimulation at first hearing, but when he worked his way into Ives' music, he began to love more and more the newness and shock he found in it. In fact, he said that this was music "I find hard not to work with it." He liked it so much that in the course of time he replaced some of the pieces and thus revised the ballet several times. Ives came like the expected unknown to him and just in time to close work on a string of composers who had enriched his fantasy: Arnold Schoenberg, Alban Berg, and Anton von Webern.

I had heard some of the Ives pieces before, but the uniqueness of his music was only revealed to me after I saw Balanchine's mind giving it balletic Gestalt. I could never wish for a better and more imaginative Cicerone through music than Balanchine's imagery which can convey through dance what no verbalization can ever do. Of course, one would have to thank Charles Ives, too, for having aroused Balanchine to come up with a visual answer to *The Unanswered Question*.

1955

The human hand has always been a symbol to me of many wonders that the Creator put into our hands. There is the hand as man's willing tool which, in fearless daring and blood-colored sweat, has ceaselessly built and destroyed and rebuilt the world in which the image of the hand is like the imprint of its towering work, its hallmark, its signature. There it is: eloquent and silent, restless and in repose; with the slightest gesture it can convey meaning and tell a story; it can write, through movement into the air, a poem that may remain unforgettable.

Ever since I became preoccupied with movement, hands assumed a telling expression for me. When facing someone, I cannot help looking first at his hands. After all, the hand is the mirror of our being. Who can forget the hand which Michelangelo gave God creating Adam? Aristotle thought men have hands because of their minds and was seconded by Kant who spoke of the hand as the "outside brain of man." How simple *and* complex is the hand with its palm full of hieroglyphics, with its four fingers stretched out like antennas which want to grasp the world, with a thumb which Newton once said, in absence of any other proof, would convince him of God's existence.

We are like actors on the world's stage (to borrow from Shakespeare) and run around with our masks which Jung called *persona.* Only the hand knows no mask, it is always the naked expression of our self. Stanislavsky—who made the actor create each role from his deep within-ness—said: "The hands are the eyes of the body," and the gesture was to him the mirror of the "inner personality." In everyday life we use the hands with the innocence of the knowing. What is so mysterious about the hand? It can only be what Einstein called "the eternal mystery of the world which we can grasp." The face may show a stereotypical smile which the ballerinas put on onstage like the false jewels of the romantic era. The hand can smile too, but the smile must evolve from the depth of a feeling. In a playful exchange, impulses move from the body to the hand and from the hand to the body. This makes us understand Cicero's astonishment when he said about a mime: "Even his entire body began to laugh."

The hand is many things to a dancer. "The hand is like a brush with which you paint a flower," Balanchine used to tell his dancers. As it moves from the body it is mirror and support, it is direction and dimension as well as spatial fulfillment. It may recreate a ritualistic image; it may create a metaphor of movement or a gesture of tradition, or it may be solely the helpmate of balance.

It has different aspects for every style of dancing. But essentially there is no dance without the language of the hands which animate the body and accentuate its movements. Even if we were to imagine a dance pattern in which the trunk and legs are in motion, but not the hands, then the hands would be the most characteristic feature of movement, most expressive in their immobility.

An entire history of the dance could be written, focussing on the hand. How different the East is from the West, the task of the dancing hand among early men is from its sophisticated meaning in our days! The Eastern dancer has retained the ritualistic features of the tradition-born movements and has taken refuge in the artistic sanctuary of a stylization which must reflect the minutest change in facial or gestural expression. How intricate—in a differing way from country to country—is the gesture language in its cultural setting and how eloquent is its meaningfulness! The Asian dancer is not, like Western man, bent on conquest of space in an active-aggressive sense and must therefore concentrate on the body as the shell of his meditative within-ness.

The stylization in ballet is quite another story. This stylized art form of a feudalistic society very soon adjusted all hand and finger movements to its growing vocabulary. It needed arms and hands partly from a technical viewpoint to create such set poses as an arabesque or attitude, and for strength and balance to achieve such virtuoso turns as a multiple pirouette. The balletic vocabulary even introduced a term, port de bras, which prescribes movement and carriage of the arms.

By the early eighteenth century the hand had begun to play a great role. Marie Sallé was the first ballerina to stress mimetic expressiveness, and Noverre extolled the gesture of the human hand. It was left to romantic excess to prefer an artificial codified gesture to spell out the obvious in pantomimic stylization. The hand was then subjugated by a grand style.

In our era of psychologized awareness the conventional gesture is out of place. Ballet has lost nothing by becoming more lifelike. And the modern expressionistic dance saw to it that every gesture of the hand had meaning and that its meaningfullness gave a heightened vocabulary to the living image of the dance.

It has become established, that the hand is, without a doubt, the most articulate instrument in the complex orchestra of the body which it accompanies in all its functions. The hand can emphasize or tone down a movement. It can take the role of a master of ceremonies and entertain in transitions between now and then, it can seemingly project a movement into infinity or cut it short with a withdrawing gesture. Within its expressive range the hand cannot have the same meaning to all dancers since it is the great individualist in each individual and has a mind all its own. Even if it obeys orders, it has the privilege and freedom to be arbiter between movement and movement, gesture and gesture. "A dance without hands is unthinkable," José Limón thought. There would be bodies without eyes moving about the stage.

After leaving Anna Sokolow's *Rooms*, John Martin wrote in the *New York Times* he wanted to throw himself into the Hudson. No other critic has more succinctly expressed the devastating effect of this dance work which gives Gestalt to the human despair in our time, to the no-exit feeling, the loneliness of man, his helplessness in a society without mercy, his bitterness toward the world moving on regardless of tears and pain. *Rooms* is a social drama par excellence belying the conventional notion that the social message is alien to the dance.

Kurt Jooss' *The Green Table* is an outcry against war, a convincing testimony against man-made madness. It came at the end of a flood of antiwar literature in the Germany of 1932, a year before Hitler began his war against humanity. This ballet has lost nothing of its symbolic meaning in the age of nuclear lunacy. It is still convincing as the curse in which man seems to delight. The central figure of death remains unforgettable the way he stalks across the stage, as if moving through time and space with steps of overpowering simplicity.

I thought of *The Green Table* when I saw *Rooms*. There a Dance of Death, here a ritual of human misery. Eight chairs, eight people. The chairs are their rooms. The rooms are as inescapable as their lives, with empty dreams, with love lost, with fear and desire in a phony, jazzy world. On an almost bare stage Anna Sokolow created a world of noncommunicativeness, the truth of life in its ugliness. "The stage is an open world," she told me. "Open to all possible experiences and only waiting for the miracle to happen that we always expect from it. What matters on stage is that it be truthful—truthful to your own self as well as to your time. This is the essence, the life breath of the theater. For only through your truth can the mystery of reality be revealed."

1956

I am sure there are quite a few very special artists in the world like Angna Enters. She had made an impact on the theatrical scene in the twenties and thirties, but today she is known to a relatively small community of connoisseurs. Is it her forte or handicap that she is a multiple talent? A fine writer, a skillful painter, a musician, stage and costume designer, and stage director. Whenever I catch her as a mime in one of her now rare performances, I am enthralled.

I get a sense of oneness of all creativity when I see her on stage. She herself feels, as she told me, that whatever she did

came about fortuitously. In my search by way of the written word to discover the classic line of life, and thus relate it to my images, I never thought one day I might try to be a writer. The writing happened accidentally, like the work in mime and painting—though now, looking back, I can see that all I did seemed to fall into logical progression consistent with my way of working—which is to plunge directly into whatever interests me.

She can only be described as a mime of sophistication and cerebration. Every gesture has its exact and exquisite place. Whatever she creates has lightness and a pastel-like quality. Moreover, she has the insight into what makes people tick, and her comments are at the same time gentle and devastating, poetic and satirical. Her excursions into nostalgia people the landscape with enchanting characters. Her *Boy Cardinal* is unforgettable.

The theater of Angna Enters takes you back into another world where time is of no consequence, where you have enough of it to develop an idea slowly, to unfold image after image like a dreamy hand would count the petals of a flower. Basically, she has devoted her life to the beauty of being, to the re-creation of experiences remote from the commonplace.

Usually, a rare touch of the beautiful is recognized only by the few. The mental palate of the many is oriented differently in its taste. Artists like Angna Enters are easily lost in a loud and fast-paced world. It would be wonderful to know that such tiny pearls of artistry will not go under in the swell of the sea, that they will stand the test of time against the masked cliché, enlightened

"Boy Cardinal"

Sketch by Angna Enters. Author's collection.

WS 82

With very few lines Angna Enters drew an hommage á Isadora Duncan which inspired me to an hommage á Angna Enters. Drawing by the author.

stupidity, the waste of the pleasantly vulgar, the smallness of bigness.

I suppose there is a place for everything in the world. The fearful thought that in a very few years she might be quite forgotten can only find solace in the hope that even then there will be—as there must—another Angna Enters enriching the life of a few who can see the uniqueness in a small gesture of the beautiful.

1957

When God made man in His image, man made an image of his own self by giving expression to his inner wonders. He may come close to unraveling the secrets of the universe, but even then he will be puzzled by the miracle that makes a flower a flower, a stone a stone, a river a river, and a mountain a mountain. Man may lift veil after veil from the mystery of Creation and, while doing it, he will not know how and why his brain functions the way it does. He can learn a craft and do with it the most exciting things expressive of his soul, while not ever really knowing why and how he did them and what compelled him to do them.

Whatever, art's main task has always been to create in man a greater awareness of himself and of others, to inspire him to feel nobly and to give his thoughts a keener subtlety and a wider scope. It is as if higher powers—call them God, destiny, or hereditary genes—had endowed a few men among us with the gift of expressing themselves creatively and a few among those few with the conviction that "art is not a pastime but a priesthood," as Jean Cocteau said.

Just as there is no universal time, to rely on Einstein, there is no universal taste. No one in his right mind—even if it is inclined to be dogmatic or dictatorial—would dare say what great art is. But one of its many criteria is certainly its lingering effect on our thoughts and lasting impact on our emotions, may it only be through a provocative phrase or a stunning image of rare beauty or impressive ugliness. It is something we can take with us that is unique and enriching in a curious way.

It is important to remind oneself from time to time that the arts do not necessarily develop in a process of constancy and logical growth. It seems that—as if due to the dialectics of Hegel—any kind of art form may or rather must create its own antithesis while still at the height of its expression. Is it the changing of the times that necessitates the artist to create with different means a different form or content, or is it the artist who, in a spirit of rebellion against the world preceding him, forces something new upon his time? However it may be, Hugo von Hofmannsthal referred in his *Letter of Lord Chandos* to the tremendous scope and the many inconceivable possibilities in which man can express himself by imitating the Creator.

I do not wish to sound as if I were endorsing works of minor stature, but any fragmentary work can make an incisive impression. The best example that comes to mind is Georg Büchner's *Woyzeck*—written in 1836—whose loose, unfinished scenes have survived into our days as a most contemporary expression of the suffering creature, man.

In comparison with literature, the visual arts and even with music, the dance is at a decisive disadvantage in this respect. It is too elusive and ephemeral for our memory to retain a fragmentary gesture. The only equivalent I can envision is a lecture demonstration or studio work. I have experienced some exciting moments in classes with Doris Humphrey, Hanya Holm, and Merce Cunningham. It seems, even as a teacher, a great choreographer cannot help being creative.

But the fragmentary must not be confused with a minor work of art. Karl Kraus once said that 999 minor poems must be written before one great poem can exist. One undoubtedly feels a strange, overpowering sensation when in the presence of a great work, but the very same work may not touch a responsive chord in someone else's heart. Also, a work may grow on us or one day we may wonder why we were so strongly impressed by something at a certain time. Circumstantial evidence may play its part.

We speak of a classic work, a semi-, minor, or modern classic, words that modify the status of a work. One would think that there are universally acknowledged masterpieces by Mozart, Rembrandt, or Tolstoi. They are acknowledged by reputation and tradition, not by opinion of the individual. There are no standards and criteria that can be applied to any work of art since its value and beauty are in the eye of the beholder. That men are so different from one another is our curse and blessing.

Since, before our time, the dance has never been notated *efficiently*, the stamp of what is "classic" about its being classic is based on relativized conjecture. All theater dance is keyed to its "nowness" and to a continued interpretation. Particularly in our time we are inclined to lift the face of such classics as *Giselle* or *Swan Lake*. There is no measure for any pure interpretation. In changing the face and Gestalt of these works we try to re-perceive them with senses attuned to our time. We nod in obligatory admiration, while questioning what is "classic" about a classic.

1958

I love celebrations. I wish one could celebrate every day. Then, one could think joyfully about the person one celebrates and about all the reasons for rejoicing. It is Hanya Holm's sixty-fifth birthday.

When, in 1931, she entered the American dance scene, it was in a formative stage. There was a restive atmosphere, a reappraisal of old values, a searching for new form and content, a trying to find one's self in ballet as much as in the modern dance. Hanya arrived to direct a Mary Wigman School in New York and she soon sensed the undercurrent of vitality—the dynamic force of the American dancers about to assert themselves—and she became part of it.

Twenty-five years later, Hanya is recognized widely for her contributions to the American theater and honored for her importance as a teacher who has had far-reaching influence, particularly on dance education in colleges throughout the nation. Hanya, blue-eyed and blonde, stands five feet two inches and weighs about one hundred ten pounds. With a birdlike expression she seems to look around questioningly and somehow warily, eager to absorb but also ready to react at a moment's notice. And yet, she quietly radiates the security of tremendous energies wisely spent, of a driving force which has carved out an inevitable path.

In her formative years, Hanya learned, she feels now, a respect for knowledge and creative ability; an understanding of the close interrelation of every branch of knowledge; iron discipline, and a belief in perfectionism. Her first twelve years of schooling were spent at the "Konvent der englischen Fräulein," a rather progressive convent for that time. At the age of sixteen she was introduced to music appreciation at the Hoch Conservatory in Frankfort-am-Main. She then attended the music-oriented Dalcroze Institute, from which, four years later, she was graduated.

It was about this time that she married a painter-sculptor, from whom she was later divorced. Of that situation she says now, "It was after seeing a recital by Mary Wigman that I resolved to become a dancer." This decision coincided with her divorce. "It was to be another kind of marriage to me," she stresses, "one to last forever. I personally find it difficult to understand that anyone completely dedicated to his art can also fully devote himself to another person. I don't say it isn't possible, and I certainly think highly of companionship. But for me, the slightest attempt to be detained, physically or by moral obligations, from what I want to do, can throw me off balance." There is such purposefulness in her that it would border on cold fanaticism, if it were not a contradiction in terms.

She became a Wigman student, and, as a member of her group, toured Europe in 1919; soon afterwards she was chief instructor and co-director of the Mary Wigman Central Institute. She was on her way; she took part in one of the first productions of Max Reinhardt's *The Miracle*, and danced the solo part in an early staging of Stravinsky's *L'Histoire du Soldat*. In the year before she came to America she was assistant director and co-dancer with Mary Wigman in the gigantic antiwar memorial pageant *Totenmal* which was presented in Munich.

It is characteristic of her that in settling down in America she did not immediately rush into creative work. She sat back and tried to absorb what was going on around her, only gradually adjusting herself to her new environment. During her first five years in New York, she devoted herself exclusively to teaching and building up a small concert company which she did not present before 1937, when it appeared at the Bennington Dance Festival in a piece called *Trend*. What became immediately clear was a fine adaptation of basic principles to a new environment. With *Trend* she established herself as an important group choreographer.

If you ask Hanya, she will tell you that you can only become— or remain—a great choreographer when you are a great teacher and continue to teach. To her, teaching is a most creative process. "Teaching means going back to one's roots. It is not essential how many pupils one has, but how much one can give, and by giving thus receive. Teaching is creative because it opens new vistas. You can constantly reach beyond the familiar, and I can say that whatever I know, I have learned through teaching."

Her group lecture-demonstrations, which explored the con- cepts of space and tension on which her teaching is based, were almost dreamlike in their lyric molding of space and mood. The distinctive movement quality of the best of Hanya Holm trained students is as hard to describe as a swoop of a wing, the flight of a bird—it belongs to the space about it. The demonstration had sections on curves, on horizontals, on verticals, on gravity and the resistance to it, on centrifugal and centripetal force, etc., and opened—as her teaching still does—a base of natural spatial laws which permits each individual to relate to it personally. Her theories of space are deeply indebted to the work of Laban and Wigman, yet, interestingly, Hanya's pupils have a lighter, more lyric air.

She told me, "I never make a student do something. I try to make him understand what I mean, and then I want him to do it as if it were his own idea, because, after all, he must carry it and make it succeed. And there is a difference between acting a movement and actually doing it. In the final analysis, it is meaningless to count the amount of jumps you can do, because one small gesture which is right and proves the oneness of purpose in what is being done will far outweigh everything else."

While Hanya will never deny that the teacher's and artist's personality must be reflected in every idea, in the largest and smallest of gestures, she nevertheless detests self-advertisement and has personally shunned the ways leading to a personality cult. Her teaching, too, reflects this respect for the individual. She insists that dancers must know people outside their own limited circle, that they must widen their horizons in every respect, for "talent implies heightened sensitivity and receptivity to experience," as she told me. Hanya wants her pupils not only to know how to dance, but also to have something to dance about. But even if they have no interest in being dancers, she thinks they should have the privilege of experiencing "a feeling for the beautiful." Because, according to her, even a movement as prosaic as walking can, if well done—which means most efficiently done—become a beautiful thing.

Since *Trend* she has experimented a great deal and has many firsts to her credit. *Metropolitan Daily*, a newspaper satire, was the first modern dance composition to be televised by the National Broadcasting Company. That was in 1938, when exposing dance movements to TV cameras was bold and daring. Her experimental work in the theater has not been limited to choreography or even direction. She has the credit of having had the entire dance score of the choreography for her first Broadway musical *Kiss Me, Kate* recorded in Labanotation—the first time show dancing has been so recorded. This notation, incidentally, made it possible for her choreography to be duplicated exactly in the London production in spite of the fact that she was not able to be there for the initial rehearsal period. And the same choreographic score has been registered, photographed on microfilm, and accepted for copyright in Washington, beginning a precedent which, it is hoped, will in the future bring much protection to the choreographer.

Hanya is never able to embark on a new artistic enterprise in which she cannot wholeheartedly believe. She must feel its relation to life. It must have the pulse beat of something she knows or can well imagine. When she was first assigned to do the choreography of *My Fair Lady*, she went to London to inhale the authenticity of the atmosphere, to get the smell and the spirit of what went on outside of Covent Garden. She recently told an interviewer: "I watch people in their daily role—in life apart from the stage. Their emotions, actions and reactions, at ease and under fire, all are noted. I absorb, then translate into dance."

Basically, Hanya's choregraphic talent has always expressed itself best in terms of theater, rather than just in concert style. "The lyric theater," she told me, "in which I am interested fuses music, drama, and dance into an entity. My early studies of the piano, of voice and painting have always helped me in my work. I also find it only natural that the choreographer should direct a production. It seems a logical development, at least it is for me." Neither film nor television—and she has worked in both media—offer the same attraction to her as the living stage, and she has directed quite a few plays and operas.

She has a sternness and devotion to principle, and standards not always easy to live up to. She can sympathize with failure, with personal troubles, and emotional difficulties, but not with self-pity and smugness, with laziness and unpunctuality and, above all, with "phoniness." Then she can be merciless in bearing down on and rejecting a person.

Broad in her theater interests, Hanya has never believed in specialization for herself on a personal activities level, either. In her concert days, she dyed her own costumes, arranged the lighting, played the piano. Earlier, when she had still more time, she enjoyed painting and wood carving. In her New York apartment she has grown plants and tropical fish, has kept dogs and cats, and still has a bird. She plays chess, is an animated worker of crossword puzzles, an excellent cook with a discriminating palate, particularly for the German cuisine; she is an ardent reader of good books, a conscientious letter-writer, and pleasant raconteur. She knows a lot about lace making, embroidery, and flowers. She can talk philosophy as well as high fidelity. She has preserved her love for conversation, an art as good as lost in our overstimulated, hectic, televisionary world. I rarely speak in her native tongue with her; she fluently verbalizes her thoughts in

English, even though her speech pattern will always have a German flavor. I rather like to talk with her, if for no other reason than that when she says something she has something to say.

It was at a party on the Eastside of Manhattan, where the celebrities of the dance world met to greet and honor Mary Wigman. She wanted to return to the places where, for three seasons between nineteen-thirty and thirty-three, she and her art triumphed in the States. She no longer performed, but she was very much in demand as a teacher and lecturer. On this trip, however, she wanted to see the people and places again, those places which were full of remembrances, those people who had become dear to her. It was to be a pleasure trip without any public appearance. But on April 16th she seemed to have forgotten that before her journey to the States, she had implored all her friends in her letters not to arrange any classes or speeches for her. In Pasadena in front of a small circle of admirers she was carried away by a buoyant mood, and what began as a little chat turned into a lovely speech (which, fortunately, was taped).

Her "welcome" party in Manhattan, arranged by Arthur Todd, turned out to be quite a special event. One rarely encounters so many of the great and greatest, whose names history recorded with luminous letters, together at one place. You may meet a well-known person of whose works and deeds you know (and know admiringly). You sit with him or her face to face for the first time. Deserved greatness always instills in me a feeling of awe, of enthusiastic respect which, in turn, creates for me an imaginary distance between us, even if occasion and space would permit us to sit quite close.

Things were different when I entered Todd's apartment that afternoon, greeted some of the guests, and was then led to the guest of honor. If love at first sight exists, why not friendship at first handshake? I will never forget that moment when I held her freckled hand in mine—probably somewhat longer than justified—, looked into her eyes (which opened like windows into her being) before I bowed to kiss the hand. That expected distance was nonexistent. After a few formal words, I felt forced to speak to her in our mother tongue, as if to seal a secret pact between us with words unknown to anyone else. Sometimes something can happen to you which you cannot immediately account for. It is as if you hear a message that has not yet been spelled out, or—if this is feasible—you suddenly discover your common archetypal roots.

1959

There are moments that remain engraved in one's memory: José Limón rushing out of Doris Humphrey's hospital room, running along the corridor without knowing where to, perhaps trying to escape a last blow which already had hit him. There was terror in his eyes, no tears; he held his trembling body erect, only his head was kept at an oblique angle as if it could not believe it was still there where it ought to be. His lips were separated, and when he passed me—I don't even know whether he recognized me that very moment—they moved convulsively, and then he broke out into a cry: "She's dying! She's dying!"

The year was late 1958. "This is sad news indeed," wrote Mary Wigman when she was told of Doris Humphrey's death on December 29th. "When I heard of it the other day, my first reaction was to write Doris immediately, until I realized she would never read it anymore. It still seems unbelievable that she passed away, as I remember her so vividly, admiring her self-discipline, and that wonderful and so noble way she carried herself, making everybody forget that she suffered from her body more than she wanted to admit."

It was more than self-discipline. She carried her pain like a secret hidden from the outside world. Even when we went down together to Nikolais' Henry Street Playhouse she would say: "I'll rather take you with me in a cab. Forgive me when I won't make it by subway." I often had a meal with her at the little restaurant, Fleurs de Lys, on 71st Street near Broadway. We then spoke about God and the world, rarely about the dance. Only once she perplexed me with the sudden question: "Which of my works do you remember most vividly?" I could have said *Day on Earth* or *Ritmo Jondo*, or *The Shakers*, but, as if I had to excuse myself, I said: "I've only seen your later work, after 1940, when I came to this country. And, moreover, I don't like comparisons." The last time I had seen her dance was in *Inquest*, but those works she had done for the Limón Company seemed to be the ones most unforgettable to me, like *Lament for Ignacio Sanchez Mejias* or *Night Spell*. Also, what she had done for The Juilliard Dance Theater: *Dawn in New York*, for instance. They were all unfogettable to me in their poetic vision and dramatic structure, in the weightiness of their meaning. I liked to watch her classes and admired her firm, almost regal way of saying to the student: "And now try to say the same in half the time."

There was a consciousness of time in her, as if she'd been listening to a watch that ticked too fast, as if, unconsciously, she had known how unfathomable the notion of time can be. The awareness of time and gravity seemed to have been her mental adversaries. While sitting in a chair, conducting classes or rehearsals, she must have felt that frightening pull of eternity disguised as gravity. She finally succumbed to the fall without recovery. She always was a very determined person; during her long illness, which she could only have taken as an unfair punishment of life, she appeared to many people as too factual and cold when, in fact, her emotions were divested of all sentimentalism.

In 1957 I invited her to a lecture demonstration at the New School, where I conducted a course on dance history. I played the role of master of ceremonies. It turned out to be her last public appearance. I often sat at her bedside during the last months of her life. She was about to finish her book—I should have said "last will"—, *The Art of Making Dances*. It must have been an excruciating feeling for her to put into words what she once experienced with her body. She had always been close to the poetic word—poetry was to her sound-turned-dance—and even though she once facetiously wrote about the "word-mongers" and about "the philosophy of life" being "a tangle of incomprehensible phrases in a book," she was most articulate. But in those days she acutely felt the rapid decay of her body, and there was constantly the physical pain mingled with the pain of the awareness that all that was left for her was the verbalization of a once experienced vision.

Somebody announced his visit. "Would you not like to get out of bed to greet your visitor?" I asked.

"I no longer have the strength even to pretend." It was one of the last and saddest sentences I heard her say.

1960

For quite some time it has bothered me that I found it somehow difficult to hear and see at the same time with the same perceptive intensity. I realize we cannot necessarily expect a sensitive ear to be housed together with a sensitive eye in one and the same body. It is not only a question of proper coordination as between the left and right hand on the keyboard, but one of two different organs and senses which are simultaneously challenged by the same artistic experience. We are facing the problem that the two different organs may become differently attuned to the same experience at the very same time. I wondered about it until Louis Horst—who surely is endowed with musical acumen and a fine visual perception of movement—told me he faces difficulties in absorbing yet unknown music while watching the flow of a dance with the same critical discernment.

It may all come down to the complex question of how the composer as well as the choreographer/dancer approach their common problems and goals. If the composer was asked to write music to the preset counts of the dancer (Petipa, for instance, detailed the counts for Tchaikovsky: "The Christmas tree grows and becomes huge—48 measures fantastic music . . . The Nutcracker is transformed into a prince—one or two chords."), it narrows the visual and aural scope. The same happens when the performer slavishly counts along with the music. I believe it is easier to follow both at the same time when the choreographer tries to capture the emotional essence of the music because then the listener/viewer can realize the movement within the music whose technical structure no longer creates too many obstacles for his attention. Then, he can answer Gertrude Stein's question: "If one really looks can one listen and if one really listens can one look?" in the affirmative: If my eyes are not handicapped by what I hear, and my ears are not unduly influenced by what I see, my vision can be carried by the music.

In other words, I do not feel that Michel Fokine was right when he over-emphasized the close collaboration between the choreographer and the composer, "when the two artists work out the content of each musical moment together." He may be right when the score does not ask for particular attention and remains a kind of background music. Moreover, besides an aesthetically direct interpretation of music through movement, we also quite often encounter an anarchic or at least undisturbed existence of sound and movement side by side, like in the case of Lucia Dlugoszewski and Erick Hawkins, John Cage and Merce Cunningham, or Alwin Nikolais' sound collages to Alwin Nikolais' movement sequences.

"Ballet music is conceived as music that is marriageable," Edwin Denby said. He overlooked to elaborate on it and to mention that there are good and bad and even indifferent marriages and that a concubinage may easily outsound and outdance all licensed marriages.

Diary Notes:
1961–1970

1961

Impresarios existed long before the (r)age of the middleman as a consequence of the demanding needs of homo consumens. An impresario is an almighty person who runs the arts as a business and who employs a number of barking press agents whom he lets loose against an unaware public that cannot help borrow bits and moments of glamour and illusion from the flame of those whose fire the impresario keeps burning.

One must be a fanatic in whatever one does in order to achieve greatness, one must love what one does to be successful. When Sol Hurok decided that, one day, the standing-room ticket in his hand would turn into a manager's contract, his career was set. It is more than likely that Hurok would have become a financial success in many other lines if he had put his mind to it. "Bread I could have earned in almost any other business," he said of himself modestly, "but caviar is irresistible." There was something strange about this young immigrant who came to the United States in 1906. He was star-struck. And to him, as it seems, caviar was a metaphor for a great dream.

Hurok was a realist, with a vision of his own greatness. When, a few months after his arrival in New York, he stood in the lobby of the old Victoria, where Oscar Hammerstein was impresario, and stared with a feeling of admiration, awe, and desire at the many pictures of great artists, he did not know who Horatio Alger was, let alone that he was about to become a Horatio Alger under the pseudonym of his own name and with the slogan "S. Hurok presents." He was still in the hardware business when, at the age of eighteen, he took over the Hippodrome for Sunday night performances and presented such artists as Mischa Elman and Efrem Zimbalist. He was still a step or two removed from caviar and champagne, but close enough to sense the realization of his dream.

It came when he managed the immortal basso, Chaliapin, and drank vodka with him, when he exclusively managed Anna Pavlova in America and kissed her hand, when he managed the unmanageable Isadora and "when she kissed me goodbye . . . I walked in a dream to my hotel." It came when he danced the conga with Katherine Dunham, when he appeared as bear trainer in *Petrouchka*, when he became the *Stammgast*, patron extra-ordinary, in the finest restaurants on two continents, with the Russian Tea Room as his favorite retreat, when he had long and serious talks with Mary Wigman, when he launched the Ballet Russe in 1933 and, when before setting off the boom in ballet, he held a first-night supper party after the performance at which Otto H. Kahn drank champagne from a ballet slipper. Sol Hurok, as the press release says, "lost about $75,000 on that first season." But this was a sound investment, for his publicity director admits that "in less than ten years he had built ballet into a million dollar business, with semi-annual seasons, spring and fall, at the Metropolitan Opera House and a tour of about 75 cities."

An impresario is an entrepreneur with his heart in the arts and his eyes on the bank account. When his eyes get too big, his heart begins to murmur and, finally to fail; when his heart beats too loud, the scales fall from his eyes in the form of dried-out zeroes. An impresario must be a psychologist who has the right answers and pills in the right doses for all the idiosyncrasies and whims of all the female and male prima donnas; he must be an organizer who brings an artist to the public and a public to the artist; he must have imagination and foresee the change in temper and taste of the audience; he must have instinct for who and what are right at the right moment; and he must be daring enough to challenge the public in the name of art to ensure the survival of both public and art.

Diaghilev's trouble was his "heart" and the ensuing financial difficulties. Impresario S. Hurok has more safely leaned towards the managerial aspects of the business. Not that he wasn't daring from time to time: he engaged Argentinita for annual tours after she had flopped in a Broadway musical; he banked on Isaac Stern's and Artur Rubinstein's futures when fame was not yet guaranteed. He brought Marian Anderson back to this country and made her native land recognize her voice in spite of the color of her skin.

Hurok wouldn't be the Russian he is if he were not in love with the ballet or dancing per se. From Isadora Duncan to Trudi Schoop, from Anna Pavlova to Martha Graham and Uday Shankar, from Loie Fuller to Vicente Escudero, he has helped and managed the dancer. He did a great service, not yet properly appreciated, for the American modern dance by bringing Mary Wigman to this country and, if nothing else, Hanya Holm and her creative contribution to the dance development in America is his living monument for this deed.

Why does history never properly credit the man standing in the shadow of greatness which he makes possible? This man has presented us with the world's most famous ballet companies, the Royal Ballet from London and the Bolshoi Ballet, the Moiseyev and Kirov companies, the Kabukis and Bayanihans, Kolo and Inbal, Roberto Iglesias and Roland Petit. One could write volumes about his managerial activities and genius, and he himself wrote two as an impresario's memoirs.

Perhaps now, when nothing can endanger his kingdom, one wishes he would sometimes be reminded that dreams have no borders, and that they live and grow best when their frontiers are constantly pushed farther and farther into yet undreamt of lands where new wonders take root and form as the realization of what they are: the magic of creation, the dream of man.

And yet—I do know of life's natural limitations whose borders are demarcated with dollar bills and the drain on a man's dreams which (un)consciously fear to turn into nightmares. Of course, we can blame him for not having helped to create an American Folklore Ballet à la Moiseyev which for a long time has cried out to be done. (And Agnes deMille was so close to him!) When, one year, the artists he presented received a series of lukewarm or downright bad notices in the *New York Times* he threatened the paper with withdrawing his ads. The dance critic was made to understand the seriousness of the situation, as I gathered from John Martin's hints. What a pity that human beings cannot help being human, that even heroes have warts. Or do they grow on all of us when we count our wishes and hopes like dollar bills?

1962

Madison Avenue blushed all over its sure-fire, Breck-shampooed head and shook the blame from it. After all, they had engaged the greatest composer of this century, its greatest choreographer, some of the best dancers, an outstanding scenic designer, and a director with many hits to his credit. They had not known, however, that the Muses are the only women who, for sure, cannot be bought or bribed and who are not easily impressed by mere bigness. They demand the magic touch of a poetic soul; they ask for mystery. They only give themselves when the spirit moves and overwhelms them, and then they do not like to be interrupted by commercials.

Now that the ballyhoo and excitement about the CBS-TV premiere of *Noah and the Flood* has died down and the trumpets of publicity have left us with little to remember except the faint echo of a nauseating clamor that wanted to bring art to TV; now that we have learned our deserved lesson—or haven't we yet?—we may go on from here to some productive thoughts.

I still hope to see one day on stage, *Noah and the Flood* as Stravinsky and Balanchine may reconceive it in terms of music, voice and movement. It will then be lifted out of its incidental character, surrounded by the phony gestures of bigness, and made to stand on the stage as a ballet-oratorio of artistic interest, musically as much as choreographically.

And this is how I imagine it to be. The bit of the hand gesture suggesting the creation of man, seemingly borrowed from Michelangelo, or indirectly from an earlier work of Balanchine, *Agon*, will have to be extended to the reality of a movement pattern. It will probably reappear as a harmonious entity within the scene in Eden which—knowing Balanchine—I venture to say will turn out as an exciting erotic *pas de deux* and/or an ironic *pas de trois* with Satan in a snake's skin.

The two final and major sections will look on stage quite differently from what the little home screen could show us. *The Building of the Ark*, with its sparse, abstract conception in which an interweaving design of celebrants comes closest to the image of building and utter dedication, stood in juxtaposition to the almost representational imagery of the *Flood*. It may even gain in contrast on the stage as the dance of *Flood* will have to gain in choreographic invention. It did not come off on TV at all. The undulating movement the dancers created seemed too gimmicky on the screen. Balanchine's obvious intention to give us—besides an impressionist painting,—the feeling that the deluge is both an end and a beginning, with the dancing couples rising above the flood time and again, was lost. On stage, all this will be far more manifest.

In the *Building of the Ark* Balanchine adhered to a similar style as in *Agon* (also a Stravinsky score), following the sharp, shifting rhythms with unexpected humor and sharply accentuated movements (What a great ballet *Agon* is!) while the *Flood* ballet had all the earmarks of Balanchine at his romantic best. These contrasting moods can be made to work when they are dramatically motivated and substantiated, when they are brought by the inner necessity of their being to the final image of a stage reality.

And thus the dance-oratorio *Noah and the Flood*, once a commercial nightmare on TV, may yet one day turn into the magic of a creative dream.

In my eyes, Paul Taylor is the prototype of the American dancer-choreographer. He has an athletic body—it is one of lyric masculinity—and a straightforward mind. You will rarely meet him without noticing an ironic twinkle in his eye. If I should quickly think of an antipode to him, Antony Tudor, who can say so much by understating what he wishes to convey, would come to mind; his ballets are full of psychologically motivated undercurrents, of tensions and pulls with built-in poeticised innuendoes. If one could speak of geographically conditioned choreographers, then I would call Antony Tudor a typically European choreographer—in contrast to Taylor who is very much like a picture postcard image of everything American, outgoing in his conceits, in wit and phrasing. And yet he can be very serious without losing sight of the fun of what he is doing, even the fun in something as devastating as *Scuderama*. His sense of humor has a charming, ingratiating, and sometimes whipping wit, surprising you, almost jumping at you from behind or from around a turn when you least expect it. Seemingly, there is a chuckling devil in him who is good-natured at heart.

Whenever I saw his work over the years I had the impression he was about to start a new phase in his way of choreographing. And, at the same time, I sensed he hadn't changed at all. But he has been trying and testing new ways to come up with something that strikes the right chords for or in him. Some of his pieces have apparently evolved from minute, incidental experiences, like seeing a girl running beautifully for a bus. From this, the intoxicatingly moving, running and skipping of *Esplanade* was born. Whenever I saw that luminous balletic piece, *Aureole*, I had the sensation of becoming a part of the lighthearted floating of the dancers, carried by their swinging arm movements, as if I were virtually an airborne creature.

As an American, with the First and other amendments protecting him, he can lash out against human brutality in a Janus-faced society: *Big Bertha* is a fairy tale of American or rather un-American life. With the help of a nickel-swallowing automaton he can crack the veneer of all surficial niceties and dramatize the subliminal realities of a clean-cut American middle-class family. Or he can thunder against the animal nature of our sick society in *Cloven Kingdom*, but not without gentle sarcasm. He can start with a serious, almost solemn mien in *Churchyard* and then reveal tragicomic aspects of mankind in a grotesque way. Or he turns things around in *Public Domain*, opening with a pleasant enough gesture, only to become gradually very serious. Or, if most artists are beastly earnest or at least erotic about that nasty business around the Tree of Knowledge, Taylor came up with a light and delightful piece, *So Long Eden*, with which he viewed man's initial mistakes with a glint in his eye. The next best to a *commedia*

"*Orbs,*" *The Paul Taylor Dance Company. Photo: Jack Mitchell.*

dell'arte prank is to put the scene in a rustic environment. After all, Paradise is a lush sylvan place, and it is there that boy meets girl. They seem to like one another (to borrow a cheap joke from Arthur Miller's play about the same topic: They haven't had much choice). Already in the fall of 1966 when we still thought little of the inevitable bane (and some blessing) of the man-made satellites, with Sputnik only nine years old, he "Taylored" and played with the *Orbs*, evoking the seasons of the planets.

Seeing Paul Taylor's company dance again, I was perusing my reviews about him and found one, written in January 1962 (pretty much at the beginning of his career) which I ended with the sentence: "May the gods (and men) who favored him refrain from destroying a unique talent that has only begun to unfold."

Well, the gods and men seem to have heard my prayer and did let his talent unfold to his satisfaction and our joy.

1963

To give ever-new meaning to the meaningful in life is the essence of all art.

I was angered by the anti-cliché that has become the cliché of our time. So I wrote an essay in defense of the future for the *Dance Observer*.

In this jazzed-up race of being-different-at-any-cost, how can we, standing in the midst of this jumble of contemporariness and up-to-dateness, separate the bandwagon opportunist from the one who cannot help being different? Particularly in a period of transition in which re-orientation and re-evaluation have become the tenets of the time?

The greatest art has always been created by immaculate craftsmen in hours of spiritual intoxication and hard work, by men possessed by the fever of forming and shaping, of giving their inner visions the content and contours of an artistic realization. But for quite some time now we have been frightened into the acceptance of the sophistication of the anti-sophisticated, of the glorification of the banal. The avant-garde has embraced the flotsam and jetsam of reality and obscured all criteria of where real art begins and the artificial reality—which we apparently have come to live—ends. One is almost afraid to call a spade a spade which the artist might present as a work of art.

I want to be involved. I am questioning and searching. I am a desperate human being, stranded in the 1960s, in a frightening and elating, a portentous and potent era. I have swallowed, with all vitamins and slogans, the realization that I am alone and lost. Now

I have become sick of being told and shown all the time that I live in a sick world. I am aware of it. I want to help and be helped. And if I must go through the experience of existence artistically, I want to be touched; I don't want to be shocked into the shame of being human and rejected through all possible theater tricks of a non-theater; I don't mind being whipped again from the stage—since I seek experience, not escape— but I want to feel the warmth of the human hand that cracks the whip. I want to feel by whatever implications, there is excitement in mere existence and beauty in being.

There is something unmistakable about a work of art. When later generations look at us they will not see the feeble, defiant scribble on the wall, "Kilroy was here," and mistake it for art. They must see an image of a danced reality, an image formed out of an inner cry and the outer chaos, and feel that the Creator must have passed by.

We have rarely had such a ready-made chance as now to compare the Bolshois with Balanchine. We could ask: Is there any meaning in Asaf Messerer's visit to the High School of Performing Arts where he gave a class or in George Balanchine's visit to the Bolshoi School, where he showed off his dancers at the barres to his Russian colleagues? Beyond the political meaning, which is for the day and as ephemeral as yesterday was, it has implications which may prove important to the growing dance generation, even if only in a few individual cases. But of greater importance is the general impression we had of the Bolshoi Ballet this season and the manner in which the Russians received the New York City Ballet.

Of all the productions the Bolshoi Ballet presented this time, the great sensation was not *Spartacus*, though it was heralded as a colossal ballet, but an unpretentious little ballet that grew out of the annual graduation exercises of the Bolshoi School, a ballet à la Harald Lander's *Etudes* (as done some time ago by the American Ballet Theatre).

Asaf Messerer staged the work and played, in a way, the master of ceremonies. It proved, if nothing else, that the sheer weight of more than 200 dancers onstage in a spectacularly mounted show can be lighter than the poetic touch of a few who, with suggestiveness and subtleness, present themselves in artistic splendor. Moreover, *Ballet School* was so successful because it gave the American audience deeper insight into the technical aspects and teaching methods of the Bolshoi School.

This ballet re-enacted the most important story of the company, the growth of a dancer from an early age to his stardom. Why is it that to see the Bolshoi School in action, to see one of its choreographers on the stage guiding the little dancer to his proficient greatness, correcting body positions, improving a line here and there, should turn out to be such an impressive theatrical experience? Probably the feeling of one who looks through a keyhole watching the private life of a great school with an even greater tradition, added to the excitement. But essentially it was the inherent drama of growth, the fulfillment of a dream and the eternal magic of theater within the theater that gave these fleeting moments their memorable quality.

More so than any time before, the stress on the physical was apparent in whatever the Bolshois did. Lifts began to outlift themselves, turns multiplied, leaps sneered at gravity, and all balances created the impression of the most difficult being just a child's play. (Perhaps this is why I sometimes thought longingly of the more lyric and less acrobatic Kirovs.) With so much emphasis on dazzling technique, the creative aspects badly suffered. Where no room is left by dizzying feats and marvels of mere mechanics, sentimentality easily takes the place of real sentiment and drama that should be inherent in movement labors and limps. This was not only shown in the massive mistake of *Spartacus*, but also in Leopold Lavrovsky's *Paganini*. True, it is always difficult to show "genius at work," but through these soul-searching, lyric lilts of torments I was not transported into any state of enchantment, though I may have admired certain moments of brilliant dancing. It is indicative of the entire basic concept that governs the approach of the Bolshoi Ballet that the obvious simplicity of *Ballet*

School achieved with the showing of pure technique what could be called the mystery of artistic creation which *Paganini* tried so hard to convey to us.

George Balanchine, a descendant of the Leningrad School, seemed to have sensed the contemporariness of the American character and skillfully blended it with the classic ballet tradition. In contrast to the Bolshoi's, who arrested their own development by channeling it into outwardness, his remained a searching spirit. For every artistic sin he commits, he makes amends with the creation of something startling and stunning that leads a few steps forward.

He, too, is master of the spectacular and the old-fashioned story ballet, sumptuously costumed against a rich setting, in which the Bolshois believe and on which the Russian ballet public was reared. Such a ballet as *The Figure in the Carpet*, a big mixed bag of too many divertissements and no direction leading anywhere— something rare with Balanchine—is little more than eyefilling waste that will fall by the wayside when, one day, the achievements of one George Balanchine will be counted. But he cannot help tossing even into these ballets moments of sheer poetic beauty or the movement-fulfillment of a musical passage.

One only has to think of his *Nutcracker* which, in spite of its threadbareness and all its infantilism, is turned into an artistic experience readily acceptable to both young and old since it does not stoop to somewhat mature baby talk, nor does it pretend that there is not sufficient childlikeness in the adult. Its fairytale is enjoyable on many levels of appreciation because of its psychological depth with the ready-made dream images and its consistent theatricality. Balanchine gives it a stage realization with all the elements of make-believe that turn the unreal into a dancing and moving reality.

But Balanchine's strength lies in the storyless ballet in which movement is self-explanatory; it lies in the dynamic use of the human body and the aesthetic manifestation of rhythmic patterns. In extending these principles he often experiments without doing it consciously. The Russians, first nonplused, finally took to the innovations of New York City Ballet's maître de ballet. One of their major critics, Mikhail Gabovich, was particularly impressed by Edward Villella ("light, jumps magnificently") and Allegra Kent ("rare charm and vital plastic lyricism. There is a flavor of Ulanova's style in this inspired dancer.") Most of his praise, however, went to George Balanchine ("he really 'sees' the music and 'hears' the dance . . . fills the 'language' of the dance with poetic meaning, giving it, so to speak, the effectiveness of verse.").

No doubt, there must have been great apprehension in Russian balletomanes to accept ballet as an art form that is not blind to a modern concept of expression. Balanchine stunned the Russians and rightly so. He is a man whose heart may be in the past, but whose mind (or is it his right foot?) is in the present. Once asked to take issue with the modern dance, Balanchine answered that he knew no difference between ballet and the modern dance, he only knew good and bad dancing. Balanchine is an artist, and as such he did not let his own time pass by without noticing it.

I can only imagine that his heart—going out into many directions for seventy-four years with an intense fervor that always wanted to light up the stars of his fancy—was suddenly so tired that it asked for a rest. His mind, original and versatile as it was, had pirouetted through life. He was not only a friend and contributor to the dance, he was virtually a literary pocketbook edition of the twentieth-century-ballet (and/or modern dance).

For all we know, Jean Cocteau—this enfant terrible of French literature—may have felt like a frustrated dancer from the early days of Diaghilev (when he designed posters for the Ballets Russes) to the last period of his life (when during the rehearsals of Le Jeune Homme et la Mort he demonstrated positions and movements to the dancers as if choreographing had been a lifelong métier of his). The inherent poetic quality in the balletic art found a responsive chord in the poet in him.

After he had failed with his first scenario for the ballet Le Dieu Bleu in 1912, Diaghilev charged and challenged him with the now

The arabesque, one of the most important poses in classical ballet, already known in the 18th century, codified by Carlo Blasis. Drawing by the author.

famous words: "Surprise me!" In 1917 Cocteau surprised Diaghilev, himself and the world with his idea for *Parade*, which Lincoln Kirstein said was the first modern ballet. With the help of Massine, Satie, and Picasso he created a ballet which no longer lived in a fairy-tale atmosphere with a spectacular sequence of heightened unreality. *Parade* was a revolutionary break with all past clichés. In fact, it was little more than a poetic montage of everyday banalities. What has become common coinage in the second half of this century was a scandal in 1917, a triumph over threadbare conceits, a breakthrough from the nineteenth- into the twentieth-century ballet. And the avant-garde movements in the field of the modern dance are unthinkable without Cocteau's imaginative daring.

He was an instigator and mystifier, an artistic snob and a serious artist, playful and penetrating. Cocteau was a protean personality who could not help opening the doors to new experiments in the dance, who could not help being fascinated by movement, which is the cause of all life.

1964

On January 23 Louis Horst left us. I have deliberately chosen the words "left us" because they mean more than one thing. Louis has left us with a heritage of American modern dance, for it was he who helped give life and shape to it. He has left us, too, the tremendous task and awesome responsibility of continuing where he left off. He was a living symbol to four generations of modern dancers, and he ought to remain a symbolic reality for those to come.

Louis, as he was known to all, liked to call himself a grammar school boy. Yet he was proud to receive an honorary doctorate from Wayne State University in Michigan this past December. I saw him in his home in the East Sixties shortly after his return from the railroad station. He showed me the gown he had worn

Louis Horst: Bust by Elena Kepalente. Photo: Lionel Rudko.

and the citation which honored him. It read: "As musician, artistic advisor, teacher, editor, critic and author, Louis Horst has influenced immeasurably the career of leading dancers who have set out on new paths of creativeness in this age-old art . . . ".

I looked at the citation and then at the newly proclaimed Dr. Louis Horst. "You must go to bed immediately, you look tired."

"Yeah," he said, "we had engine trouble. It was a bad trip. I'm pooped. It's almost noon, now, and Doris (Rudko) will be by for me soon. I've got a one o'clock class at the Neighborhood Playhouse. And you've got to finish the editorial. I want to take it to the printer."

I sat in the cubbyhole of the apartment which served as the

office of the *Dance Observer* (a small monthly magazine, devoted to modern dance, which Louis had kept in continuous publication for thirty years). A few weeks away, on January 12, Louis was going to celebrate his 80th birthday. The typewriter keys plunked: "This is a month of celebration." (We did not know it would become a month of mourning.) "The *Dance Observer* and Louis Horst are one. The editors wish to congratulate him for being thirty years young at the age of eighty." The *Dance Observer* was Louis' brainchild, probably born out of wedlock with and for Martha Graham in the name of the modern dance. That the magazine should not get into any alien hands of however kindred spirits, Martha's decision was that the *Dance Observer* must die with Louis.

He drove off with Doris that noon to teach the student actors at the Neighborhood Playhouse. He couldn't, he wouldn't, stop. He always had a heightened feeling of responsibility, as if he personally carried the modern dance on his shoulders. And in some ways he did. He had taught for decades not only at the Playhouse, but at Bennington College (twelve summers), at Connecticut School of Dance (sixteen summers), Columbia Teachers College, at Mills, Barnard, Sarah Lawrence, The Juilliard School of Music, and The Martha Graham School. There is hardly a modern dancer in the country who hasn't gone through his classes of pre-classic and modern dance forms and hasn't learned the ABC—that is, the ABA—of dance composition from him. All this, plus what remains in the minds and hearts of those thousands of students and scores of leading dancers, plus his two books, are among the things he has left us.

Not long ago Louis got very angry with one of his *Dance Observer* reviewers: "If you have to write an unfavorable review," he scolded, "I demand constructive criticism. We are here to keep the modern dance going." I asked Louis whether he knew where it was going. Louis shrugged. "What difference does it make where it goes? The main thing is that it's going."

In his lectures Louis has always been quotable: "The new dance does not depend on beautiful line, unearthly balance, or sexual titillation. The movement is abstracted to express, in esthetic form, the drives, desires and reactions of alive human beings", or, "An idea is touched upon in the briefest fashion, like an insect which lights briefly on a leaf before flying on to the next. It is suggestive."

Louis was much loved, but he was also feared and even hated, usually because of his sarcasm, of being a severe, in some eyes, a ruthless, taskmaster. He could not tolerate phoniness. After a concert at the "Y" he said, "These kids take toilet-flushing for music and structureless immobility for dancing. To rebel, to be way out is fine. But they don't know how far they can go and still be with us!"

That was Louis. He blended acute sensitivity and esthetic creativity with sound horse-sense and biting wit. For the last ten years of his life I wrote reviews for his magazine and every second month I had a lead article in it. All the praise coming from him was wordless acceptance. Only once, when I had written for him the essay, *In Defense of the Future*, he called me up at midnight saying "Marvellous job—that essay!" Before I could even say "thanks" he had put down the receiver. "He was terrible today, you can't please him," said a young dance composer, leaving his composition class in New London. Next week she reported: "He made me rewrite it three times. Now I know I've got it right." What infuriated him most was to see a former student give a bad performance. Then he would say "Did you see that? And she took my classes!" Or if he was satisfied, but not completely, he would always remark "It's not enough to be good. I've always told you, a great work of art reveals itself through its mystery."

Any work of art that makes you go on dreaming about it, that sets off a chain reaction of thoughts in you, has achieved a rewarding, if not ultimate effect. That is what Lucas Hoving did to me with his ballet *Icarus*. To translate this eternal dream of man into a danced movement sequence seems to border the impossible. Our flight to the sun can only be insinuated by physically and spatially limited leaps into the air. Hoving succeeded in giving man's longing the needed "imaginary" wings. The logical highlight of this dance work was its dénouement in having Icarus coming crashing down to earth, his wings burnt.

Everywhere we face a natural limitation in unlimited space. Earthbound man has always dreamed of flying. Sunday means escape from everyday drudgeries. Icarus wanted to get to the sun because, blinded as he was, he wanted to escape himself. He did not know that everyone carries his whole world with him on his back. His world is not bigger or farther than his inner vision. The end of the horizon is always the same, wherever he may stand.

We all have something of Icarus in us. A secret longing—of which we are not aware, and if we are aware of it, it remains inexplicable to us—often asks for what we do not have, wants us to be there where we are not. The desire of Icarus tortures us since we know only too well about the melting of his waxen wings as soon as he came closer to the sun.

Moderation can be a measure of infinity through the knowledge of our limitations. If we feel we need more and more and must grasp the world in its remoteness, then this feeling comes about because we are empty within. Look through the window. Too many have not yet learned that to look is not to see. To see means to be a poet, Ibsen said. The one who has learned to see, can see the whole world through his window; so many who have journeyed around the world, return with an empty stare. Why do so few of us try to find wonders while digging the depth of our being? Certainly, it is less comfortable than to race around and stay with the surface.

We should be aware of the madness of a bigness growing through the mere impetus of its own bigness, we should be aware of the known and unrecognizable cartels, syndicates, and professional prophets of all parties who sell promises with built-in damnation at clearance. We must try to free ourselves from the chain of numbers, from all unreal reality, to be able to live again with a tree as a symbol of life. What, in the last analysis, is really important is usually hidden in the apparent unimportant.

We praise quality, not quantity. Does not an epigram often contain more knowledge and wisdom than a short story, can a short story not say more than a novella, a novella more than an oversized novel? The Japanese painter knows that he does not have to paint a forest, not even a tree, only the branch of a tree, in order to evoke in us the wonders of spring. Does not our critical eye sometimes say about a work of art that less would have been more?

Michelangelo saw in the omission of everything superfluous the secret to beauty. Did not Shakespeare have his Hamlet say that brevity is the soul of wit? Did not Leonardo da Vinci maintain that a small room disciplines our mind? We can learn more from the essence of littleness than from the widest dimension of bigness which ultimately loses itself in infinity. If we feel like escaping all narrowness, then the shortest route leading to it runs toward our own within-ness. There, and only there lies for everyone the wonder of human greatness.

Coming home from the theater I have always felt grateful if my mind could take with it a beautiful scene or even a telling sentence, the light tune of a song, the lovely melody of an aria, the image of a danced gesture which will remain unforgettable. Lucas Hoving's *Icarus* has made me muse on the big dream in us to reach for the unattainable and to embrace on our way there what we cannot really grasp. Certainly, we should always test ourselves, respond to challenges (even to those we create for ourselves); but in doing so we should not fail to re-discover our self time and again in the light of a new idea, of newly won territory. This will of necessity keep our dream from crashing beyond the measures of our vision.

1965

This winter Volume 10, Number 2 of the *Tulane Drama Review* was, in its entirety, devoted to "Happenings." Perusing this issue was quite some happening to me. Its contributors are people who have been far-out in the avant-garde movement. A feature written by Yvonne Rainer refers to "Some retrospective notes on a dance for 10 people and 12 mattresses called *Parts of Some Sextets*." This event or happening was performed at the Wadsworth Atheneum, Hartford, Connecticut. I saw it at Judson Memorial Church in New York.

One passage in her account startled me very much. It was an artistic credo of flaming negativisms. The performance puzzled and pained me—particularly since, exactly two years previously, I had seen Yvonne Rainer at Judson Hall and then believed in her as a novel artist, someone who might lead somewhere, which briefly gave me hope. I wrote in *Dance Observer*:

February 15, 1963

Cool, man. I admit I'm a square. Well, upbringing, you know, last and lost generation and so. I'm not stuffy, but in any show you've got to see what's being shown, and in Judson Hall there is standing room only if you want to see something from the torso down. And, man, there was a lot to see. Ten numbers, two solid hours.

I'm digging a good deal of it. I'm all with you against a crazy cracked-up yesterday, against the forms and norms of middle-class ideals with Whistler's "Mother" over the fireplace and against this nutty, rotting universe, kiddo. But you can't let me down and be just different out of spite and because it's smart and everyone else does it now and even gets grants for it. If you spit into the face of whatever it is, you've got to take good aim and you can't just ignore structure, dynamics, rhythm and meaning, baby.

Phyllis Lamhut is a likeable dancer; that girl has stage presence, choreographs vignette-like images with taste and tight structure. She knows her limitations, and that's her forte. She is precise, restrained, with a feeling for form that makes her almost old hat among her colleagues. Whether it was her *Touch Dance*, *Recession* or *Shift*, I could sense the mood, I could touch a shape, I could feel something there. But in her *Group* she tried to jump on the bandwagon of the dance of the absurd and fell flat on her nose. With the exception of the first section it was a bore.

Albert Reid's *Shade Cool To Rest Under, Fruit Sweet to The Taste* pleased my visual palate. I was in it and with him (sure, he's an engaging dancer with a fine figure) in spite of the fact—or perhaps because of it?—

that many an image was, no doubt, on loan from Merce Cunningham's artistic collection. In his *Dumb Show* he tired me with posing and staring while Barbara Tucker, his partner, had a few moments with which she pleasantly filled space and time and, oh boy, was I glad that she finally stepped out from her inner withdrawn-ness, although to little choreographic purpose, while Gertrude Stein's accompanying words overwhelmed this piece with her wit.

"Chance" gave William Davis his chance to show us in *Crayon* how far one can go and get away with it because despite its improvisational character it was of one piece and held my attention. When he came back with Barbara Lloyd (a lovely dancer with a quivering sensitivity) and did his *Field*, he went far afield, went out on a limb—or was it limbo already?—, attuned to wave lengths lost to my auditory sense and intellect.

I dig Yvonne. Her nuttiness has method and Gestalt. There is a male will in her wedded to a fantastic caprice. There is something fresh about her, I mean both connotations: refreshing and forward, bold and obtrusive. In her *Duet Section* with Trisha Brown she has taken a model as model, put sense into posing and caught the tragic aspect of clowning. Her *Ordinary Dance* is extraordinary as an autobiographical outcry, in its dramatic fusion of word and movement, a telling story told breathlessly by Yvonne who, however, did not lose her breath nor the dynamic pulsebeat of the dance nor her audience. *Ordinary Dance* roused me from the stupor into which you fall when you protest against madness with another kind of madness for more than an hour and a half.

Before I went to this recital I thought that a square has four angles which are right. When I left I was convinced that all is relative.

Everything still is. And so was certainly my short-lived attempt at trying to speak for those who wrote mockingly on their banners "avant-garde"—a threadbare word by now if there ever was one. These dancers did not want to stop the world in order to get off because they were enraged about its readiness to embrace all trivia and trash and, above all, the bomb. Most of them wanted to play with the emergency brake and shock the world with a new hoax.

In March 1963 I went so far as to conform linguistically to the ambiance created by these then young dancers. Yvonne Rainer asked me at that time why I chose this obviously imitative tone and mood in my articulation. Stunned by her question I only then fully realized that I used this vernacular as a crutch to help myself narrowing the gap between a fading yesterday and a seeming tomorrow. Though I knew of the great risk involved, I half-heartedly bravoed what I hoped would be a new trend.

Did I also want to say yes to an uncertain daring as so many critics have done over the decades only to avoid finding themselves isolated from the rest? I doubt it. I clearly remember that I was impressed by this young dancer who called herself Yvonne Rainer. I hoped that she would be able to unfold and succeed. I saw in her a rare talent that one encounters only once in a while and I envisioned the possibility she might fill a ready-made vacuum.

She had betrayed my hopes. She had insulted my eyes with vagaries and vulgarities (such as stag movies accompanying a non-dance or the exploitation of nudity for the sheer pleasure of shocking whatever square would still hold on to established aesthetic tenets). A series of bad artistic experiences may at times corrode one's patience and beliefs. What else could have lured me into a trap of exaggerated hope? And there was, no doubt, something in Yvonne Rainer's stage presence that conveyed, if nothing else, a sense of otherness.

Not only a critic can fail an artist—so many claim to be misunderstood, and some are— but also the artist can fail a critic. If one day they shine brilliantly despite a critic's scorn and doubt, they have proved the fallibility of human judgment. If at a later date they fail to live up to the critic's measure of their potentialities, they only prove that a critic is only human. The difference in Yvonne Rainer's artistic gesture captivated and fooled me as much as the fury of her fallacies made me mourn the loss of a maybe fine artist gone astray. She proclaimed:

No to spectacle no to virtuosity no to transformations and magic and make-believe no to the glamour and transcendency of the star image no to the heroic no to the anti-heroic no to trash imagery no to involvement of performer or spectator no to style no to camp no to seduction of spectator by the wiles of the performer no to eccentricity no to moving or being moved.

Breathless with bilious spit she threw herself into a torrent of negations. Yvonne Rainer taught me a serious lesson. I learned to say no to raging nonsense in the sixties and to an artistic expression of nonart. Some artists hanged themselves on the rope of their own spit.

Ever since, I promised myself to be on the lookout for a few yeses to break through the din of this age of confusion. We may again be moving closer toward new cataclysmic events. This may be one of the reasons for the arts to reflect a stronger awareness of the forces that desperately try to counteract the finality of these many noes with which we have had to live for quite some time.

1966

Notes on Inspiration
  José Limón said:

My first requisite is an idea. I cannot function with abstractions, or with what is called absolute dance. I work out of the emotions, out of human experience, mine or those about which I have read or heard. Certainly there has to be a deeply felt motive or subject . . . .

  George Balanchine said:

I approach a group of dancers on the stage like a sculptor who breathes life into his material, who gives it form and expression. I can feel them like clay in my hands. The minute I see them, I become excited and stimulated to move them. I do not feel I have to prepare myself. All I know is the music with which I am at least as intimately acquainted as a conductor of a symphony with his score. Of course, the contours of an outline, though sometimes only vaguely, exist in my mind—certain visualizations from listening to the score.

The thought of finding the source of inspiration and discerning how much of that inspiration becomes a part of the creative process has always fascinated me. Every artist would probably have a different explanation for how inspiration and creation work within him. Mary Wigman, who thought a great deal about these phenomena, envisioned both as an entity divided into two parts: the intoxicating moment of conception and the ecstasy of the work process. For her the initial spark—from wherever it may have come—must continue to glow through the sober considerations of craftsmanship.

For a long time Frederick Ashton was obsessed by the idea of a ballet on Arthur Rimbaud, one containing things that could hardly materialize onstage: the poet's short existence full of wild adventures, a series of hallucinations, a dreamworld hiding and saying everything. Ashton read and reread Rimbaud's enigmatic poems, works painted with colorful sounds. He listened to Benjamin Britten, who had set some of the poems to music. The moment of conception was over, Ashton lived with a vision, was haunted by it, but something—let's call it hesitation, or was it fear of failure?—kept him from starting to work on it. He needed a catalyst, someone who would make him do it. It was Lincoln Kirstein, a minor poet himself. The ballet was Ashton's unique *Illuminations*.

There are astounding contrasts in the way inspiration finds fulfillment. Birgit Cullberg confessed in an interview that her ballet *Medea*—a great success in 1950—was inspired by a feeling of powerless fury and a merciless wish for revenge. At that time she had gone through a divorce. In her feverish anger she took revenge onstage. Poor Jason!

Another interview, this one with Jerome Robbins, shows the intricacies of inspiration from its fortuitous angle. *Dances at a Gathering* came about when Robbins began to work on a pas de deux for Eddie Villella and Pat McBride. His imagination, fueled by Chopin's music, caught fire, and the movement ideas overwhelmed him. It was mere joy for him to let things flow and find their own form.

Sometimes inspiration works as if by relay. Immediately after World War II, a book-long poem, *The Age of Anxiety*, was published by W. H. Auden. He wrote it in despair over the alienation of man from himself and from his fellowmen, over the emptiness around us and the fear of the void within us. Auden took his cue from the Existentialists who had taken the absurdity of life as their point of departure. This poem inspired Leonard Bernstein to compose his Symphony Nr. 2 which, in turn, led to Robbins' version of *The Age of Anxiety*, choreographed for The New York City Ballet.

A similar inspirational pattern followed Stéphane Mallarmé's *L'Après-midi d'un Faune*. Mallarmé's reaction to Claude Debussy's musical setting was "This music enlarges the emotion of my poem and makes the scene much livelier than any color could have achieved." Nijinsky's ballet *The Afternoon of a Faun* had a far more direct inspirational source in Léon Bakst's enthusiasm about a choreographic tableau, a Greek frieze in movement as a two-dimensional ballet. This idea came to him while journeying through Greece with Diaghilev. Also, Bakst seemed to have suggested the archaic steps and poses for Nijinsky's choreography, in which he tried to imitate the ancient Greek images. (Dame Marie Rambert tells us that he was very intent on achieving this imitation; he reiterated to his nymphs "No expression in your face, you must look as if you were asleep, with open eyes—like statues!")

This famous, scandal-ridden production offers another facet of inspiration: a dance work leading to another choreographic conception. Robbins was able to give a totally modern face to the subject of the *Faun* and Debussy's score by limiting the story to a pas de deux and transposing it into a dance studio. What a stroke of genius it was to have moved the almost identical story into a narcissistic ambience, with a slight kiss on the ballerina's cheek as a substitute for the nymph's scarf! Robbins practiced a similar trick in *The Cage* whose point of departure was the second act of *Giselle*: the female being out to destroy the male—as is found with certain species of insects. It is, next to Stravinsky's *Rite of Spring,* the most devastatingly exciting ritual in the theater dance.

There are a few sources of inspiration which seem to be prefabricated; they are a part of our mental life: the Bible, mythology, and Shakespeare (this sequence seems to be quite accurate). Historic material limps far behind (with the exception of Martha Graham's output, if you take for instance the apotheosis of the pioneer spirit in *Appalachian Spring* based on historic source material). To all this the nineteenth-century ballet is an exception. Its roots are in the melodrama, in the transcendental, in the fairy-tale world. In the course of the century it also got its material from folklore and exoticism, as a throwback to the eighteenth century. The fairy tale took the place of mythology which held a life-sustaining power for the balletic libretti through the centuries.

Quite a few poets inspired the choreographer (Lorca, Dickinson, Dylan Thomas, Tennessee Williams), but no one exerted the same magic attraction as Shakespeare. How many versions there are of *A Midsummer Night's Dream* and *Romeo and Juliet* and *Othello* (from Viganò to Limón)! It seems most difficult to reshape *King Lear* and *The Tempest* choreographically. Myra Kinch tried it, with Ted Shawn as Lear. He thought one must have lived a long time, must have braved many challenges in life to be able to dance this role. But Erick Hawkins as a young man did it in Graham's *The Eye of Anguish* and he remarked that it is not enough to report on the tragic, on the neurosis of our time—this is without any value. Only if the dancer grasps the ritual of tragedy can he really give Gestalt to this part.

The Tempest was already danced in 1834 as a full-length ballet at the Paris Opéra. About this production of *La Tempête* Gautier said in a sarcastic tone "The best one can say about this ballet is that it is a ballet."* It was choreographed by Jean Coralli, the man, who,

---

*Rudolf Nureyev choreographed a one-act version of *The Tempest* on December 2, 1982, with the Royal Ballet at Covent Garden. He used the incidental music which Tchaikovsky composed for the play. Nureyev handled this difficult material extremely well and harvested many kudos.

some years later, gave *Giselle*—together with Jules Perrot—its stage image. This production, however, was important for Fanny Elssler's debut in it at the Opéra.

Hamlet has been a favorite theme for a surprising number of German choreographers after the second World War, and it's all been pretty much experimental stuff. Could there be any connecting link between Hamlet's ambivalent character and the German mind feeling an urgency to close the gap between yesterday and another tomorrow? The only British *Hamlet* was choreographed in 1942 by Robert Helpman. It was a one-act ballet with Margot Fonteyn as Ophelia: a kaleidoscopic sequence of the events in Hamlet's life, shaped in nightmarish flashbacks.

It could be that Shakespeare's work penetrates the secret of our being, revealing to us the poetic uniqueness and dramatic oddness of our existence. Perhaps he edges closer to us again in our century. "The time is out of joint," is being said in *Hamlet*, and this relates acutely to our own era. In the interchanging game between inspiration and ourselves, we must not overlook the role played by the sociocultural climate of the epoch. For the medieval artisan there was no self-glorification in his art, it was a spiritual experience in which the divine was celebrated for the weal of the community. One can probably see the *Reigen* as a symbol of it. The Renaissance created the personality cult. From the fifteenth century on there was no longer any limitation set for the scope of man's imagination.

Perhaps one could refer to inspiration as a time-bound phenomenon. Did Isadora Duncan not have to appear on the scene to bring disorder to the traces of balletic development at a time when it was in bad shape? Was it mere coincidence that her soul-searching experiences coincided with Freud's probing of the soul? Some artists have been on a confrontation course with inspiration. Ruth St. Denis, for instance. Was it really the goddess Isis on a cigarette poster that triggered an instantaneous notion of what she wanted to do? Can inspiration issue from such a banal experience and turn an insignificant actress into a fascinating dancer overnight? (Was not at that time a general trend to escape

Ruth St. Denis in one of her ecstatic gestures. Author's collection.

to the East noticeable, with writers and painters such as Pierre Loti and Paul Gauguin?) Or did the goddess Isis foresee she would have to found a school from which would emerge inspired dancers changing the face of the dance world?

A scene that took place in Russia early this century shows how coincidentally inspiration can work. A young, not yet famous ballerina asked a colleague of hers to choreograph a solo for her which should not be longer than five minutes or so. The man was

Michel Fokine, a mandolin enthusiast who just had been busy practicing Saint-Saens' *Swan*. He looked at her delicate figure and immediately thought she would be a perfect swan. "How about this music?" he asked. She also thought it might be fun to impersonate a swan. Fokine told in an interview how it worked on the spot, that it was almost like an improvisation. He showed her what he meant, she imitated his movements behind him. Then she danced it alone, and he merely corrected some of her gestures and positions. The immortal solo, *The Dying Swan*, was born.

We can never know what may actually lead to an artistic accomplishment, or how and at which point the spark of inspiration is ignited. In the last analysis, it is a spark filched from the Creator; for the result of this spark, the artist may be tortured by his own critical pangs of conscience, judged by his fellowmen, and honored or damned by those who follow him.

After the conclusion of each work one should not wonder about how one achieved it. One should accept inspiration as something that just happened to come one's way. One should leave to the chance of destiny what happens to it. The work speaks for the inexpressible about it; its spirit is the measure of all things and of all being. Nietzsche said about the process of inspiration "One should accept it without asking where it comes from." Martin Buber added "Maybe one should not ask, but at least one should say thank you!"

1967

There is the well-known prejudice that ballet is a nice and gentle art form, destined to beautify our hours and to make us happy with its visual virtues. This has been the case most of the time. Even in its most Dionysian moments ballet has kept its Apollonian face. Basically it stayed away from pronouncing any social message, it hardly ever wanted to get involved in the reality of everyday experience.

As a matter of fact, despite its feudal origin, ballet survived the two great revolutions, the French and the Russian, with grand jetés. And it was especially in these two countries where the modernization of ballet dragged its feet. But being attuned to the twentieth-century-spirit does not yet mean coming to grips with reality or attempting to send a social message across the footlights. This was essentially left to a few barefoot dancers.

Of course, we could cite Kurt Jooss's *The Green Table*. But Jooss combined "modern" and classical ballet; he spoke in the idiomatic language of expressionism prevalent in the twenties with a balletic accent. He created it one year before Hitler seized power, it was the greatest indictment of the future to come, well comparable to the many anti-war novels that appeared at that time. Mary Wigman reacted to man's past and future madness with the production of *Das Totenmal* in 1930. These were the most decidedly social statements at that time.

In those years the modern dance in America was still in its infancy, and neither in the late twenties nor in the thirties was any serious social statement made by any of the young dancers. These American dancers were not motivated to cope with these problems; they never felt the immediacy of danger. None of the important dance works done in those days even reflected the social upheaval caused by the Great Depression. Was the dancer's mind too much preoccupied with his ego or the folklore of his environment or immersed in the struggle to find himself in his own new craft? Was it safer to deal with mythology and history far removed in time and distance?

Wigman grew while taking issue with man in his time. Balanchine choreographed Brecht's *The Seven Deadly Sins* in 1933, a ballet showing man's greed and hypocrisy. Tudor came somewhat late. His *Echo of Trumpets* depicted the cruelty in the devastation of a city by militant forces. It was, however, a weak echo of trumpets. The best social comment came from Robbins in his musical *West Side Story*.

Cunningham rebelled against the zeitgeist. His was far more a protest against the form and content of the then prevailing dance concepts than a social outcry. Those who followed him, the dancers of the Judson Dance Theater, jumped from excesses of nudity into the political arena as a protest against the bourgeois square and the Vietnam war. Limón came up with a noble gesture against man's inhumanity with his *Missa Brevis*. However, Anna Sokolow's *Rooms* remains for me the highlight of social protest. She has always had her finger on the pulse beat of the time. *Rooms* creates the no-exit feeling of man, his lonesomeness and despair. I also remember Sophie Maslow's *Poem* as a reflection of the Beatnik generation. In it, she caught the spirit of a lost youth, its powerless fury, a longing that cannot be crushed. But this work did not have the incisive power of *Rooms*. Then, of course, some black companies (it's gradually become a must for all of them) dramatize their racial problem; they are at their best when their personalized outcry is muted into a generally valid social statement.

After all, dance can express what plagues mankind. That it is so rarely the case must be because the mere joy of movement has, by itself, a liberating quality and escapes with us into a world in which we can easily forget the world in which we live.

1968

All her life Ruth St. Denis tried to bring some light into the darkness of our day. It may have started as hesitant hope, but as soon as she was immersed in the incense of Eastern spirit and had captured the mind of such a philosopher-poet as Hugo von Hofmannsthal*, her hope turned into faith and faith forced upon her a missionary valour with a touch of defiance. Not everyone can believe in a Providential choice, or that the course of his life

---

*Hugo von Hofmannsthal wrote about her: "In her motionless eyes stands a mysterious smile: the smile of the Buddha statue. It is a smile which is not of this world . . . . It is a smile from which the soul has flown to another world . . . ."

has been mapped out long in advance and with a higher purpose
to it—but she could.

She not only danced, she also wrote, and could use words like
the Eternal Now, the Church of Divine Dance, and the Eternal
Presence in a most disarming mood; she saw such words as Beauty,
Art, and Nature capitalized, whether in print or spoken, and
would see herself working in "the Lord's vineyard of Beauty." The
spiritual manifestations in life were her brothers and sisters. And
there was a majestic magic about her. She came right out of the
ambiance of an art nouveau world and never quite lost that touch
of endearing flourish, borne on the flight from reality. But to call
her unreal would do her a bitter wrong, for she remained real in a
totally unreal manner.

When she was in her eighties I had the pleasure of coming
closer to her while helping her compile and prune some of her
writings, mapping out with her synopses after synopses with which
she tried to solicit the help of politicians to do something for a
dignified living of the artist. And in one of her "current
biographies" which she sent out to her friends and "to a few
chosen enemies" (I loved her humor), she could write:

"High over the heads of wrangling political ambassadors sails the
benediction of Beauty. (That is a good sentence. I just made it up.)"

We spoke at the same panel on the Sacred Dance Movement at
Riverside Church. She was praising the gesture of poetic piety,
while I was trying to assess the question of artistry in the sacred
dance and expressing my fear about the great danger involved that
something phony may be used to heighten something holy. I also
will never forget the day when I appeared together with her in a
small downtown theater and she spoke of some kind of freedom
of the soul. What she spoke about did not matter as much as the
way in which she delivered a theatrically exciting performance,
projecting her white-haired beauty, wrapped into a flowing
costume which she skillfully manipulated. When she raised her

arm more than her voice, her seemingly elongated body reached out in gentle ecstasy.

When Ted Shawn once praised her, saying, "She conceived a whole new system of movement, a revolutionary school of dance . . . ," he certainly shot beyond the target. She was far more a prophetess than a pioneer, the saleswoman of a dream rather than a dancer. She happened to stand at the gates leading into a new world and knew how to open them. She had the advantage of being beautiful (no minor merit in the process of succeeding) and of having a magnetic personality. Ted Shawn was the better teacher of the two, and that they both had a school and some outstanding students was historic coincidence. What, however, was not coincidental was Ruth St. Denis' contagious inspirational spirit, which had a unique claim to greatness for whose real fulfillment those to whom she gave birth had to be indebted.

1969

All that has been going on onstage this season has the quality of pleasing, rarely of exciting, mediocrity which may be what our time asks for and deserves. There are still many issues of general nature more dramatic and significant for the development of the theater than the plays or dance events themselves. The latest Ford Foundation report gives us a rather dark picture as to future subsidies for the theaters. It also calls our cultural explosion a myth, a fact I have always suspected. The good mediocre fare, with its popular appeal, will show rewarding results at the box office. The unusual creation—even though it may be faulty—needs subsidy badly.

Off-Broadway and the legitimate avant-garde is needed to keep the theater from turning sterile. The young and unproven need attention. Attention means a chance to be heard and seen, and this takes subsidies. Nowadays there is not much difference between drama and dance, as evidenced by Clive Barnes, who was appointed as dance and daily drama reviewer by the *New York Times*. I happen to like his reviews because—among so many badly written reviews in all papers—they are at least highly readable and, without any pretenses, passionately personal in their relatively good judgment. Some prejudice is thrown in for good measure. New York has always been the Mecca of the dance, but Barnes has greatly helped to put the dance on the map of America. He may one day be crucified for it.

The role of a critic is often a critical and mostly a crucial one. Both Barnes and I have put great hopes in a young dancer-choreographer called Yvonne Rainer, who created a storm that spilled over the proverbial tea pot. To spite the squares and heterosexual majority she ran some dirty films during one of her non-dance creations sponsored by the Ford Foundation. In one of my reviews I called her presentation "pornographic Kindergarten." Barnes not only attacked her, but also and mainly the Ford Foundation for having lent its ear and money to the producers' choice of Yvonne Rainer. This caused a storm of protest which will continue for some time, since, in his defense, Barnes asked to end all "subsidy of mediocrity." Money should "only go where it will do the most good" which excludes the "unproven," who, in Clive Barnes' opinion, will find in not being supported "a fine incentive . . . to prove himself."

This is a well chosen clarion call against mediocrity, which is now and supposedly has always been, rampant, but if heeded—and after the Ford Foundation's latest report there is no doubt that it will be heeded—it may easily have the sound of a death knell for some struggling young artists of great potential. For instance, there are several organizations, supported by Foundation money, which give the yet unproven artists badly needed guidance and a platform to prove themselves.

What Yvonne Rainer did in a prankish mood was only a logical consequence and extension of the near-orgies of The Living Theater's *Paradise Now* and of Richard Schechner's *Dionysus in 69*—which both received a friendly nod, though with some reservations, from the dance and drama critic of the *Times*. The news about *Paradise Now* being filmed, a non-play whose pulse beat entirely depends on spontaneous audience participation, made me shudder. By its very nature, its cinematic version must belie the very message it pretended to have and can only glorify the phony and the spiritual depravity of our time.

We must not forget that we live in the Philip-Roth age of *Portnoy's Complaint*, whose author made a million dollars on this book before it was even published. It is an apotheosis of spermatic filth, it sees the tests in life's testes, but it is well written with the inky bile of self-hatred. It is a potential potboiler for the movies and, perhaps, television, since it proclaims—while celebrating sex—that sex does not pay. Well, even at the risk that *Portnoy's Complaint* will be dramatized for the stage, and it very well may be, and that Yvonne Rainer will come up with another spit and spite, let us not draw a line between the proven and unproven artist because, too often, mediocrity hides behind the former and a great talent may wait to unfold in the latter. Companies and individual artists need the patronage of Foundation money which, in the last analysis, is the money of the people, whose everyday existence should become more meaningful through the arts.

Publishing more and more books exposed me to being at the receiving end of criticism. One must learn to live with the strangest reactions, reactions evolving from convoluted minds. A critic blasted my biography of Hanya Holm: "I must be critical of Walter Sorell's biography of Hanya Holm. He knows his subject well—perhaps too well. I can sympathize with his problems, yet I can't help wishing he had tried harder to cope with them. Friendship is a beautiful thing, but we are talking about biography which aims at a kind of truth."

This statement implies that I have not spoken the truth or perhaps not "nothing but the truth, so may this critic help me!" It is true, and I have never denied, that I have known the subject of my biography. (By the way, how can you write a biography if you are not pretty familiar with your subject?) I also do not deny that friendship is a beautiful thing. I have appreciated knowing Hanya. I have not yearned or asked to write this book. I was asked to do it. After having done some work on Mary Wigman, I was considered by Bueno de la Torre, senior editor of Wesleyan University Press, to be the most likely choice for this task. I have tried to be as objective and factual as possible and have used the assessment of many other people, such as Walter Terry, Alwin Nikolais or Don Redlich, people who have not only watched the constant growth of Hanya's accomplishments, but also knew her intimately well from working with her. My critic poked fun of the too frequent use of my tape recorder.

None of the other critiques were negative. For instance, John Martin said in the *New York Times*:

It is good to have Hanya Holm rescued from the mysterious and invisible status of choreographer and brought into tangible focus both as a person and as a master and teacher of movement. Her vast knowledge and intuition in this field—how to produce movement in the individual body, how to set it in its proper spatial and musical relationships, how to manipulate it into communicative form—have done much to shape the concept of the creative dance in this country and have provided it with an authoritative basis as a professional art. In treating of this crucial but less familiar area, Mr. Sorell's book performs its greatest service.

Of course, there is no book (as there is no work of art or performance) which you cannot condemn for some reason. A student of mine at Columbia University evaluated Goethe's *Faust* as the greatest bore in dramatic literature. If you are set to do so, you can easily send Dante's *Divine Comedy* into its literary purgatory.

Criticism—an unavoidable part of the complex game of life—is often confused with the art of finding flaws and faults. I am convinced that you can find fault with anything the human mind, hand, or body can create. For years I have conducted classes in criticism. My point of departure has been integrity, my aim to reach a balanced account of appreciation as much as depreciation. Criticism is one of the most crucial exercises we can indulge in—

and usually it is, to a great extent predetermined by the critic's mental make-up, by his artistic background, by his likes and dislikes.

The creative effort is an act of faith in oneself and in one's art, it is a deed done; something is put into the world that has not existed before. Out of reasons, even unknown to himself, a critic may feel compelled to kill this effort. The critic must live with his conscience. Some critics lock their conscience conveniently into the closet of their minds.

1970

Martha Graham's company danced at the Brooklyn Academy of Music. It was an important event for more than one reason. After forty-four years as a performer Martha did not appear with her group anymore. Moreover, some of her major works of the thirties and forties were revived and proved how essential it is to keep more of her dance creations alive. It is no longer a startling statement to say that her intensely and consistently poetic approach and attitude give her work the stamp of greatness, but it was a thought I took with me from these performances.

She, like very few other choreographers, has been able to create the visualization of "the interior landscape" of her characters in their own divided self and in relation with their world. She makes us hear the fearful and hopeful pacings of their hearts. A great deal of their lives—and they are mostly famous heroines—is remembered from the past or projected into an uncertain, sometimes historically established, future, but all this, focused on a pertinent nowness on stage, is highly dramatic in its lyricism and beautifully lyrical in its drama.

Two of Martha Graham's most ambitious works were revived. Both dealt with figures of literature. *Letter to the World*, first done in 1940, was a breakthrough into a then unconventional balletic dramatization in which Emily Dickinson, in her dual appearance as

Martha Graham in Lamentation. *Drawing by the author.*

the one who dances and the one who speaks, is caught in the light
of her inner world. She is remembered as a poet of brief lyrical
bursts of singing and capricious lines uttered with emotional
intensity and sarcastic fleetness.

It was a stroke of genius to personify Emily in two images, the
one who lives in the landscape of her silent suffering and the one
who makes this life bearable by escaping into the quick motion of

poetic lines. Jean Erdman portrayed the one who speaks, and she spoke well, indeed, accentuating her words with humorous quirks of movements which created the needed counterpart to the wistfully tragic existence of Emily Dickinson which Pearl Lang danced with great intensity and beautiful feeling. She was consistently creating the drama of Emily's inner landscape with the frightened wonder and resigned incredulity in her gestures and movements. Of all the dancers who stepped into Martha's roles I felt that Pearl Lang was more her own self without falling into the pattern of imitation.

Jane Dudley protrayed the terrifying figure of the Ancestress as she did in 1940 and pretty much repeated her striking charac-terization. At certain points she is overpowering in the drama she enacts in Emily's life. In this work as in *Deaths and Entrances* each minor part is vibrant with movement which is clearly defined for each character. Graham's sense of theatricality can best be seen in the weaving of patterns and in the skillful blending of contrasting elements, of repetitions underlining a thought-feeling but stopping in midair at the right moment.

This has become particularly clear to me while seeing *Deaths and Entrances* in which the experiences of the Brontë sisters are visualized in their real unreality. With time denied its division into years but given a vision in depth, the real and unreal fade into the sight of inner realizations. Little objects are magnified by awakening memories and dreams, fears and hopes. They play an especially potent part in the symbolism and meaningfulness of the movement.

Mary Hinkson took over Martha's role, and she was able to recreate this difficult part beautifully, almost intuitively reliving Martha's breath and pulse beat. As Hinkson proved in *El Penitente*, she has a high degree of malleability, easily feeling her way into a choreographer's visions. Because and in spite of such—shall we call it imitative—quality (which does not take away anything from her astounding abilities as a performer) there were moments in which I was longing for Martha Graham to be there on stage. But there were also passages in *Appalachian Spring* in which I felt that

Martha Graham in Acrobats of God. *Set by Isamu Noguchi.*
Photo: Oleaga. Author's collection.

Ethel Winter had brought an inimitable glow to the role of The
Bride. Moreover, Matt Turney, undoubtedly a wonderful dancer,
simply has not the emotional format and personality to do justice
to *Phaedra*.

There are some of the Graham works which will never be the
same without the Martha of the forties and fifties, but this should
not deceive us into thinking that these works should not be
revived. I am not certain that all the revivals we have seen were
equally significant. However enticing *Every Soul Is A Circus* is as a
lighthearted excursion into humor, one of Martha's fortes, her

efforts in this direction were crowned by a far better and more mature work: *Acrobats of God.*

This year is very likely opening a new era for Martha Graham, resigning finally to the biological facts of life at the age of seventy-five and accepting herself in the part of the proven choreographer of her conceits. *Acrobats of God* may have been her most fitting final farewell, a role very much tailored to suit her personality. Probably this is one work which should not be recast and only kept alive in the memory of those who were privileged in having seen Martha in it.

Diary Notes:
1971–1984

1971

It may have begun with George Balanchine's invitation to Martha Graham to join him in choreographing *Episodes* in which Miss Graham did the first part and Mr. B. the second, now the only section still in the repertory of the company. If memory does not trick me, both parts went well together—and that Martha Graham's choreographic contribution was later discarded may have had purely technical reasons.

It is amazing to see how much the modern dance could influence the classical ballet which had its twentieth-century face lifted through the impact of the barefoot dancers crying out for self-expression. The modern dance's *raison d'être* is the unlimited inner freedom to express thought-feelings and to take issue with the world within and without. It is neither psychologically nor technically equipped to mount a classical ballet. Even though I heard Balanchine say that he did not see any difference between modern and classical dance, that he could only see a difference in good or bad dancing, I take this statement as a generous gesture on his part. Ballet, an art form with a century-old tradition, can afford to play with the idea of trying a production of a modern dance work. But when the two get really together, one finds that there is a very noticeable difference in attitude, in nuance, in acting and technique, in the execution of a gesture weighty with meaning—which all contributes to a different dance experience.

I am inclined to think that it is a basic philosophy of life which underlines the discrepancies more easily than their points of likeness and oneness. The dances never look quite the same when done by a modern dance or ballet company. And all this has little or nothing to do with the fact that nowadays most modern dancers go through a balletic training and a number of ballet dancers began their careers with modern dance companies, or that modern dance has moved closer to ballet technique and ballerinas roll on the floor, the fourth dimension discovered by modern dance.

Since modern dance has always been financially weaker than

ballet and needed exposure to a more general, i.e. non-dancing audience badly, one can only applaud a ballet company's policy to incorporate modern dance pieces in its repertory. The Joffrey Ballet triumphed with Kurt Jooss's *The Green Table*, not only because it is a timeless creation, but also because the choreographer was one of the first to fuse "modern" and ballet successfully. From the very beginning, Jooss approached his creation with the vision of using modern's dramatic expressiveness with balletic technique.

Merce Cunningham's *Summerspace*, when re-choreographed for The New York City Ballet, achieved a fluidity and precision it has never had with his own company, but it also lost some of the innate casualness which is a vital feature of Cunningham's work. But in its total impact it fared pretty well.

José Limón's *The Moor's Pavane* and *The Traitor* have become a part of some ballet companies, also of The American Ballet Theatre's repertory. We have to be grateful for that because the former is a masterpiece in composition, dramatic impact and choreographic texture—a creative totality rarely achieved by modern dance works including ballets. The latter is less tightly structured, but creates courageously and successfully a dramatic tableau of the greatest story ever told.

Limón has a very personal way of communicating the inner drama of his characters. There is a certain grandeur, with a touch of the archaic, in his gestures; there is an intensity in the rapport between the dancers on an emotional and intellectual level, and there is a specific ambience created through emotional communication of the dramatic intent through facial expression as much as the body's movement. At their best, his works—such as *The Moor's Pavane* and *Missa Brevis* (which might have been a better choice than *The Traitor*)— reach out for a "mystic communion with heaven" (a phrase culled from one of Limón's essays).

It may be due to insufficient rehearsal time—I fervently hope so—that little of all this has been accomplished so far by the staging of Limón's works by The American Ballet Theatre. The dancers learned the steps and learned them well. With each performance the dances will undoubtedly become more fluid. But these are prerequisites. It seems the dancers knew what they were doing—but not the why's and how's.

In *The Moor's Pavane* they dance rather well with one another, but the piece's dramatic impact will only be conveyed when they can get the feeling of dancing against each other while being together, when pauses and accents will gain the sharpness they need, when the stately flow of the Pavane will almost seem to give way to the volcanic power of the underlying emotions.

I still feel—that both ballet and modern dance can only gain from such unions. But the ballet dancer will have to accept the idea that it isn't necessarily technical proficiency alone that helps recreate the poetic essence of a work originally conceived in terms of the modern expressionistic dance.

Asking my students what they know about Helen Tamiris, I see their blank stare. No reaction. Five years after her death she is really dead. Not even forgotten. Not known. How fast time can pass us by! How great is the ignorance of our past!

All the more will my memory have to love her, to cuddle her in my thoughts, this lovely creature who was precious to many and most important for the modern dance, for whose independent development she had been fighting valiantly and with the spirit of a desperate heart. How often did she call for action:

We have produced a rich, creative, new Dance-Art. The masterpiece of the past must cease to be treasured memories and re-emerge as performed, living realities. New works should be commissioned. Our skilled dancers, performing in the works of a variety of choreographers, will grow and flourish. We must consolidate efforts of the last thirty years. In this way we will move into the future of modern dance as a genuine expression of America.

She feared that the accomplishments of the first three generations of modern dancers could be destroyed by the very means which were once so fruitful: by ignoring the "common tie that binds all the creators of the modern dance." She overlooked that the modern dancer would—and perhaps could—not yield an iota from the copyright on his or her individuality. Martha Graham's famous advice to the young dancer was that she had only one competitor, namely herself. But she cannot help going out into a competitive jungle life in which she must fight for approval and fear defeat. On second thought, Graham's maxim envisioned the inner struggle of the dancer aiming at and utilizing in her work all the potentialities of her individuality, thus barring the way to any common, cooperative action. When Helen Tamiris had a vociferous adversary in her "call to action"—then the voice came from the camp of Martha Graham.

I remember Helen Tamiris as a spontaneous, magnanimous human being who could see the woods despite their many trees—without denying the beauty of each single leaf.

Zürich. It is not necessarily world-shaking news when a ballerina takes leave from the stage and her career. But the way in which she takes her last bow and asks the divine engineer to have the spotlight dimmed on her, sheds light on her personality. How many fanfares will the press agents let loose to proclaim far in advance that the irrevocably last performance of the world-famous "so-and-so" will take place "then" and "there".

Gaye Fulton has never received the same intense public attention as a Fonteyn, Fracci, Ulanova, or Makarova—to name only a few. But she danced herself into fame in London, Washington, and particularly in Zürich where, for many years, fourteen altogether, she was the *ballerina assoluta.* Therefore, it was only fitting that she chose the Opera in Zürich as the place of her farewell performance.

Did the papers announce it? Was it made known to all her fans? No, nobody knew about it (except the Direktor of the Opera who wanted to turn her last performance into a festive event, a gesture she declined). She appeared in one of her favorite parts, one which seemed to be cut to measure for her: Caroline in *Jardin aux Lilas*. The evening she chose was a closed performance for a well-known Swiss enterprise called Migros. After the second intermission it was announced that this would be the last performance of the British ballerina Gaye Fulton. As simple as this.

What a character to be able to leave all the sham accoutrements of fame behind her at a minute's notice and hardly any notice to her public! Did she recognize the relativity of fame? Or was this last step onstage emotionally uncomplicated? No one who has ever gloried in applause can easily do without it. And yet, she took her last bow with a gesture of routine as ever before. We shall hardly learn the truth about what she felt that moment. Was it a gratifying feeling of triumph over herself? In withdrawing from the stage she may only have wished to find out who that real creature was behind Caroline and Clara, Cinderella and Miss Julie, Desdemona and Romeo's Juliet, Odette, and Giselle, and all the other fictitious realities onstage. Whatever she may find out will probably remain her secret, even if she should decide on writing her memoirs one day (which doesn't seem likely). All I am left with is the impression that she is one of those rare creatures known as *Mensch*.

1972

The day on earth is short and seems even shorter when memories of a great artist who was a great human being are crowded into a short memorial performance. The performance opened with the Chaconne from the Sonata in D Minor for unaccompanied violin by Bach, who meant so much to Limón. Bach and Michelangelo, Shakespeare and Goya, were the men whose creative gestures reconciled—in Limón's mind—man and his deeds with man and his dreams.

Limón, who shunned the trivial and had an enviable flair for everything monumental and magnificent in life, could not have been honored better than by a performance of Doris Humphrey's *Day on Earth*, a work she created for him in 1947.

On this occasion it mattered little how good the performances were. They were adequate and, for the older ones who still remember José in it, Letitia Ide as the woman, Miriam Pander as the young girl, and Melissa Nicolaides as the child, the performance was able to recall the great moments of this simple, but all-embracing work of man's day on earth, his first love, his life with his wife and daughter, the playful joys, the heartbreaking pains, as it was once danced by the man in whose memory this *Day on Earth* was performed.

This work extolls what José Limón strongly believed in: the beauty of being and the dignity with which to express one's feelings and thoughts in life and on stage. Doris Humphrey's spirit greeted Limón's with that greatness of simplicity which, in the eyes of Limón's idols, has always been the simplicity of greatness.

This, I suppose, was why we gathered there: to think of his day on earth and to remind ourselves of our debt to those days of his.

José Limón moved in an inimitable, intense manner, with a sideways attitude, as if an animal in him would wait, lie in ambush, then move, jump or run toward its goal, full of the awareness of the moment, clearly stating what had to be said. He was tall, and his body, despite its leanness, appeared strong. His legs were long and well formed, his hips compact, his chest deep and his shoulders broad. His arms and hands were leading the motion. In moments of tension of great emotion he would thrust them out straight, as if pushing a huge and weighted object: the elbows seemed elongated, the hands flexed back at the wrists. Those hands of his were an eloquent voice of his body. I felt as though they would open and complete each gesture and movement. They were the first strings in the orchestra of his body. His hands not only breathed like his lungs, they also breathed the spirit of his thoughts.

His hair was soon turning gray and thinning, but I remember most clearly his restless, deep-set eyes, questioning, framed by dark

José Limón and Lucas Hoving in The Traitor. *Photo: Arnold Eagle.*
Author's collection.

circles. His was an unforgettable face, somewhat hollowed, but strong and vital and yet it was marked by an unearthly quality. His was a timeless face, as if a sculptor had tried to model him after the image of an Aztec prince. This was where his great nobility came from, from far in space and time: a Renaissance man having suddenly risen from Indian soil. José Limón could lift his arms, standing in the lofty fifth position of *Concerto Grosso*—or he could crouch low, head to the ground like a wounded animal, arms hugged tightly to his torso in fear and despair, as in *The Moor's Pavane*.

His nobility was best mirrored by his courtly gestures toward women, but also toward men; his entire bearing had a touch of otherness. He was a living anachronism. But behind a beautiful facade of formalism lurked the image of violence and men locked in mortal conflict. He needed drama to soothe his own clashing feelings, to unshackle his controlled anger. He freed his *The Traitor* from its mere religious connotations, lifting the theme to a level where betrayal itself was put on trial. Though he had broken away from the Catholic faith which had a strong hold on him in his youth, and had forsaken the conventions of the dogma, he returned to religious topics time and again, in such works as *The Visitation* and *There Is a Time*, unconsciously proving his suprareligious ties. What *The Moor's Pavane* is on secular terms, *Missa Brevis* is in the name of faith.

One easily throws around such epithets as "a classic of the modern dance." But, in my book, both these works tower above anything else that modern dance has brought forth in many a decade; they are masterpieces in form and content. The effort that went into everything that preceded and followed these works seems to be justified by them.

Alvin Ailey staged a short one-act play without words in the open-air Delacorte Theatre in Central Park. It was a theater piece rather than a ballet, even though two dancers, Bonnie Mathis and Dennis

Wayne, were featured in what Ailey called *Shaken Angels*. It was a sordid picture of our time emerging from the love-hate relationship of a man and woman. He was lost to dope. While she expressed her horror and despair, we saw him engrossed in the ritual of applying the needle in a repellingly realistic manner. He then pursued her with the apparent desire of forcing her to join him. She resisted. She tried to escape through all exits of the theater. He finally dragged her back to the stage, where he pushed the needle into her arm. A short pas de deux of frightful agony ensued. She died—no doubt of an overdose and shock—in his arms.

It was magnificently acted and danced. But some people booed. They could not take the naked stare of reality. That night, according to police reports, a burglar broke into the apartment where the two dancers slept, a man who desperately needed money for the stuff that kept him going. The dancers woke up and struggled with the intruder. Bonnie Mathis was stabbed in the arm. Dennis Wayne, wrestling with him, was stabbed six times. Bleeding, he dragged himself into the adjoining room where he had hidden a gun. He could still reach for it. Two shots felled the burglar. Both men were lying in their blood. Bonnie phoned the police who arrived accompanied by an ambulance and the wild screams of the siren. Curtain.

When I read about it, I looked up to the imaginary gallery, anxiously, desperately, waiting to hear thundering boos. The neighbor's radio blared forgotten tunes of an old operetta. A car hooted impatiently to get nowhere fast. I wanted to shout down that this is exactly where the world is going. But I was stunned, staring at the paper, seeing Bonnie Mathis' face in front of me, her pained expression when Dennis Wayne pushed the needle into her arm—or was it when the burglar stabbed her? I wanted to say something. "I love you . . . I loved you in . . . !" What roles she played, how magnificently she moved, what drama in her expression! How beautiful was the fury in his face, how mad each gesture with which he groped for the needle to push it into her arm—or was it the gun he groped for? Only a Shakespeare could

have found the right lines for these actor-dancers in this drama of
an everyday-reality.

There he sits in front of me, his eyes denying the time and distance
they have measured: Charles Weidman, one of those handful of
dancers who, in the early thirties, went out into a wilderness to
find themselves.

Was it much different from our time? Yes and no, he thinks.
The difference was in the time itself. It was a positive time, one
that said yes to human values. Despite the economic depression, it
was a time full of vitality, one which did not know such words as
"copout" and "dropout." There was that urgent need to express
oneself, but also to express the time in which one lived.

"Sometimes," he said, "you felt you could not help being
creative." Belief, future, and belief in the future were not yet
foreign-sounding notions. Weidman shrugs and gestures as if he
wants to say he cannot understand how any artist can be creative
without being a true believer. In those true-believer days you
ventured to do something new because you were convinced that
the past had passed. At that time there were no grants for the
dancers. Their struggle in those days helped to create what is being
taken for granted nowadays.

Charles hopes to get Doris Humphrey's *New Dance* and *Theatre
Piece* filmed. With his deep devotion for the past he is constantly
reviving some of the old dances. On his way through the country,
touring mainly the Midwest and South, he and his company will
stop at the Lexington "Y" for one evening.

With wistful sadness I recall the many evenings and afternoons
which I spent there. It was a spiritual home to me. It was like a
haven to which you could be sure your ship could find its place,
you could cast your anchor. The "Y" was once a magnetic word.
In the thirties Dr. William Kolodny became the new Education
Director there, and, with his unflinching support, it was at the "Y"
that dance history was made. Weidman's return may have a
nostalgic touch. (But everywhere in the theater now we can feel a

yearning look and clandestine groping for the past. Why don't we openly admit that at least something must have been good about the old days?) It was at the "Y" that Weidman worked on *A House Divided,* his Abraham Lincoln opus, "upstairs in the hallway between classes," he remarked. He taught there a great deal. There he premiered his Thurber piece, *Fable of Our Time* and *War Between Men and Women.* I remember it as if it had been yesterday, but it was quite some time ago when I—as a male—could still indulge in being a female chauvinist in a romantic manner.

At the "Y" I saw him first do *Lynchtown* (which was my visual introduction to the racial question), I saw him in *Flickers*—and how I chuckled when he did *And Daddy was a Fireman!* His humor was then so simple, good-natured, and convincing that he made me forget that I, a sophisticate, was not supposed to laugh about such things. I cannot forgive myself for having come too late to these shores in order to have seen him in *The Happy Hypocrite,* a delightful Max Beerbohm concoction about a corrupt roué whom love turned into a human being behind his mask. I was told it was a masterpiece of miming. Charles has a great sense of timing, and is a fine mime in a gentle humorous way.

Doris Humphrey played a decisive role in his life. They became partners in more than one way. Did they discuss the works they did together at great length? "Not at all, we were attuned to one another in such a way that we could choreograph on the spot. I lost Doris three times, and three times the loss was painful, even though it was different. In 1938 I lost her love (but she always told me, art is the only thing that matters, so I stayed on, and we continued to work and dance together). In 1948 I lost my partner in her when arthritis crippled her. In 1958 we all lost her." Then, after a pause: "In 1948 when she could no longer dance I did not have enough pieces for a full-length program, so I took Doris' *Shakers* with me on tour. A great work. So is the *New Dance,* uplifting, a healthy dance which should also be done by a ballet company."

For years now he has worked in a tiny studio in the Village. It is in such a miniscule studio that one must first overcome a claustrophobic feeling. But then Weidman talks to his small audience, and you feel at ease and at home. His gestures, the timbre of his voice are inimitable. He knows that spatial limitation can be a creative stimulus, he knows it from way back when everything they did was stripped to its most essential. He can accept the fact that he can barely seat thirty people and thinks the almost ridiculously small dancing area is an artistic challenge. Deep within he is still a pioneer.

Weidman enjoys the thought of now being able to return to the past—for however fleeting a period it may be—to show a new generation what it once meant to be fighting for an idea called modern dance American style, to revive some of his and Doris' dances and perhaps to get them on film—for another generation to see what the Nineteen Thirties were like. Just as a reminder of how it all began here, as a memento to the past, to the present and future. This is all so much idealistic thinking. I doubt that this or any future generation will honor George Santayana's wisdom that those who do not know their past will have to relive it. This and seemingly any future generation are much too busy doing their own thing. We have lost the capacity for rebelling against the past, we rebel against now, and our ambitions and dreams feel secure in today's void.

1973

New York. The houselights were dimmed. The stage was in demi-darkness. Somewhere in the corner I discovered a shape on the floor, small, in some kind of an embryonic position. Vivaldi's *The Four Seasons* began to fill the air.

What followed were minutes of motion-filled stillness until the shape slowly unfolded like a bud in spring. With deliberate pacing she liberated her body. The dancer, so it soon became clear, had decided on creating a maximum of universal experience with a minimum of movement. Like an Asian dancer, she confined herself to a small area. I thought of the concept of a Japanese painter who, with a few brushstrokes, conjures up the beauty of awakening spring. And more than that—he can open up your own dream of spring. That is what the dancer did for me.

From season to season her basic costume was slightly changed, with the help of a dresser on stage, in Asian fashion. What did not change was her choreographic notion. The quintessence of a feeling was drawn in the air with the sureness of a line, a small gesture. So pattern after pattern of simple lyricism followed season after season; the simplicity had depth.

The theme, in its obviousness, could have easily tricked the dancer into a descriptive or sentimental phrase now and then. But in their distilled form, in their suggestiveness, the movements remained rich without spilling over into emotionalism. *The Four Seasons* were a celebration of being, an emphatic yes to a life that is born to blossom so that it may grow to die. The place was Alice Tully Hall. The dancer, who choreographed and danced the work to the measure of her thoughts and the scope of her feelings, was Emily Frankel.

Vienna. There are many autumns in one's life; there are many deaths. There may be fewer springs and resurrections. But there is poetry in all seasons, even though with a difference. Autumn's poetry is rhythmically less jubilant than the one associated with spring; on the other hand, it is more intense in content. Everything becomes more meaningful when we can hear the wind brush the branches and whirl the leaves to the ground.

I remember the wind and the leaves which came falling down, turning and dancing in the air, pirouetting their farewell to the once secure heights from which they looked down with hope in their eyes and wings on their mind. I saw them lying there, hopelessly brown and withered, some of them turning around in sadness before a gust of wind picked them up again to sweep them from the ground and make them dance and dance a fantastic bourrée. I remember watching them in the gardens of Schönbrunn and wondering for the first time about the beauty of movement, about its rhythm that seemed as natural as it was casual.

I must have been twelve or thirteen years when I first learned to see, to say yes to the secrets of the silent movement that I found all around me. Without wanting to unravel those secrets I gradually realized that their meaningfulness was hidden in my own dream of their meaning. I became prepared to see the dance of life, to embrace its minutest and it broadest gestures with love in my eyes. This was my first step into the world of dance, into a world of bewildering awareness.

I had to think of it when I perused *The Dance Perspectives*, No. 52, an anthology of twentieth-century dance poems titled, *The Dance, The Dancer, and the Poem*. Jack Anderson edited this issue, and I could sense the tortures of frustration and the joys of a collector's intoxication that must have stood by his side all along. It is pretty much the same feeling which the initiated reader has when he reaches page sixty-four and the last poem in this rewarding collection. Robert Creeley praising *The Rhythm*:

> It is all a rhythm,
> from the shutting
> door, to the window
> opening.
> . . . . .
> The rhythm which projects
> from itself continuity
> bending all to its force
> from window to door,
> from ceiling to floor,
> light at the opening
> dark at the closing.

It is the continuity of the rhythm in which I have come to believe, the rhythm going on and on beyond its visually perceptible space between window and door, between light and dark. What I hope to experience within the space is not that it be filled but be fulfilled, that the rhythmic movement may not only have beauty (I do not think of any pretty prettiness), but its beauty may have the meaningfulness that lingers on and reaches beyond the fulfilled space into the dream locked in our being. If I cannot continue the dream over a poetic line or the visual line of a movement—neither has been.

Jack Anderson quotes in his prefatory essay, "Dancing and Poetry," Eliot's *Dialogue on Dramatic Poetry* in which the problems of contemporary theater are discussed. It is questionable whether we can praise twentieth-century ballet for having revived "the more formal element in drama for which we craved." Eliot, in classic fashion, has friends gathered who, over a glass of wine, speak their minds, and the one reference mentioned was prompted by the speaker's admiration for Diaghilev. But Diaghilev, without being aware of the scope of his deed, did much more than give the drama its formal element. At a moment in history when the creative minds of men were in a state of desperate ferment, anticipating with a feeling of frightened wonder the cataclysmic events to come, Diaghilev blended the cross-currents of the proved and the surprisingly new artistic statements into a challenge.

Eliot speaks his own mind when he has one of his friends say "The ballet is valuable because it has, unconsciously, concerned itself with a permanent form; it is futile because it has concerned itself with the ephemeral in content." The fact is that the intellectual of our time has turned his back on the theatrical arts in principle because he has come to distrust its cerebral power and integrity. For all we know, most of them may have done so during many past periods, perhaps with the exception of certain Romantics in the mid-nineteenth century. But only those men of letters who see the poetry in visual terms can love and serve the dance. Gautier and Marianne Moore painted with words. They could see the lasting poetic image in the ephemeral.

This is also where Eliot errs. Dancing is not necessarily content per se, but content visualized and expressed through the poetic translation of the artist's experiences. Louis Horst comes to mind. He had another word for it when he asked from the dance creation the ultimate, that is, the secret of the dancing soul revealed. He used the term "mystery." What else can we expect from the arts but the revelation of mystery? What else can we expect from a fully consciously lived life but to find through awareness its poetry? Those who have never sensed the poetry of life will never know of the mystery that can be hidden in a work of art—damn it, even the mystery in the art demystified. Did not Gertrude Stein say that art is art is art? Well, she would have done so, had she not thought of the image of the rose.

New York. We live in a fast-paced world. We are restless. We crave for excitement and the drama in order to top the excitement and drama of our everyday life. We love to run away from ourselves. It has now become routine and a matter of principle for many choreographers to create fast-moving ballets. They make the dancers rush across the stage, throw their bodies around like muscle-flexed weight, whirl past our eyes with frenzied haste.

Rush, rush, rush. The way we are haunted by speed in our daily existence has become a way of choreography. Speed has always been the trademark of the Alvin Ailey dancers. With them it is an intensity that seems to come from deep within, as if they were propelled by a devilish mechanism in their soul. With Gerald Arpino of the Joffrey Ballet it is far more surficial, superimposed. He possesses a built-in speed, he knows how to phrase and make ballet enjoyable. But too often he runs. If he wants to, he can probe the depth in a beautifully measured way, as he did in *The Clowns*. But why this constant fastness in pushing an idea? Arpino is not alone in this. He only is an outstanding example and must be cited because there is great talent in him that he himself is often wasting.

Speed is not only an American phenomenon, we suffer from a worldwide jet-syndrome. I am speaking here of the inner haste which is a sign of insecurity, of having to prove oneself. In the recklessness that goes with it may lie a death wish—the death wish of a civilization. But whatever it may be, expressed in the arts, it is inimical to the poetic image. And what is even worse, the fast-moving choreography has dulled our feelings and receptivity. Our audiences have become less and less attuned to the reality of the unreal, to the sensitive and tender statement, and the clamor is on for the ever-faster choreography.

This accounts for our lack of understanding of a work like *Watermill*. In a way, Jerome Robbins appealed in it to our subliminal world and tried to connect it with our consciousness. Or let me say, he was as down-to-earth as Asian symbolism is, in which time is almost brought to a standstill and movement slowed down through the act of meditation. Robbins caught some phenomena of nature and made them be the wonder they are and be alive as if somebody would tell about them, slowly, very slowly and suggestively in the manner of a haiku. Robbins created something that could be seen as the reality of a dream, a plastic rendering of visualized elusiveness. What it all suggests is as simple as nature and time, as living rhythm or rhythmic life. But essentially *Watermill* is about the mystery of being and the poetic magic surrounding and expressing it.

No wonder that those who yesterday had seen Arpino's latest and daringly whipping movements were stunned and infuriated, bored and perplexed by this work. Those of course who grew up with Erick Hawkins' art philosophy and movement vocabulary were better prepared and could yield to the inexpressible, to a world in which time is of no duration and esoteric elegance is wedded to the sensuousness of sensuality. I can feel mesmerized by these movements of utter tranquility, or I can feel as if he would gently massage all my senses. But whatever I experience I am always with him in an imaginary creation through which I am guided with a few suggestive gestures.

I was fascinated by *Watermill* and I have mostly been intrigued by Hawkins' works. I think Leonardo was right when he thought of the quiet as being stronger than the storm. Perhaps what no fairytale ballet was ever able to do to me, Hawkins and Robbins did. They took me back into my childhood and returned that part of my innocence to me that I never wanted to lose: the ability to wonder.

I have tried several times to *Cuddle Up* to the Beach Boys and our time. But by now I'm sure I've missed another of those many bandwagons which had passed me by for some time. In the driver's seat I saw Twyla Tharp. I was told that there is a Tharp cult, and that her *Deuce Coupe* is tremendous fun and turned into a runaway hit of the ballet season. I could not help watching the press making it a runaway hit. That I did not see so much fun in it must be my fault.

The idea for *Deuce Coupe* was to juxtapose "the ballet vocabulary . . . with another vocabulary loosely based on the social dance of the past ten years." I did not admire her as much as I sympathized with Erika Goodman, who did the balletic steps, and did them with classical composure in the midst of an organized chaos of frugs and go-gos. I was prepared for a great deal of "twisting, sliding into or shrugging delicately out of," of "loose-jointedness and slammed-into passages." It really was all there; it had some clever elegance—which social dancing, when elevated to a theatrical fare, often has.

There the case rests. The fan-fared ballet *Deuce Coupe* was one of the many put-ons and hoaxes of a fast-moving time. As soon as the contrasts between the classical ballet and the pelvic gyrations which were on display in the dance halls in the sixties were established, the idea turns out to be the non-idea of the century. "It doesn't add up to much," as one of her staunch supporters whispered into my ear during the standing ovations Miss Tharp received at opening night.

Perhaps all generations have been "lost." We have always dubbed an earlier generation as lost. In our lostness we accept skill and smartness for greatness, and there is a lot of skill in Twyla Tharp's wriggles. We are hungry for sensations and are grateful for finding a hero or queen of a passing fad to which we can bow in the general tumult of a few insignificant days. To stress the sensational and ephemeral accents of this ballet, Miss Tharp invited "graffiti painters in action" as a kind of décor, this crowning her idea of contrasts. When I saw the Tharpists rise to their feet, shouting bravo, Daniel (5:25) came to my mind with his inspired thought, "Thou art weighed in the balances, and art found wanting." I just wondered that no one saw the handwriting on the wall:

Zürich. There is a great deal to be said in favor of continuity. Also, continuity of work. And yet, it seems to me that, from time to time, we ought to step back and close our eyes in order to rest and replenish our inner strength, to gain a new perspective on life and the arts expressing it. In a wider sense of the phrase, we ought to take a vacation from sameness at certain points. As is the case with all vacations, there is a question of economics and one of opportunity. But it also needs some courage to leave the scene of one's activity for a longer period of time.

Switzerland has always seemed to have been a safe place to withdraw to, to find one's inner peace, to replenish one's creative strength (as proved by a surprisingly large number of artists), to be able to reflect on God and the world. On this island—figuratively speaking—one seems to be far away from the world's ills. Perhaps only seemingly though. But since we all run around with our personae, pretending with the help of our masks that we are what we think and hope we are and the way we wish to present ourselves to the outside world, little can be said against living one's illusions to the hilt once in a while.

How can I express the feeling of such isolation—just short of being total—from the international or New York dance scene, if only for a few months? Is it a feeling of deprivation, of emptiness, of a sudden letdown, as if one were uprooted from one's routine existence, an existence such as I have lived for many decades? I found out that, so often, one does not really have to see all the things happening in the world. The main thing is that one could. Whenever I returned to "where the action is," I found the scene virtually and factually and, above all, spiritually unchanged. Sometimes in life it suffices to look out of one's window and dream of one's journeys through the world. Emerson, I think, said something to this effect. Knowing the dance world, I decided to look out of the window and dream of the dancing everywhere from time to time. I am certain that suddenly the noise on my street corner will shake me out of my dream and force me to see what's happening right in front of the window or around the corner.

Moreover, we may all need a state of self-sufficiency forced upon us from time to time. It may easily create a feeling of content—perhaps a kind of happiness to which we no longer are attuned, and this happiness, within its set limitations, can be a blessing. In this self-imposed isolation I have learned to look at things with different eyes. In this relative stillness I have gained a wider perspective on the things remembered.

Ascona. Mary Wigman is no longer. Summer after summer I dreaded the thought that one day I would no longer be able to hold her freckled hand in mine. Summer after summer I could observe how her body disintegrated, aching in its agony while breaking into bits: Bones, which were used to take much punishment; muscles, once so lithe, refusing to obey; lungs fighting their own breath with violent spells of coughing; the heart sometimes forgetting to beat while recollecting those many minutes when it was asked to stand still for a fraction of time before the curtains went up. Her mind never weakened; it was strong to the very last minute when, facing a merciless void of no-light, it asked for the final curtain to come down.

Her legacy—her thoughts, her dreams, her accomplishments clearly expressed in essays and interviews, or loosely sketched on shreds of paper—is in my hands. She strongly believed in what she had done without overrating her importance as the first pioneer in the modern dance. I have never heard her say an ugly or only slightly derogatory word about her colleagues; she liked to talk only of those aspects of the dance scene which delighted her and which pleasantly lingered in her mind.

She believed in herself with an ironic twinkle in her eyes. She knew her limitations and the limitations of the modern dance. She had the courage to stop dancing while still at the height of her abilities. "Great" names were of little importance to her. When she viewed a ballet or modern dance recital she never looked at the program bill for the dancers' names, she told me—she wanted to judge a work and the dancing as it unfolded. A name with a well-known sound to it could unconsciously influence one's judgment. In the theater as a member of the audience she wanted to recapture the state of the innocence of the child.

While writing this I received a clipping of an interview that Martha Graham gave to Anna Kisselgoff at a time when Wigman's death became known. Miss Graham did not refrain from making certain pronouncements and using words spoken over Mary Wigman's grave, who may have smiled but also wondered at those words:

I was afraid of the German dance until I saw Wigman dance. Then I realized I had nothing to do with it. It was an entirely different world. The gestures were completely different. It was a dance of thrust, of a colonizing nation. The image of Barbarossa, which Germany still holds.

Methinks the lady protests too much. By the way, John Martin, champion of the modern dance, wrote in his book, *The Modern Dance*, in 1933, "At its highest point of development we find the so-called expressionistic dancing with Mary Wigman as an outstanding practitioner. This class of dance is in effect the modern dance in its purest manifestation. The basis of each composition in this medium lies in a vision of something in human experience which touches the sublime."

Certainly, I share Martha Graham's disgust for the Prussian spirit and, out of personal experience, I can add my loathing of any chauvinism, any exultation of a hollow patriotism, racial madness, and an ecstatic feeling of superiority. In many of her dances Martha Graham extolled beautifully the spirit of the American pioneers who bravely conquered a continent while wiping out the Indian nations. I do not possess any particular historic-political wisdom, but I know that only ruthlessness (whatever language it may speak) leads to power, and America's industrial power built up in the last centuries has Coca-Colonized all of Europe, if not the greater part of the world. While I am writing this, Frenchmen hoisted a swastika flag on top of a church spire in Nancy, and no one will dispute France's cultural domination for many centuries. A cultured people then, famous for their blind belief in their own gloire, well-known for their xenophobia, bourgeois pettiness and shabby treatment of those refugees coming from the land of Barbarossa's successors.

True, movement never lies (as Miss Graham said), and it may be shaped by the spirit of a nation, although it always is the creation of one man whose spirit might oppose his nation's spirit. If nothing else, it is highly debatable whether Mary Wigman's dance "was a dance of thrust, of a colonizing nation." Moreover, and sadly enough, these words were spoken when Martha Graham's dead colleague had not yet the time to turn in her freshly made grave.

1974

Paris. Dreams can be productive. After having seen André Tahon's marionette theater, I spent a lovely and lively night with weird sequences of childhood images, with clowns, mimes, and marionettes toppling over each other, haunting shapes wrapped in flaming colors. Now in broad daylight I have forced my thoughts to focus on the reality of the unreal, to explain the inexplicable and bring order to the miraculous and mysterious.

I cannot help thinking that the childlike and the sophisticated join forces in the marionette. As a child—as all children—I had the ability to see the real in the imaginative and the imaginative in the real. A child triumphs over the adult in seeing the real with its inner eye, with its belief in the poetic wonder of being. The child's imagination is free of the fetters forged by man's thinking in terms of Realpolitik on whatever level it may be. We, adults, have come to accept the facts of life, with the result that we conveniently finger the beautiful and recognize the most sublime by the reversal of its pornographic connotations. I have always wondered for what reason Creation tricked us by uniting organically the basest and the most sublime in us, if not for the one purpose of teaching us to separate the functional from the beautiful as much as to see the beautiful in the functional and vice versa.

This needs a great deal of belief in the innocence of belief. The former was akin to the romantic movement in the nineteenth century, the latter is basic to our own desire to return to a myth of sophisticated simplicity in a Miróesque or Paul Kleeish manner. For the adult it is always the question, or rather the problem, of how to accept the reality of illusion as a viable point of our de facto existence in a blown-up and distorted make-believe world.

My first contact with the reality of the unreal was the marionette theater. Richard Teschner was a painter. He was also a man possessed. He believed in making color come alive through movement. He was also madly in love with the utter grace of motion in the ever-changing light of theatrical deception. He did not believe in the word, only in the magic of color, movement and music. His figures moved on a tiny stage with beautiful self-evidence, as if animated by God. But everything seemed magnified. I saw flames burning in their own red, devouring space in a dancing mood. There was the frightening dragon fanning the fire which was about to reach the beautiful princess for whose rescue a brave knight gave his life and who was finally saved by a divine figure called Buddha. At the age of six I could have hardly known who Buddha was, or that dragon. But fire and knights were symbols of the realities in our daily life, symbols of a fairy-tale world which, later, were to people our adult nightmares.

All that had happened in Vienna—not here in Paris—quite some time ago when I was little and when Vienna was still the capital of a huge monarchy whose realities were sheer illusion. Teschner taught me that I can only feel safe and happy when I believe with him that the beautiful princess can return to safety and happiness in her castle. He taught me to believe in the miracle of make-believe. He made me sense the excitement of the theater, of movement in space, of color in motion. Today I know I can only love the ballet because, as a child, I learned to love the marionette theater. I do not doubt that, without an early experience of marionettes, the poetry of life and the beauty of ballet may be lost on us. There is always the danger that our inner eye will remain blinded by and too much tied to the nakedness of everything real.

I thought of Richard Teschner when I saw the Parisian marionette theater of André Tahon. He gave his hand puppets spherical heads, mostly without distinct features (these were left to the viewer's imagination). This does not mean that his imaginary creatures, human, animal, and inanimate, were not imaginatively visualized. In contrast to Teschner, he relied heavily on the word. He created a charming figure, called Papotin, an emcee whose witty *conference* gave this puppet theater the touch of a Parisian nightclub which in no way distracted from its marionette character. Tahon's show was full of entertaining gags and was enchanting on a higher sophisticated level. It was disarmingly witty even when the entire group of puppeteers stepped in front of their stage, revealing the mechanics and tricks of their visual surprises.

They played no matineé because Tahon does not wish to appeal to the child but to the nostalgic memory of the child in man. Perhaps the improbability of the animated characters' exploits and experiences symbolizes what, in our waking dreams, we would like to be or to do ourselves. The more improbable and symbolic the marionette is—while still being reminiscent of some real being— the more easily we can believe in it. (This is the very same thought, by the way, that Gautier expressed about his ideal concept of ballet.) Our imagination's willingness to decipher the code of analogies and symbols, to embrace allusion and illusion with the heart of our mind and to see the poetry between the lines and gestures, is crucial for all performing arts, if not for all the arts.

There is something intrinsically suggestive about the art of the marionette, as there is about ballet. The margin of error and failure which always exists with any live performance is replaced in the marionette theater by a larger margin of the viewer's imagination. An increased aesthetic distance is created which works to the advantage of the child, who accepts the puppet as something of his own size, certainly smaller than the grown-ups and even smaller than himself. He does not have to look up, he feels co-existent, on one level with the puppets. We may very well imagine that, for a child, existence is play in disguise, with the grown-ups being giant puppets, larger-than-life figures, whose movements are dictated by routine reflexes, predeterminable as recurring impulses like love and suppression, with carefree or inhibiting gestures. Long before the world of Ionesco came into being, the child must have visualized our reality as bizarre, grotesque, and absurd, regulated by strange conventions and the tyranny of purposeless purposes.

Life may be little more than a gray-haired platitude for the child, and all he has to learn is to play its game. Only a child can experience glorified make-believe. Blessed state! When we see a puppet show, we may relive unconsciously moments of a total relapse into childhood. Blessed moments.

The mime is a cousin to the marionette, twice removed. First, the "as if" has become alive with a soul; second, the final truth of "the purest and most intimate grace"—to follow Heinrich von Kleist in his *On the Marionette Theatre*—must be abstracted from reality by the mime, illusion must be created out of "nothing there." Etienne Décroux taught me how to walk up nonexistent stairs, and Jean-Louis Barrault did it to perfection in André Gide's version of Kafka's *The Trial*.

The mime is the magician of the gesture. He is a master mask-maker. How does Marcel Marceau define the mime? He "is man and object at the same time, wind and the man walking in the wind . . . child and balloon . . . "

In comparison with the marionette, the mime is at a great disadvantage. The marionette possesses—to come back to Kleist again—total innocence; it has total freedom, being free from all self-consciousness. In the marionette's realm a violin, for instance, may bend and turn and dance, a servant may attend to your needs with six hands, a lover may actually lose his head at the sight of a girl, and a lovely girl may become a swan right in front of your eyes.

The marionette could destroy the ballerina by being her utter fulfillment, by being the purest poetic form of the absurd, the *ne plus ultra* of surrealism. The marionette can step from the frightening vision of Kafka's waking nightmares, it can inhabit the dreamland of Chagall's weird world of colors and of flying, or upside-down, figures. Alwin Nikolais' amalgam of marionette and dancer reaches beyond the dancer's self-consciousness. And yet his limitations are still as human as those of the dancer. The marionette has none. But the essential criterion for marionettes remains the essential criterion for the dance; its suggestive power: to remain fragmentary while creating the poetry of all genesis.

There are mimes and mimes—but also pantomimes. Marcel Marceau is one of the last great mimes. He does not express meaning through gestures instead of through words. He expresses feelings by attitudes. With him the subtlety of the smallest nuance counts. The subject challenges the entire body, which is turned into an intensely expressive instrument by the nature of its being and by what it is while on its way to becoming something else.

Charlie Chaplin, the greatest comedian of our century, in my book, is a pantomime. He is always involved in mastering props which trick or overwhelm him. He reflects the little man's struggle with obstinate objects in a devious, devilish, and deceptive environment. There is quite a bit of the traditional clown in Charlie Chaplin, W. C. Fields, and Buster Keaton. It is symptomatic for the clown to create the difficulties over which he stumbles. This is his tragi-grotesque fate. The clown blows reality up to gigantic proportions, the mime needs to reduce reality to a symbol.

The saying that Raphael would have been the same great painter he was, even if he had been born without arms and hands, can be applied to the mime. Cicero once said about a mime of his days that "even his very body began to laugh," and David Garrick supposedly exclaimed, "Look at the character and expression in Carlino's back!" when he saw one of the great Harlequins of the eighteenth century.

As long as we are with that period: In order to liberate the body from all conventionalities and their stereotypical gestures, Marie Sallé, Noverre, and Viganó undoubtedly went to the other extreme, and each in his own fashion. The age of exoticism and the artificialities of the minuet cried out for the noble, sensitive, and self-expressive gesture. Of course, no one can lay down a dictum of final rules of what ballet, or dance in general, should be. And yet a single consistent line of sentiment toward the principal ideas of what ballet should be and how it can be presented unites these three dancer-choreographers. By giving the articulation of

Marcel Marceau created a very personalized and articulate character whom he called "Bip." Author's collection.

human emotion full reign, all three prepared the way for Romanticism, which turned out to be the very antithesis to their ideals. Isadora Duncan and Michel Fokine, both deeply involved in the neoromantic trend of their time, renewed the efforts toward a heightened sensibility of self-expression. The "dancing gesture," however, achieved a degree of inner freedom only at the end of the twenties and during the thirties with the growing awareness of our psychic mechanism. What Viganó extolled as "the movement of the soul" had to wait for its fulfillment as "the movement of man's psyche."

Noverre knew what he was talking about when, in one of his *Letters*, he said that the gestures are "the lifeblood of dancing." The struggle—beginning in the eighteenth century—between virtuosity and expressiveness is still on and, more often than we would think it possible in our time, the gestures remain bloodless in newly choreographed works. Are we not justified in assuming that at this point of the development of the artistic dance the gesture is an intrinsic part of the choreographic concept, meaningful in its spatial description even there where a balletic movement needs the dancing hand as a helpmate of balance?

It is a truism—and as so many truisms only too true—that the torso has a different function from arms and hands, but all three have vital tasks to fulfill; every style of dancing puts varied demands on each part of the body. Nothing can ever be predetermined. Every theme dictates its own needs. Moreover, every individual has his own personal gesture pattern, which has to be subordinated to and/or absorbed by the part he is asked to dance.

Characteristic gestures can become the trademark of an artist. To choose three from the modern dance: Paul Taylor's swinging arms have extroverted qualities but are—very likely—overcompensations resulting from his athletic physique; as his counterpart let us think of Murray Louis, whose staccato hand movements, neurotically shooting out of his wrists, have always fascinated me with their playful, witty, narcissistic manner; Alvin Ailey's arms and hands move ecstatically from the body, as if trying to recreate a ritualistic image, as if widening the spatial dimension through articulated invocations. Their gestures are unmistakably their very own.

The hand has always been many things to the dancer, but as far as expressiveness is concerned it can best mirror the state of emotion and reach the spectator more intensely and faster than, say, his facial expression. The dancer's register of expressive means is of course different from but also far superior in scope and artistic nuances to those of the mime. However, the dancer can never hope to attain the purity of grace and innocence of the marionette. It will always remain his problem to find the ultimate gesture coming closest to the unfolding of an emotion, its drama and beauty, or the revelation of the mystery of reality. What a pity that the dancer cannot step out of his own character or shed his self-consciousness! At least, the artist should have the privilege—if only for the duration of a performance—to return the apple with his awareness and knowledge to that legendary tree. On second thought, would not such assuredness of perfection quickly bore us?

1975

The dream of a total theater has been with us in one form or another as long as the notion of theater exists. Even to the ancient Greeks theatrical spectacles (with speaking actors on cothurns, the singing and moving chorus, the deus ex machina, masking and costuming) must have appeared rather total. The comedia dell'arte gave, in its extemporizing way, its spectacles—however abortive—the feeling of theatrical totality, with each of the actors doing practically everything onstage: from poetizing to acrobatics. But it also seems that in no histrionic environment was the idea of totality ever totally fulfilled. This is probably the most wonderful thing about creative homo sapiens—even in the moments of the most consummate accomplishments there is always some room left for greater perfection. Mallarmé rightly chided Richard Wagner for having omitted dance and poetry in his total theater concept. Appia and Craig dreamt of it from the scenic designers' viewpoint. Craig—envisioning a super-marionette endowed with all theatrical magic—wrote in *The Masks*, in 1908, that "the ideal theatre would focus all the arts in a magnificent over-powering unity of impression." In a variety of ways, Diaghilev can be seen as coming relatively close to it with some of his balletic adventures. But among all the total-theater dreamers Alwin Nikolais holds a unique position.

At an early stage of Nikolais' career I have tried to characterize the immediate impressions his work conveyed:

Alwin Nikolais does not offer us dancing per se as we have come to understand it in terms of any expression through movement . . . We cannot very well speak of choreographic notions—although the end products have in their imaginative, raging freedom a clearly designed pattern—, but rather of pieces of fantasy whose rationality lies beyond human life and its problems.

He denies the emotional essence of modern dance by erasing the dancer's personality . . . He only permits the theatre to function on a magic level of his own determination where the conflict lies in matter, not in man.

If Nikolais is at his best, the painted movement sensations on the stage are a triumphant flight from reality into the realm of a theatrical wholeness, if at his worst the magician out-tricks the artist in him and lets the audience in on the secret that imagination and creativity are often unreliable bedfellows whose magic lies in a combination of a few intangibles.

At that time I was puzzled about the improvisational quality of his work when, at the same time, I realized that he was a serious explorer of technical phenomena and that his gimmicks were so tricky as to demand very thorough rehearsing. With the passing decades I have got used to the variations on his basic concepts and accepted Nikolais, the painter, the supreme master of light and projection effects, the skillful electronic sound mixer, the

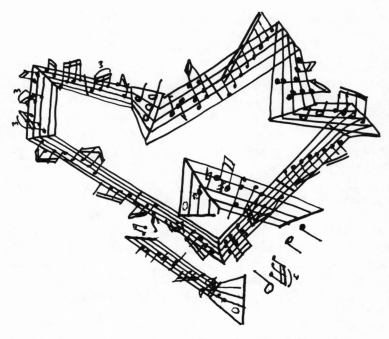

Drawing by Alwin Nikolais. Author's collection.

manipulator of prop-bodies and body-props, in short, the magician of his kind of total theater. I took in my critical stride that, from time to time, he failed to illuminate the poetry of his conceits in spite of all the magic effects he did let loose. On the other hand, I admired a work like *Tent* (despite its tedious beginning), since he seemed to have been able—as I found in 1971—

to create in this piece poetry in and of the theatre. Mere technical tricks gain visual power of exalting beauty and their surprises create evocative feelings . . . Much of Nikolais' work has always been playful and seemed to be done for the sheer enjoyment of fragmentary visual marvels combining moving bodies and props in a sea of wondrous light images and projections, supported by the rhythm of electronic sound effects. These fragments were usually flowing into one another and causing an

"Tent." Nikolais Dance Theatre. Photo: Brynn Manley.
Courtesy Alwin Nikolais. Author's collection.

inevitable totality and, when achieving poetic heights, a total inevitability. These creations, caught on the flight of a multi-faceted fantasy, mainly have had one specific frame of reference on which Nikolais' imagination concentrated.

Of course, there has always been this specific frame of reference, and one could argue about that "muchness of sameness" which may be the trademark of any artist, his recognizable signature, but which strikes us much stronger when it is so unique and inimitable as in Nikolais' work. He undoubtedly gives his critics a hard time, forcing them to verbalize the visual diversions he is able to evoke with shapes, sounds, lights, projections, and motion, one depending on the others. Dance critics, conditioned to viewing and expecting to see "dancing", have always been a bit uneasy about reconciling the theater experience he offers with what is considered legitimate dancing.

Nikolais was a musician and puppeteer before he became a choreographer, and with choreography being his Achilles' heel, it has always been there he can most easily be wounded. In his *Foreplay* (1972) he indulged in a greater amount of "pure dance." He had divested his moving shapes of their body masks and prop-like accoutrements. Eight years later he created another work in which the dancers also appeared as human figures: *The Mechanical Organ.* Its point of departure, with ten dancers lined up in profile, could have allowed it to go any way, but the road it took was prepared for a pedestrian build-up of movement upon movement from the easy stroll to the more complex exercise. It probably set out to become a celebration of the human body in motion, but, with the exception of one clever scene with the company on stools, it did not brush any wings of angels on the way out of its classroom exercises. It seems that when his dancers are not concealed, his choreographic notions may more openheartedly reveal a conceptual bareness here or weakness of idea there.

Since Nikolais' work was so different from anything else in the dance field, one looked for roots of his ideas or historic points from where he could have departed, when it was quite obvious that without the mad advances in our technological age there would and could not have been a Nikolais Dance Theatre. "From the point of view of mathematics, dynamics, dispersion of visual and auditory events and energies I caused the whole upset to dance dynamics," Nikolais wrote. But he thinks that technology, in a certain way, has always been with us. "Technology is just something to be fed, to be used . . . and this feeding involves choice." Naturally, technology per se "never originates anything," as he maintained, but it becomes the cause of our choice with which we feed it. "There was little acknowledgement of external source of heritage," he claimed.

Mary Wigman, whose art was so decisive in Nikolais' life, believed that "art grows out of the basic cause of existence." Many artists, like Nikolais, had turned in their creative gesture against "the stimuli derived from neurotic frictions," which had become a bane for the modern dance in the latter half of the forties. Nikolais fed the computer of his mind with the furious determination to ban emotion from the expressive vocabulary of his art. And to do this radically, "the self as the sole germinal point of all value" had to be eradicated. "Being relieved of one's flesh is really the most wonderful attribute of man because it allows man to identify with and become something else, something beyond," he once said in an interview. The most logic reply of his computer was: with the self you must eradicate the habit of the human body. And so he did. Nikolais called himself a mystic and, going one step further, I would describe him as an "alchemystic."

I have often envisioned him as a madman, with almost Mephistophelean zeal and ease, working in the laboratory of his waking dreams, melting his dancers in the furnace of his mind only to re-animate them into shapes of his fancy, hauling down any available space from heaven, brightening it with his own light devices, crazily and stunningly colored, with all the most beautiful projections on and behind his moving shapes, changing their appearance at will, fleshless figures revealing the reality of the unreal. A new magician, like a new Daniel, had come to us, trying to drown and to deceive our senses in and with his sound and light collages while playing with his live hallucinations wrapped in props and masks and moving them like mobiles in disarming charm, in total freedom from any psychological or balletic need to pretend whatever dancers wrapped in emotion feel called upon to pretend.

In the fifties a trip to the Henry Street Playhouse was always like a holy pilgrimage to me, where I tried to recapture the unfulfilled dreams of my childhood in an age in which science-fiction became a daily reality. Nikolais could still ignore the reality for me and, often enough, make my dreams come alive on his stage. Only somewhere in a remote corner of my mind (or was it in the heart since I, with my weakness for mavericks, liked him quite a bit), I questioned whether his magic would not one day turn out to be a limitation to his art, whether this remarkable illusionist would not burn down the furnace of his fancies.

Several decades have passed since he appeared on the dance scene, which has changed greatly, while so far Nikolais has gone on to do his thing, to explore the potential of his kinetic vision, the sensitivity of his light perception, the scope and marvels he pursues in motion. He is a fortunate man. He did not find the philosophers' stone as yet, but his alchemystic instinct makes him believe that he is on the way to it, which simply means to the source of whatever it may be. The critics may chitchat about this and that, write superficially or profoundly about what we think we see or see what we think we see. Meanwhile, he moved from Henry Street Playhouse to L'Opéra in Paris. He made it because he seemed to have told himself day and night, in paraphrasing a famous saying, "Right or wrong, my way!"

When anyone steps into a new direction, questions arise in those watching him. Usually they are moot questions, but occasionally one is voiced. Perhaps it is safer for us, the bystanders, to watch the artist walk his tightrope. Of course, there are precedents to what Nikolais did. I do not wish to imply that he borrowed from here to there, or leaned on this and that. These precedents are of interest historically, they indicate that, enclosed in a specific environment, the artist in man cannot help but follow his instincts testing himself and his time. On a practical level, Loie Fuller was as much obsessed with light in its incipient stage as Nikolais is today. On a metaphysical level, Stéphane Mallarmé's concept of the dance and the ballerina was a lyric synopsis for Nikolais' work. Mallarmé did not believe in the dancer as a human being or in any emotional statement through dance. He pleaded for the elimination of the dancer's humanness because the human factors only distract from the potential miracle that unfolds in the dancer's motion. In his poetic eyes the dancer becomes "l'être prodigieux reculé au delà de toute vie possible" (the prodigious being withdrawn beyond all possible life). In effacing herself—

Mallarmé always envisioned a ballerina—the dancer lets her motion create its own intrinsic meaning. In a poetic nutshell this is Nikolais' credo. He summed it up in his own terms when he said: "One of the major characteristics of our current dynamics is our capacity to transcend the literal and to replace it with an abstract metaphoric language."

About two decades later, Jean Cocteau sought a solution for a total theater based primarily on movement, but it was dancing with a cerebral approach which "combines classical steps and new gestures." These new, intellectualized gestures enlisted the help of total masking of the dancer which left no room for showing any emotion. He not only wished to transform his dancing characters, but wanted to transfigure them and, depriving them of their mere humanity, to make them superhuman. The characters ought to be subordinated to the décor and the ballet's general concept. The real dancers should be reduced "to the size of puppets" next to "décor-men," such as the managers in *Parade*. Rolf de Maré's Ballet Suédois was also very much interested in experimentation and opened its doors to Cocteau's exploring mind which, in his ballet *Les Mariés de la Tour Eiffel*, tried to achieve the sophistication of simplicity by depicting the absurdity of life in a grotesque way. His two narrators appeared as phonographs. Avoiding a true-to-life story he had his dancers wear masks and endowed them with the spirit of artificiality. Cocteau's was a step into an intellectualized direction, but he predicted that "this new genre, more constant with the modern spirit, remains unexplored land, rich with possibility." One of those possibilities became Nikolais' work.

In the twenties, there were two artists who experimented with the theatricalized effects of moving planes and objects. Their aims and means were different, but not the source of inspiration. Alexander Calder and Oskar Schlemmer are Nikolais' cousins— and not too far removed from him. Calder was first interested in circus images before he created those strange shapes and constructions moving in space, held together by balance and harmony. Calder did not know what to call these things and asked Marcel Duchamp who immediately responded with the word mobiles. About them, Calder wrote in 1951:

I think that . . . the underlying sense of form in my work has been the system of the Universe, or part thereof . . . a rather large model to work from.

NIKOLAIS: I began to establish my philosophy of man being a fellow traveller within the total universal mechanism rather than the god from which all things flowed. The idea was both humiliating and grandizing. He lost his domination but instead became kinsman to the universe.

CALDER: What I mean is that the idea of detached bodies floating in space, of different sizes and densities, perhaps of different colors and temperatures . . . and some at rest, while others move in peculiar manners, seems to me the ideal source of form . . . I would have them deployed, some nearer together and some at immense distances. . . . Then there is the idea of an object floating—not supported . . . this freedom from the earth . . . .

NIKOLAIS: I don't care about the physical presence of someone as much as I care about his transcendence . . . I want my people to be free of themselves . . . to transcend and be anything they want to be. That's what art is about. Art is always exploring freedom.

Then there was Schlemmer working at the *Bauhaus*, dehumanizing the dancer, creating—what he called—*der Tänzermensch (Man as Dancer)*:

He obeys the law of the body as well as the law of space; he follows his sense of himself as well as his sense of embracing space. As the one who gives birth to an almost endless range of expression, whether in free abstract movement or in symbolic pantomime, whether he is on the bare stage or in scenic environment constructed for him . . . the *Tänzermensch* is the medium of transition into the great world of the theatre . . . the metamorphosis of the human figure and its abstraction . . . .

Schlemmer decries that the materialistic age of ours has lost the genuine feeling for play and for the miraculous . . . In this time of crumbling religion, which kills the sublime, and of a decaying society, which is able to enjoy only play that is drastically erotic or artistically *outré*, all profound artistic tendencies take on the character of exclusiveness or of sectarianism.

This is where Nikolais' philosophy comes in which turned against the dancer's subservience to the figure, against "his reverence to himself—uglies and all. Man was now stuck with a sex–dominated libido." Schlemmer went to the far end of the other extreme denying the need for man as co-actor. The architect L. Moholy-Nagy (who also worked at the *Bauhaus*) explained their aims toward the achievement of a total theater with the words "Theatre is the concentrated activation (Aktionskonzentration) of sound, light (color), space, form and motion."

All this creates the impression of a total dehumanization process, and the very first thing that Nikolais was reproached for was the dehumanization of his dancers and his choreographic approach. José Ortega y Gasset had written a remarkable book about *The Dehumanization of Art* in the mid-twenties, the time when Schlemmer worked at the *Bauhaus*. He wrote in defense of the new trend, then in its first flourish, to dehumanize art and to avoid living forms. He recognized that everywhere and in the most different art forms the twentieth-century creative spirit shows a deeply imbedded dislike of the past and a growing hostility to traditional meaningfulness, expressing "contempt for the old monumental forms of the soul and unhuman attention to the micro-structure of sentiments, social relations, characters."

But Ortega does raise the question of whether there can be an art that does not in one way or another make some reference to actual objects. He realized that this leads to the suppression or rejection of any artistic responsibility to, what Ortega calls, a "lived reality." What he could not foresee was that, in the process of ignoring and denying all "lived reality," art would have to become nonart one day.

Nikolais maintained that Ortega "saw this 'dehumanizing' of the physical body as a positive thing." Not quite so. He merely accepted it as an expression of our time, he saw it from an historic viewpoint and did not come to its defense out of love for it, since there is not one enthusiastic or approving statement about it in his book. He simply explained in a wider frame of reference why a new aesthetic eclipsed all human elements. When Nikolais continues to say in the same breath and interview that "being relieved of one's flesh is really the most wonderful attribute of man because it allows man to identify with and become something else, something beyond," he is much closer to Mallarmé than to Ortega. A circle is closed.

It is risky to categorize talents and it is even more dangerous to throw around the epithet of "genius." But whatever weaknesses and flaws one can find in Nikolais' work, no one can deny his persistent and multi-talented pursuit of a unified theatrical spectacle based on the body's motion. He certainly anticipated the psychedelic craze of the sixties by more than a decade. Long before the modern dancers began to work with multimedia, Nikolais had worked with them and perfected this idea on his terms. In the early fifties when Merce Cunningham escaped the catharsis of the psychological drama in the modern dance, Nikolais had already labored on the diffusion of its dénouement. If at that time the concept of nonliteralness began to entrench itself, Nikolais went his own way in giving nonliteralness a very specific image.

1976

New York. Whenever I entered one of my classes in Dance History I shuddered at the thought that perhaps in one or two more generations a future teacher will face a class of students who can no longer write because they have lost the ability and will to read. By now already a frightfully passive trend is noticeable. The young ones want to be told and—more than that—shown visually what dancing in the past was all about, they do not readily like to acquire knowledge through their own research and reading. But dance books are being published and magazines on the dance issued monthly and quarterly. For an elite? Or are the masses of dancers, choreographers, balletomanes, briefly dance buffs, also readers in an age growing progressively electronic?

I had the unenviable pleasure of running a dance bookstore in the early sixties for a short while. The enviable end of it was to talk to the dance-interested public, to watch them look at books, browse through all kinds of dance material. It was then that I gained better insight into the reading habits of the dance world. Without exposing myself too much to the reproach of generalization, I believe I can safely speak, with regard to their reading habits, of three groups of those involved or interested in the dance. Besides the balletomane who collects not only all sorts of memorabilia but also everything that is issued between covers, hard or paperback, with a not entirely selective passion, we meet those who believe in the classical ballet as the alpha and omega of dancing—and they are mainly interested in the dance picture book. This is more than understandable since the dancer hopes to see herself or himself and the dancers they love, and who serve them as paragons, in one or another pose in the book. It may almost sound like an apology, but the fact is that photography is still one of the most essential documentations of this visual art form. Not to be omitted is a muted reference to the narcissistic trend which, obviously playing its role in the life of all artists, has a unique part in the daily work of a dancer who must live with his mirror image many hours a day.

Of greater scope and depth is the attitude of dance teachers, ballet masters, and choreographers toward the written word. Once they all were dancers who, due to the merciless toll of age, injuries, or an early realization of their re-creative limitations, turned from dancing to related activities. They are aware that their knowledge must go far beyond mere trade literature. Profound teaching demands a heightened understanding of everything connected with the physical and mental aspects of a human being and, above all, an understanding of oneself, the overt and latent potentialities of one's craft. Every creative process emerges from far-reaching life experiences, briefly, from a philosophy the sources of which lie in the poetry of reality as much as in the reality of the poetic word.

The reading habits of teachers and choreographers are as often eclectic as restricted to a certain type of literature or philosophy. Glen Tetley is a good example of the former reader, and a list of books, as he wrote me, "would have to include everything from the Bible through medical journals, gardening catalogues, books of mythology, archeological manuals and, above all, travel diaries of all centuries." Glen Tetley did not forget to refer in his note, still held at the Württembergische Staatstheater Stuttgart—whose ballet company he headed at that time—, to the one book "which has very often influenced me, Noverre's *Lettres sur la Danse*," a book he carried around the world for many years, also as far as Stuttgart. Even though John Neumeier also admitted to "reading a lot and in many directions," his reading habits are far more channeled in the direction of the poetic or rather literary when he says, "a few names come to mind immediately—Shakespeare comes first. Rilke is also very important for me, as is the poetry of St. John of the Cross, Lorca, but also Chekhov." But even the choice of his favorite novelists show the literary gourmet in him: "There has been a lot of inspiration and comfort in the novels of Jane Austen, Graham Greene, Evelyn Waugh, and Antoine de Saint-Éxupéry."

This attitude toward purely literary reading material is playing an even more important role with the modern dancer, who so often is his own choreographer. I only know from hearsay that Rudolf Laban was a voracious reader whose thirst for knowledge embraced everything from religion and philosophy to literature and science. According to such range of interest one can well imagine the bookshelves of this man for whom the notion of movement became a philosophy of life. Mary Wigman—who turned Laban's theoretical dreams into stage reality—was strongly influenced by the revolutionary upheavals in the world and in the arts during World War I. She was riding the wave of expressionism and felt close to the experiments of painters like Emil Nolde, who brought her together with Laban. And her library reflected her interest in painting. She loved to read poems and plays and found pleasure in books describing faraway and exotic countries. She read both English and German books, and there was hardly a dance book she did not know.

For Kurt Jooss, dance has been theater mirroring its era. Situation and characters, drama and message seemed to have been more important for him than any aesthetic effects of dance itself. He told me that he has always read much poetry aloud, together with his wife; she brought closer to him the poetic world of Stefan George, while he tried to convince her of Rilke's greatness. Jooss has always had a weakness for first editions and very old books, which he collected. However, he found the strongest sources of inspiration for his choreographies in the magazine *Weltbühne*, edited by Carl von Ossietsky, and in Kurt Tucholsky's political writings. It was Tucholsky whose moral integrity and struggle for human decency were directly responsible for *The Green Table*.

Anna Sokolow's social awareness comes to mind. But her concern with and insight into the feeling of the young generation has always been drawn from life. She never needed political essays or poetry to sharpen her awareness of daily life, although she seems to be partial to Lorca's poetry, which meant the most to her. The books, however, to which she returns time and again are the biographies and autobiographies of great artists. "They mean so much to me because I not only want to be informed about the artist in *his* time, about how artists at different ages and at various places became what they were. Above all, the question has always interested me of how a human being becomes an artist or what makes an artist an artist."

Her fascination with the word, "with its power to stimulate and evoke images, is undeniable," Nancy Wilson Ross wrote in her introduction to *The Notebooks of Martha Graham*. The repertory of a choreographer indicates the avenues of his thinking, the directions from where his inspirations come. Miss Graham's entire oeuvre makes the range of her interests obvious, and the random remarks made in her notebooks attest to how strongly she must

Kurt Jooss' The Green Table *as produced by the Robert Joffrey Ballet Company. Photo: James Howell. Courtesy Robert Joffrey Ballet Company.*

have been "attracted to and enlightened by symbolism and classical mythology, by legends from everywhere, by the passionate dramas of the Bible, the mysteries of the Asian sages, theories, thoughts, insights of Carl Gustav Jung, Heinrich Zimmer, Joseph Campbell, James Joyce, St. John Perse, T. S. Eliot, Dante, Rilke, etc." Bosch and Blake have added to the imagination of her visualizations. How strong the interrelation of the arts can be, the constant mental interaction of influences, overt and latent, can be inferred from a tongue-in-cheek passage of her *Notebooks*:

> I am a thief—and I am not ashamed. I steal
> from the best wherever it happens to me—
> Plato—Picasso—Bertram Ross—the members of
> my company never show me anything—except you
> expect me to steal it—
> I am a thief—
> and I glory in it—
> I steal from the present and from the glorious
> past and I stand in the dark of the future as
> a glorious and joyous thief—There are so many
> wonderful things of the imagination to pilfer—
> so I stand accused—I am a thief—but with this
> reservation—I think I know the value of what
> I steal and I treasure it for all time—not as
> a possession but as a heritage and as a legacy—

Doris Humphrey's reading habits were in no way less literary and selective than Martha Graham's. Humphrey was passionately interested in poetry, which can be readily seen by the choice of her subject matter. She often returned to inspirations that came from lyric passages; but, as a rule, verbal imagery was for her a point of departure to free her own fantasy, to ignite her imagination. Doris Humphrey is only another example of the many modern dancers for whom the literary word has been a necessary stimulation. There seems to be one and the same motivating drive which makes the poet verbally articulate and which makes the modern dancer express through his body: the truth of an experience turned into the Gestalt of his inner vision.

The dancer's life is one of total physical dedication. Not everyone has the strength to recuperate from his physical state of exhaustion through mental nourishment. Some dancers who are very "literate" could claim that they do not find enough time to read. I spoke about it with Violette Verdy who had made this claim. In my book she is one of the most articulate, profound, and knowledgeable ballerinas. In the last few years she has devoted the few of her free hours to Indian philosophy. For Violette Verdy this philosophy, concentrated on the self and rooted in the depth of self-awareness, is the only counterpart to an excessively active life in which she finds herself caught. She also feels a far-reaching personal gratification in her work with yoga and the thoughts of this tradition-bound *Weltanschauung*. Whenever she can free herself from her outward-turned life, she studies Indian literature or converses with someone who is also on his flight from the self-inflicted pressures of an over-accentuated activity which, in its final analysis, despite all its direction runs its course aimlessly.

Miss Verdy is not alone in her quest for the ultimate answer to our modern life. Hanya Holm has always had great interest in modern theological writing, befriended, as she was, with the well-known theologist Paul Tillich. Moreover, what fascinates Hanya are the wonders of nature and their description in books; they also are the real things behind and between the words. She said "what, for instance, is time as such, what are the driving forces in the universe, the ultimate meaning of what man creates? These questions interest me. Books must stimulate me to go on thinking, even though I may get to totally different results."

I had a unique experience speaking to Dame Marie Rambert in London about her reading habits. She took pride in having one of the finest private libraries, but the most astounding library treasures were in her memory. She spoke seven languages fluently and could quote many of the great poets in their native idiom. When I talked to her she was close to ninety years young. "I wake through many sleepless nights and while away the time by reciting my favorite poets in the dark." And as examples she quoted passages from Goethe's *Faust* and lines from Dante's *Divina Commedia*, followed by a Shakespearean sonnet and verses from Pushkin's *Onegin*. She interrupted herself. "Still a few years ago I loved to walk with some of my Russian dancer friends through Regent's Park and we recited Pushkin and some Polish poets. I also have a weak spot for Dickens. Do you want to hear *Tale of Two Cities*? Of course, there are the French poets. Whose mind can resist being captured by La Fontaine or Hugo or Rimbaud? Oh, God, Baudelaire," she added quickly and with emphasis, as if she had perpetrated a crime almost forgetting him. Then she rushed through many poetic cascades.

Out of context Dame Marie suddenly asked me where and when we had actually met for the first time. I thought it was at Jacob's Pillow in the mid-fifties. "No, it must have been in July 1959," the old lady corrected me. I expected her to ask me now about the poets we had discussed at that time. I was almost sure that they were Heine and Hofmannsthal, but I preferred not to test my memory in Rambert's presence.

There are fulminant figures in the dance world, as there probably are in every other art form. And there are quite a few for whom the poetic word, a singing line of prose, and a clearly perceived and articulated thought have meaning beyond the word itself. But there are many more dancers out of step with the printed word and for whom literature is a remote world. These dancers can be encountered here as much as in Europe. During my stay in Switzerland I discussed this problem with the Bern teacher Alain Bernard, who, by the way, has probably the most complete private dance library in all of Europe. "With some exceptions," he told me, "the dancer is not a great reader. I certainly have experienced how little today's dancers know of the past, above all, the immediate past. This ignorance is frightening. I believe that we can blame TV for that. People no longer have to think, to acquire knowledge. Everything is done for them on a trembling little screen."

Fortunately, there are always examples with which the contrary can be proved. The word may have lost much of its traditional values ("A rose is a rose is a rose," said Gertrude Stein in order to give the rose a new poetic image, while James Joyce made his verbal somersaults). And yet, the world could not get along without the word-become-poetry. From the anonymous poets of the Bible to the poetic cry of the last 'ism,' the word has constantly revealed new dimensions of our existence.

1977

With the first press releases I received many years ago, announcing Maurice Béjart with his Ballet of the 20th Century, I also found a button saying that "Béjart is sexier." I immediately asked myself "than what?" Than Balanchine, Joffrey, or Feld? Or the two nude dancers involved in a gentle pas de deux in *Oh, Calcutta!?* Next question: Does every artist get the kind of publicity he deserves?

Perhaps Béjart did. Whatever the real truth behind the truth may be, his company filled the large house of the Brooklyn Academy for almost three weeks. The impact of his ballets on the European youth is astounding. This makes me believe that Béjart is a phenomenon of our time—like the fortunately defunct Living Theatre. I am fascinated by this problem. For many, Béjart seems to be the answer to a need which spells escape with a capital E: be it to India, Revolution, Buddhism, or *art nouveau*. For the despair of our anger with the world and ourselves he offers the sincerity of insincerity. Béjart borrows from all current forces at play and integrates them in his ballets, which are never only one thing.

I don't think one should ask from Béjart more than he is able and willing to give. He was told that his Ballet of the 20th Century cannot be compared to any American company. He is, in fact, light years away from what is being done here (which in itself could add spice to variety). As if he were not of this world (while being very much so) he seems to hark back to former centuries. His preoccupation with basic geometric patterns, with symmetry, remind one of the very beginnings of ballet. His predilection for the statuesque moments may, for all we know, go back to Viganó.

I don't think he should be compared with anyone at all. He is unique in his longing for the over-sized design, for poetic theatricality, and choreographic images which come best to life as spectaculars in huge arenas. This may partly explain his preference for the big gesture—even if it has little meaning—and his success with the staging of mass scenes. He is simply lost when it comes to any detail and choreographic finesse. He shows a certain inability to structure a solo with meaningful patterns and gestures, but somewhat improves when facing the problem of a pas de deux. His conceits, like French embroidery, often have touches of coyness and cuteness.

One other basic feature in Béjart's work is his total involvement with the idea of the ritual. All dances are basically ritualistic, as Jerome Robbins once wrote. But while other choreographers accept it as a fact of life and keep this knowledge in the back of their minds, Béjart works with it as a point of departure wherever possible. This approach works creatively in at least two of his ballets I saw, in *The Rite of Spring* and *Bhakti*.

I considered his *Rite of Spring* a successful ballet. I remember having talked to Balanchine, who also thought that at least the first part of it has quite stunning qualities. It certainly is, in the shattering brutality with which it hits the virgin mind, a ritual expressive of the awakening of spring but it also takes into account the male as a bird of prey swooping down on the female in an obsession with and glorification of his virility (in the truest D. H. Lawrence sense). Béjart created a dramatically powerful movement design for this ballet, however geometric or linear it may be.

It must be stressed that one of the outstanding features of his company is the strength of his male dancers, a fact that helps the *Rite of Spring* to be as effective as it is. *Bhakti* is less impressive as a ritual, but it has many poetic moments of astounding beauty. This ballet reveals some of Béjart's weaknesses and fortes. He thinks strongly in terms of the theater, and when he fails he does so because the showman is stronger in him than all his knowledgeable sense of theater. He knows what sells, he knows too well what is en vogue. So he mixes East and West, Wagner and Buddhism, and then one of his poorest concoctions, almost the epitome of Kitsch, *Les Vainqueurs*, is born.

We may grant him a great deal of imagination (which is not necessarily identical with choreographic inventiveness). As character so easily defeats genius, his lack of taste sometimes defeats his imagination. He is, no doubt, a well-read and educated person. One only has to read interviews with him or see him on television. He is a strong, hypnotic personality who has come to believe he can afford to believe in himself. Sometimes he reminds me of the messianic madness of Julian and Judith Beck of The Living Theatre, and Béjart's *Messe Pour Les Temps Present* is the balletic counterpart to Beck's *Paradise Now* and other "*Mysteries*". Béjart is much cleverer than the Becks, who preached revolution and anarchy. Béjart only wants to bring ballet to the masses. He does create little Woodstocks here and there and loves to end his ballets with an apotheosis of love.

His *Firebird* is a kind of balletic wolf in sheep's clothing. Partisans in blue jeans—jeans have become a fighting symbol for a better future in his eyes—raise their fists, even though it says nowhere that these are communists. One of the partisans metamorphoses into a firebird, then dies, then rises in youthful freshness and determination like a phoenix from the ashes of yesterday's calamities. The implication is clear, but you can never definitely say it is a political statement. Walter Terry referred to Béjart's *Firebird* as "a modern-day Prometheus." I did not miss the Russian fairy tale. I was disturbed by the obviousness, the simplistic approach with not enough excitement and variation in the choreography. There was his chance for another *Rite of Spring*, and he missed it.

Another salient feature of the Béjart ballet is most disconcerting: Not his simplicity, but that he makes a virtue of simplicity.

Sometimes he succeeds in finding moments of poetic beauty because simplicity is basic to it (as in the second section of *Actus Tragicus*). But more often it is an excuse, a way-out for his limited vocabulary. By being elementary, householding as he does—however skillfully—with the choreographic means at his disposal, he reduces the art of ballet to a self-explanatory level which is frightfully close to non-art, non-ballet. (An articulate lady behind my seat: "I love it, it's so simple, so clean. The other modern companies set my teeth on edge, they always try to make me think.")

Béjart has the gift of a visionary without the technical means of putting his visions into a strongly focussed and structured ballet. A case in point is his *Romeo and Juliet Suite*, to music by Berlioz. He had the great idea of condensing the sequence of the entire love story in a single pas de deux while letting the drama of the Capulets and Montagues killing one another unfold in the background. A great and challenging concept. But while little occurred to him choreographically to make the love duet come alive, his male dancers having their hands on each other's throats only heighten a simplistic image to the point of absurdity. If he'd had Tybalt facing Mercutio and fighting it out in the background, while the star-cross'd lovers embrace in innocent passion, slowly gliding from ecstasy into growing awareness of despair, it could have been a great experience. But feeling on safer ground with a mass scene and ensnared by the ritualistic mania, he has about twenty men killing one another. This contradicts all logic in the case of *Romeo and Juliet*, except perhaps if it were choreographed for a stadium with more than ten thousand people watching it. (But then the subject matter would have been wrongly chosen.)

He is an ambitious fellow. In his repertory he has *Notre Faust*, his free translation of Goethe's *Faust* into a dance drama. In a most informal way he uses key sentences or sometimes merely key words from this poetic play. They were in French and in the original German. To be better understood on Broadway, some of the French phrases were translated into English. The tri-lingual presentation was too reminiscent of Babel (all the more since

German and English were spoken with heavy accents), but it gave *Faust* an international touch.

In order to spite Goethe, Heinrich Heine had once written a ballet scenario in which Mephistopheles appears in the disguise of a ballerina. Béjart surprised with a series of metamorphoses which, in a way, seem to be significant, almost in a Kafkaesque manner, and do make sense. At the very outset when Faust voices his doubts about

> Habe nun, ach! Philosophie,
> Juristerei und Medizin,
> Und leider auch Theologie . . . .

the play of metamorphoses begins. Instead of telling my version of it, I let Béjart give his:

To start, everyone is on stage. It is a small cast—twelve boys and myself and eight girls. All soloists . . . they play all the parts. They change costumes, and they come back. We found authentic church clothes in museums and galleries . . . they are two- or three-hundred years old.

The music is an interesting mixture, the Mass of B Minor of Bach, and all the demonic parts I made on Argentine tangos . . . I dance mostly the tangos. It's half funny, half parodic. I dance tango like Gene Kelly would dance tango.

I found out that *Faust* was like a religious ceremony for Goethe, so the story happens inside a ceremony, which is like a magic black mass. They put on those enormous church clothes, and when they use the crosses and chalices—everything is real.

I start as old Faust. Then young Mephistopheles arrives. When Faust wants to become young, we change personalities . . . Every time young Faust wants to meet one of the three women he falls in love with, he never meets the woman, because the woman is dancing abstract. And I myself put on the costume of the woman and act the role for him.

I put on a mask like in the Kabuki, and I have huge costumes like in the Noh theatre, and do very little movements—slow movements—at the same time the girl is dancing. It was in my mind to use the old religious theatre ceremonies where the man takes the woman's role. It is something that I have been thinking about for a long time.

He succeeded quite brilliantly in the first part. What was happening on stage was electrifying in the finest theatrical tradition. But the second part, with the exception of one or two ideas, was less impressive. Perhaps the surprise had worn off by then, perhaps there were a few empty stretches when my mind had time to wander off and to think of some Goethean lines. It was probably too big and daring an artistic endeavor to swallow both parts of *Faust* and hope to get away with it without giving the artistic devil his due.

It is not easy to do justice to Béjart. He may not be important as a choreographer, but he creates ballets with a difference. He is very much important as a phenomenon of our time. We may not like his choreography. We may not like the difference. We may also dislike the time in which we live, the success of its failures, its phoniness, its non-art. But there is little we can do about or against it. Except perhaps comfort ourselves that everything is out of joint, and that time has the wonderful and frightening habit of passing.

1978

New York. What we know under the misnomer of "the modern dance"—the German word "Ausdruckstanz" comes closer to the truth—is the expression of the artist's self, the confrontation of his being with himself. In trying to discover himself he was supported by the vast scope of the yet unknown in him, a plenitude of joys and torments forced upon the strength and fragility of his body.

He—or rather she—was born as a recitalist. Historically, the solo developed from the sociocultural habit that well fitted the bourgeois homes in the nineteenth century. Poets, musicians, and dancers, were invited to entertain the host and hostess and their guests and to while away the time of an afternoon or an evening. But the artists who took up the torches to light up a new world of expression dared to face the mercy and anger of the gods. In the process of finding themselves they had to go back to the beginning, to the innocence of experience, the tree of artistic knowledge. They were alone with themselves and the vastness of their chances and crossroads. They wanted to rediscover Paradise while staying outside of it. Isadora Duncan sought the road to her soul and discovered the innocence of her body. Loie Fuller, caught in the frenzy of billowing drapery, discovered the Promethean splendor of light. Ruth St. Denis wanted to escape the reality of herself only to find the within-ness of the spirit.

These soloists discovered the Absolute of self-expression. They learned by finding, they found by learning. The solo is a two-front war; you wrestle with yourself and your audience. You must demand the most from yourself because you demand the most from your audience. Were they madmen who rejoiced in their daring? Perhaps. The artist took it upon herself to divorce her art from the norms set by tradition, and in doing so she divorced herself from the public. She had to reconquer it. But this divorce was already proclaimed by the nineteenth-century artist in other fields, in literature and, above all, in the visual arts. Dance followed suit.

There was, in these artists, a mystical belief that destiny had chosen them, that they were performing destiny. The expression of this new dance was the revelation of one person alone on stage. And it remained so to this very day. To choreograph for a group of modern dancers is a concession to tradition (which the modern dance actually doesn't have) and to the public—a flight into theatricality. The genuine expression was the unfolding of the individual: the splendor of her thoughts, the beauty of her feelings translated into the movements of her body. To have thrown away the accoutrements of ballet, to have negated the technique and principles of the classic ballet could only have been realized by one single individual again and again. For the first time since early history the naked truth of an experience could become a stage reality. It could only be told by a soloist.

The ballet dancer has a chance to be alone on stage in divertissements, but then she (or he) is limited by the conventions of the craft and only granted the opportunity to prove technical proficiency. In a way, the one exception was the fortuitous event when Fokine choreographed *The Dying Swan* for Pavlova. The solo has become a way of life for the modern dancer, his justification for being what he is. The fact that all the great soloists, from Mary Wigman, to Martha Graham, to Pauline Koner, turned to choreographing for groups was unconsciously necessitated to keep the "species" alive and consciously forced upon them by the need for a broader basis of activity.

For some time I thought the solo recitals were no longer fashionable or needed. Pauline Koner was one of the last dancers who could bring it off beautifully, followed at some distance by Daniel Nagrin. I was convinced it could no longer be done, because there was no great dance personality with something new to say. Then Ze'eva Cohen changed my mind somewhat. She taught me that a successful solo tailored to the creative dancer's need and expressiveness was not necessarily limited to the same performer.

Miss Cohen was seen in solo works by several choreographers, and from number to number she surprised me more and more with the ease she slipped from one choreographer's spirit to the next. She presented five pieces, and she was only choreographically responsible for the last one. Some, not all, of the works she danced I had seen before, in the main executed by their own choreographers. It was fascinating to observe what Ze'eva Cohen could do with someone else's material, how her forceful personality gave it different highlights, another dynamic feeling, more drama here, and stronger lyric overtones there. The range of the original works performed by her is stupendous: From Anna Sokolow to James Waring, from Jeff Duncan to José Limón, from Deborah Jowitt to Daniel Nagrin. Only a truly dedicated artist being creative in her own way, can recreate someone else's dream image, and only a fascinating performer can come really close to the spirit in which a solo was conceived.

I admired what I saw. Whenever one doubts that something can still be done, somebody emerges as if from nowhere to prove one

Ze'eva Cohen in 32 Variations in C Minor. *Choreography: James Waring. Photo: John Budde. Author's collection.*

wrong. And yet, I will go on cherishing the memory of certain soli I have seen in which a creative mind has expressed itself in its unique native way.

Zürich. "We are longing to go home and do not know where to," wrote the German Romantic lyricist, Joseph Eichendorff, in the eighteen twenties. He could not better have described man in the 1970s. Perhaps we should envision Romanticism as a never-dying power without which man cannot exist. Has any generation ever stopped defying reality or trying to escape it in some devious ways and disguises, often in fear of its own daring? In his self-contradictory manner man has always longed for his Arcadia, but it was not before the mid-eighteenth-century that his point of departure became a philosophical postulate and his journey to the destination of the unattainable turned into a worldwide malaise, whose major symptom was the air-borne ballerina. We honor the memory of the romantic who dared to put the naked feelings of his tragic ecstasy on the map of history by spelling his era with a capital "R".

Is romanticism—upper or lower case—outdated in our scientific era? Not at all. Now that we are able to turn the moon into a tourist attraction—if we only want to—, we shall need dreams for something even more remote and magic. We are frightened by our own fear of the future because there may be none. All the more do we need to run away from a reality which holds up a mirror to all possible marvels while preparing the seed of destruction.

When we escape to the theater, a spontaneous sputum of creative negligence will not do (and still there is so much of it in what calls itself the avant-garde). As the true neoromantics that we are, we need to be shown the excitement in mere existence and the beauty in being. We cannot help, ever so often, being shocked into shame of being human and responsible for the sores of our portentous and potent era. But the paroxism of negation, the depths of hollowness, are signs of our time, and they have been with mankind in one form or another through the centuries. So much that is little more than a feeble and defiant scribble on the wall is taken for art. Shall we take it for the Mene Tekel of our time or already as its epitaph? If escape we must, we want to be told at least one truth of the many truths; we want to face the revelation of life's mystery or some aspect of it; yes, even a romantic and escapist needs to be shown the image of a heightened danced reality, an image formed out of an inner cry and outer chaos.

Bertolt Brecht once said, "What kind of a time is this in which it is a crime to speak of trees!" We ought to add: Because it is the time it is, an extremely sordid state of affairs, let us also speak of trees. After all, the tree is but a symbol of our belief in the creative will, a symbol of our hope that something will and can last if not hit by lightning, lightning from above or man-made lightning.

New York. Has the jet age made the world smaller? Our imagination has become slave to advertisement slogans; without ever becoming aware of it, our thinking has lost its independence from a world at odds with itself. But there are—or were not so long ago—some minds unmoved by the torrents of fallacies. For instance, the French mystic, Simone Weil, said that it is immoral to reach a destination without having made the journey. One can go all the way—slowly, I would suggest—to reach the opposite point.

The world of Alexander Calder is a whole world in a nutshell, created by the playfulness of the child in a great artist. If images of sculpture have ever danced, his do. I saw a short film in which he played with his own figures made of wire and metal, and he played with his toy-like circus in total oblivion of the world. The *Kunsthaus* in Zürich had a representative show of his mobiles, works that move, forced by the mood of their own balance. I remember vaguely that one afternoon a few modern dancers used part of the exhibition and danced around Calder's mobiles and stabiles. My recollection tells me that his work as a stage set did little to enhance the dance, nor did the dancing bodies give Calder's witty and playful scuptures more weight, or rather, more airiness in space.

I was reminded of it when I witnessed a tribute to Calder on Broadway. The "Orchestra of Our Time" presented Satie's *Socrate* and used a reconstructed mobile set which Calder did for the 1936 production at the Wadsworth Atheneum in Hartford. Satie and Calder are kindred souls. If there ever has been a musical expression of highly polished sophistication in the guise of childlike and sometimes primitive naiveté, then it can be found in Erik Satie's work. When *Socrate* was first heard in Paris in 1918 it was described. as "variations on monotony." Its rhythmic repetition conveys the feeling of white music and reminded me again of Satie's reverie on a plate: "How white it is! No painting ornaments it; it is all of a piece." At certain points I envisioned images of one of those white paintings which are just white-on-white, but there were other moments in which I felt the monotony radiating a deeply felt sensation.

While the orchestra played and the singers voiced Plato's words, Calder's mobiles were seen in the background. For some time they did not move, but then when they were set in motion, beautiful in themselves, strangely enough their beauty paled, their wit seemed stale. Most often when two media meet, one of them has to give way and bow to the other. There was not even that eccentric incongruity between mobiles and music, that incongruity Satie loved so much; he could not even have said about it what he once voiced about one of his scores, "this work is absolutely incomprehensible, even to me."

The decline of quality goes hand in hand with the decline of Western civilization, as predicted by Oswald Spengler during the years of the first World War. It is a gradual process of everyday corrosion, and, being daily witnesses to it, we are never really able to notice it. Commercialism has a dictatorial hold on us and forces all expressions of our time—the artistic and nonartistic ones—into the channels of the mass media. By virtue of its nature, commercialism must court the quick and garish, it must flirt with the lowest average to achieve the highest harvest. It is honest about helping and offering the arts to a larger audience, but by putting its signature underneath, it determines the point of departure as much as the direction. It not only controls the artistic product itself; it determines the entire approach to the work process. In other words, the artistic intent becomes cheapened.

What now passes as culture is seen with eyes trained to see the trash of our fast moving days. These eyes have lost the ability of measuring themselves in the mirror of the past. A dancer-choreographer who had twirled herself into the foreground of attention could refer to Beethoven as "that old European shit." It remained uncensored and was spoken in a television interview on NET. Some younger people I queried found nothing reprehensible about it.

We wonder about the dance explosion in our era. Ancient Rome—before it was sacked—abounded in dancing schools. History does not tell us whether the ancient Romans considered this phenomenon as odd or ominous.

1979

New York. It has been a long way from here to absurdity. . . .

To see the postwar period in retrospect, or in whatever fragmented form our memory may assist us in looking back without anger over the last three-and-a-half decades, we may easily find ourselves in a state of wonder about how much our confusion and despair resulted in a disarray of artistic expression. The significant signals pointed to the dangers in the development of a society which was divided in itself and devouring its natural resources while making the best of a reigning consumer spirit. Man's efforts remained directed toward accelerating the use of the growing scientific advances in all possible ways without giving much thought to means and consequences.

One of the major trends was to endow the "machine" with godlike power which necessitated to shift all priority to "thought" in order to feign mastery over something that obviously slipped out of control. This only increased the already latent estrangement between the function of our brains and the state of our feelings and with it our estrangement from our self. Our attitude toward criticism grew ever stronger than our impetus to create, so that our minds were more often enriched by what critical writing could do for us than by the rare cases of an unforgettable creative experience. This became most obvious in the fifties and sixties. But in spite of our keen interest in analysis and criticism we lost the most important feelings, those for truth and dignity and the passion for asking what things mean and what meaning means. And thus all became meaningless.

The world becomes too easily what we think of it as or wish to see it as. With the artist's growing estrangement from himself and society, his antagonism turned into cynicism in the postwar world; his castigating laugh about a world as a malleable model shaped by man's greed and glut and most insincere sincerity could be heard everywhere. Jean Cocteau knew why he saw our greatest danger in our over-cleverness. He only reminded us of Goethe's warning that "knowledge can only be true as long as it is not in excess of man's feelings" and, at the end of last century, Nietzsche prognosticated our downfall when he warned us that "man ought not to know more of a good thing than he can creatively live up to."

The artist at odds with himself faced a society which, in the process of proliferation, could not help but reduce scientific knowledge into bits of information. The highfalutinness of mere gossip became the accepted standard of dispersing information, particularly through the mass media. Modern society no longer has the ability to grasp that what *is* is only real in so far as it is symbolic, and man's mind—more inquisitive than curious—feels satisfied with the facade of appearances. Thus, the experience becomes fragmented, dissolving reality into incoherent images. Great art, or what we accepted as great art until now, mostly arose out of outside stimulation, but out of inside inspiration. The outside world is nothing until the artist transforms it by magic. It is the magician in him who discovers the invisible and turns it into the visible for us.

We have been trapped by the crazy confluence of all the commercialized din, the air-conditioned nightmare of our lives (in the words of Henry Miller), by the neon-lit phoniness advertising the artistic "musts" as they are determined by press agents and defined by a number of critics and by the entire fabric of a society with its televisionary look, with people being out to outdo each other as well as themselves, who, in their motion-madness discovered that speed can cover up for the nonexistence of content and meaning. Some artists aped and mocked their own time, making skillful use of reality through overemphasis of its excesses and playing sheepishly on all keys of its insanity. Some escaped into nudity or escaped to India to find salvation in meditation with gurus. The Beatnik generation saw the writing on the wall, the Hippies added their graffiti. It has been a living theater dramatizing their protests against the life of our own making to the cathartic point of nausea.

Of course, there is no era that could not articulate its dilemma artistically, and if it were only to shock with its replica of an obvious reality or the desperate new. But, fortunately, there has always been one or another artist who can envision the poetry of life and give life to his poetry—in whatever medium he may find his expression.

All great events in world history are registered by the arts. The artist anticipated the traumatic changes caused by World War I long in advance with many way-out "isms", violent in their deviation from the accepted, indicating mankind's unease within its social fabric. With Dadaism the artist's creative mind went berserk and jumped into the face of the ill-established world with vitriolic vehemence, declaring aesthetic bankruptcy due to the total collapse of all ethic principles of mankind. Alongside the dadaists, the expressionists cried out in terrified despair. When Dadaism—which, to this very day, has never really left the art scene—had spent its first fury in the mid-twenties, it metamorphosed into surrealism. After having castigated himself, man escaped from the nightmare of his reality—always with his built-in nostalgia ready to go into action—and gave Hieronymus Bosch's fantasies the Freudian lyricism of the colorful unconscious.

A strain of Dadaism can be detected in the work of Cunningham who, however, was skillful enough to create for himself a highly *aesthetic* and polished veneer with which he covers the anti-aesthetic base from which he operates. In the work of those who took off from him and can only vaguely formulate an anti-aesthetic aestheticism, the self-destructive and self-defeating trend becomes more often revealed than not. Surrealism has left its mark on the mainstream of the ballet. Frederick Ashton's *Illuminations* is probably the most outstanding example of a successful surrealistic approach. A great many surrealistic moments are manifest in dance works which strive to achieve a super-reality, an imagery lying beyond the images of the phenomenal world. The dance's elusive quality, its inherent spontaneity, the release of the dancer's dormant sensibilities, and above all the poetic allusion of the slightest gesture are basically surrealistic.

Historically seen, Diaghilev's heroic theater scandals—*Afternoon of a Faun* (1912), *Rite of Spring* (1913), and *Parade* (1917)—are the same expression of revulsion about the established way of doing and seeing things as we find at the source of Futurism, Expressionism, and Dadaism. These scandals were strong accents in an era of political and spiritual upheaval, as was the emergence of the modern dance in Germany. The revolutionary was of an explosive nature in the years of 1913 and 1917. It was reflected in Mary Wigman's dances and remained very much articulated in German and Russian theater, literature, and painting. America was rather removed from the horrors during and after World War I, and when some Denishawn dancers broke away from their past, they did it in a totally different mental climate. This is one of the reasons why the classical modern dance in America—despite its seemingly revolutionary stance—retained a neoromantic flair. For more than two decades the modern dance had the historic task of finding a new way of artistic expression, of impelling the balletic mainstream to put on a twentieth century face, and, in a true Hegelian way, to engender its own antithesis.

The mood of the twenties was characterized by a roaring turmoil of a Prohibition-drunk America whose intelligentsia exiled itself to the Left Bank of Paris, while the Europeans tried to rebuild a world which had collapsed and buried all old values in its debris. However ludicrous and inhumane mankind's attitudes were in the twenties and thirties, the idea of continuity was still all there. But the forties after World War II, when the atom bomb had been dropped over Hiroshima and Nagasaki, erased the artist's belief in posterity. Even if the creative man never questions tomorrow, he cannot help sensing his lostness, he can no longer get rid of a "le-déluge-est-avec-nous" feeling. In the pivoting year of 1952 the systematic wrecking of the past began on both sides of the ocean, although the French artists indoctrinated by their philosophes Jean-Paul Sartre and Albert Camus, were better equipped to declare a profound moratorium on their humanistic world than their American brethren who never really took to the ideas of Existentialism and rather borrowed those from Zen Buddhism. It seemed as if there had been a division of labor and a two-front conquest of the vanquished over the victors.

The French had brought home from their battle and main enemy the concepts of the German philosophers Martin Heidegger and Karl Jaspers (who had been strongly influenced by Sören Kierkegaard) and seized upon Franz Kafka as the tortured soul and perfect paragon of lived Existentialism.

Bringing home Zen notions to a sober, commercialized American society that had started to Coca-Colonize the world was a daring action which could but create confusion and consternation. Pollock stumbled into action painting, Cage invented Zen-inspired indeterminacy. The shock was all the greater that a ballet-trained dancer like Merce Cunningham, who preferred modern dance to ballet and was Martha Graham's partner for years, had left Graham to turn against all principles she stood for and to join forces with John Cage. A few years later, another partner of Martha Graham, Erick Hawkins, embarked on his very personal safari into an imaginary East.

It was in the early fifties that a new kind of modern dancer spearheaded a new era of a nonliteral dance (with Alwin Nikolais' experiments as a sideshow). On second thought, I am not sure whether the dance was then in the forefront. The Cunningham version of it seemed in tow of the painters, from Duchamp to

Rauschenberg and Jaspar Johns, and it was, above all, under the influence of the magnetic personality of John Cage. But whoever may have been the driving force, these were the experimental artists who formed a new solid front against literal and psychologized art.

The time was apparently ripe for negation and experimentation. Some of the creative minds had to say "no" to the past, a "no" that swelled to a vociferous, though a more and more articulate, sound from year to year. Peter Brook, a raging genius of the theater, summed it all up when he said: "All through the world in order to save the theater almost everything of the theater still has to be swept away." They were the sweepers and form-smashers who taught us to see life and art with new eyes, to see the very things the way they are, to reduce life to art and vice versa. Already in the twenties Bertolt Brecht tried to exclude the notion of illusion from a theatrical experience. He did not expect the audience to go through pity and fear in cathartic ecstasies, he wanted the public to be objective, cool observers of the scene— like a juror at a trial, who ought to bring home a verdict, as Brecht would say.

There is a thin-edged parallel in this objectivized attitude with Cunningham's approach to choreography. In one of my newspaper reviews I expanded this thought: "An evening with Merce Cunningham is a unique experience, puzzling here and perplexing there, but an exploration of time and space in a new fashion. He seems to have done for the dance what Bert Brecht did for the theatre: He has created an epic theatre dance."

Merce Cunningham must have liked this comparison since he quoted it among the newspaper clippings in his brochure published in 1963. This statement is probably correct as to the cool and analytic attitude which both Cunningham and Brecht expect from their audiences. Neither wishes us to enter their theater with emotional expectations; they want us to let things happen to us the way they happen. But there the comparison ends. There is hardly ever any social comment in Cunningham's works and if so only by the faintest insinuation and the farthest stretch of one's imagination. He feels that the dance has no message to deliver, that a dance work has no other content but the inherent essence of the movement itself. John Cage once defined theater as anything you can see and hear, viewing "everyday life itself as theater," the idea being that any art presented should be as "unstructured" as daily life, without any focal point, as if projected by the many Happenings and Events. This finally leads to the concepts of bombarding all our senses and of audience participation. Perhaps the artist had nothing to show but the "thing" itself; he had nothing to say since he discovered that we were unable to communicate.

The fifties were beset by the sudden realization of noncommunicativeness which, in fact, has always been our most hourly guest. We experience it in our private lives as much as in our conduct with the world at large. How often do we face the difficulty in reaching out to the person closest to us and how often have nations resorted to warfare because of their basic lack of communication? This is not a new problem. Adam must have had difficulties in talking to Cain and Abel, and at certain points of their lives my grandparents must have acutely suffered from it. But it was left to our growing awareness in the wake of existentialist despair to celebrate artistically man's psychological impasse with man.

Noncommunicativeness also brought to the fore a greater insight into the awkward but insoluble gulf between the young and the adult world; the term "generation gap" suddenly rose to the prominence of a cliché behind which a frightening reality kept hiding. The "new" artist removed himself so far from society that he could not help taking a position that was an articulate juxtaposition. In his excesses over the years he had finally nothing to offer but spite and spit, most often couched in polite contempt, whether he went conceptual, minimal, Performance, Pop, or environmental. But he kept the lively arts lively, and his inspirational paroxysms caught fire all over the world.

But not all noncommunicativeness was doomed artistically. I am not thinking of John Cage's famous piano piece 4'33", whose artistic secret's key was never touched by the pianist who waited together with the noncommunicative instrument for the allotted time to pass in the hope it would do as it did, and in the expectation that we could catch the sounds in the stillness. I am not thinking of painters who filled their canvasses with the bareness of their genius (with a dot or dash somewhere on white or the minute shading of white on white or black on black), or like Rauschenberg and Jaspar Johns, Warhol and Joseph Beuyhs, who added to the reality of life their monumental hiccoughs and the shock of a twisted irony that impressed the critics and curators who were testing the public, its patience and threshold of gullibility, its ennui and willingness to buy the idea that the emperor wore beautiful new clothes. I am rather thinking of a couple of iconoclasts in French literature.

Jean Cocteau, who did not want to "be enslaved by obsolete formulae," had made the first sally in this direction when he tried to heighten poetically the banal and commonplace, while Cage and Cunningham went one step further and presented the very thing that is as the thing that is, with the advice for the audience "to let it happen to you" without looking for meaning of poetic substance. In the very beginning, when this new trend crystallized in the early fifties, the American artist on the way to non-art received intellectual sustenance from the French writer-philosophes who gave articulate expression to W. H. Auden's *Age of Anxiety*. Their despair was deeply rooted in the existentialist thinking of Sartre, Camus & Co., who, weighing the meaning of life and man in his time, felt justified in equating "Being and Nothingness," as Sartre did. Sartre came to the conclusion that "man is a useless passion" and that "hell is other people," while Camus philosophized about the senselessness of man's Sisyphean labor and metaphysical anguish, conditions leading to the absurdity of the human condition.

Eugène Ionesco, a father figure in the theatrical realm of Absurdity, believes that it is society itself that stands between human beings and creates the chasms across which there is no communication or, at best, where there's only the echo of empty clichés: "No society has been able to abolish human sadness, no political system can deliver us from the pain of living, from our fear of death, our thirst for the absolute; it is the human condition that directs the social condition, not vice versa."

His first play, *The Bald Soprano*, is a parody of the linguistic commonplace in which we dwell. The tragedy behind the frightening humor of this play, is the mechanical aspect of our existence, which is wiping out our identity. The chairs in his *The Chairs* become real, haunting symbols of nonpresent human beings, giving Gestalt to man's inability to find meaning in his existence. It pictures the frustration of man in making himself understood and of the artist who, when called upon, can barely stammer meaningless sounds while facing a nonexistent audience. Was there ever drawn a more devastating image of absurdity and futility?

In the early fifties, the greatest form-smasher of them all was Samuel Beckett, who became the high priest of minimalism when he ended his theatrical journey with a huge mouth onstage uttering gibberish nonsense. But in the year 1952, when Cage introduced the Happenings at Black Mountain College, Beckett gave us the classical play about the era of noncommunicativeness with his two tramps, lost in a desolate landscape of life, *Waiting for Godot*. When the tramp Vladimir says to the Messenger of Godot in the trembling breath of mankind: "Tell him, tell him that you saw me," he expresses the desperate hope of being recognized. In contrast to the more radical art movements in the States, and despite his sense of futility, Beckett's voice cried out from the dunghill of all absurdity and human waste "Eli, Eli, doth thou not see that I am, I am?!" Man may have always been confronted by the unanswerable question, "Who am I?" What had been added in the fifties was man's traumatic fear of himself. The artist in him blamed society for it.

I may be considered as a conservative critic who feels the need to conserve the treasures of the past. But there it ends. I am also eager to discover the revelation of the new. And yet I must have often sounded rather square and queer to many of the so-called avant-gardists in the sixties when I lashed out against the hoaxes and put-ons, against the fads and faddists that had been fêted by critics who seemed to have been studying the schedules of the latest bandwagons—when they were leaving and where they were going.

"The cult of the anti-cliché had become the cliché of our time," I shouted, believing in Baudelaire's dictum that a critique ought to be written with passion and a bit of poetry and, above all, not by a hunchbacked mind. The greatest art has always been created by skilled craftsmen in hours of spiritual intoxication, by men possessed by the fever of forming and shaping, of giving their inner visions the content and contours of an artistic realization. Some of the greatest innovations belonged with them. Van Gogh's color explosion, Frank Lloyd Wright's dynamic forms, Isadora Duncan's soul-searching, liberating gesture, and Martha Graham's percussive beat and angularity certainly went against the taste of their time, but not against the taste of art itself.

Even if non-art somersaults itself into ecstasies, the result is still non-art. Wherever I could, I have tried to make this clear. For there is no difference between

an eighty-four inch club sandwich of sliced car grille, billboard faces, and boiled spaghetti, as exhibited in a museum, and a dance creation in which the performers play ball as if in a gym for twenty or more minutes only to numb the audience into accepting a love duet which follows it with the illogic of real life blending the most absurd of Ionesco with the sexiest of the Kama-Sutra and Brecht's detachment theory thrown in for good measure. And, are we supposed to take it as a comment upon our time when a dancer excels himself in static positions sparingly interrupted by frantic attempts at movement? Is it a touch of irony or an elating inspiration when two dancers carry radios which, for the purpose of accompaniment, are tuned to a certain wave length that, one night, may let you hear Mozart, and, on another, a news broadcast? Or what should we think of a dancer running around in circles onstage, while showing a stag movie? Must the art thus become a hoax to the score of the flushing sound effects of a water closet?

I admit I had little patience and much disdain for artists who denied dignity to any creative expression by insulting, mocking, or parodying the meaningfulness of meaning. I am with Braque and Picasso, who believed that art must disturb. I go one step further and say that art, among other things, ought to shake us out of our complacency if, at the same time, it gives us some substance to hold on to and lets us discover, somewhere, a spark of elation.

The critic has to judge from within the artist. In September 1959 I wrote about the New London Dance Festival for the *Saturday Review of Literature* and said about Merce Cunningham: "His *Antic Meet* is a crowning achievement in making the absurd lovable. In *Rune* he can say a great deal through surprising imagery in the most unrelated form."

You may not think that an artist is doing the right thing for you, but you cannot help acknowledging that his artistry—even if irritating—is to be respected. James Joyce and Gertude Stein, both in their very unique ways, gave me a hard time in the twenties and thirties, but I recognized their peculiar genius. Oskar Kokoschka, with whom I grew up in Vienna, had early gone through an expressionist-experimental phase as a painter and writer for which, in my own formative years, I could not muster enough under-standing or liking, but I have always felt intuitively the genius working in him. Having grown up with this century I could list many examples.

They have proved to me that my understanding and tolerance has grown with me as much as has my instinctive feeling for how far an artist can go without losing me on his way. I have always tried to keep at a certain distance from what- and whoever it may have been in order to gain a better perspective. I have always hoped to match the artist's dignity with my reverence for the created work. When John Martin, dance critic for the *New York Times* for three decades, was honored with the Capezio Award, he apologized for all the hurts and injuries he may have caused certain dancers and choreographers. I sing psalms of praise on behalf of humility and shrink in horror when I detect arrogance and an overbearing gesture. One cannot help doing wrong in life, but let us not blame life for it.

Sometimes a postscriptum can be an important afterthought opening a forgotten window.

I have become acquainted with Ludwig Wittgenstein and his precisely verbalized philosophy in the late twenties in Vienna and then met him again in the late thirties in London. I understand that the school of logical positivists take their wisdom from his. More often than not I felt bewitched by his intelligence, which seemed to render the most simple thing difficult and the most difficult thoughts seemingly simple. There was something of Nietzsche's prophetic power in him, but there was also an ironic twinkle in his right eye and a verbal smile around his lips when he turned master juggler with words, making sense of the nonsense dominating the world.

While reading John Cage, who sees this world with similar eyes, I remembered a sentence Wittgenstein wrote in his *Tractatus Logico-Philosophicus*, one that could have been written by John Cage: "In the world everything is as it is and happens as it does happen. *In* it there is no value—and if there were, it would be of no value."

Wittgenstein's dictum, "Ethics and aesthetics are one," makes one think twice about Merce Cunningham's choreography and realize that perhaps indeed living, as well as thinking and the form of movement, are strongly interrelated. And in a certain uncertain way Nietzsche already anticipated the direction of the Mercistic trend when he said "I have at all times thought with my whole body and my whole life. I do not know what purely intellectual problems are."

"Since Stravinsky liked your version of *Rite of Spring* which you re-choreographed in 1920 so much better than Nijinsky's had you made decisive changes?" I asked Leonide Massine, whom I interviewed for the benefit of my dance history class at Barnard College in the late sixties.

His answer was surprising. "No, I don't think I did. I simplified most of the extreme archaic movements, the bent wrist and ankle movements. I tried to avoid what may have been Nijinsky's mistake—if mistake it was—to stay rhythmically too close to the score. I let myself be influenced more from the angularity and the broken lines of cubism and leaned heavily on the round dances of the Russian peasants which I knew well. Stravinsky may have liked anything done only slightly differently from Nijinsky's musicality and ability to choreograph. I had not seen Nijinsky's *Rite*, but have known about it as much as one can know second-hand. I am not sure that my changes were really an improvement. As some people who saw both versions said, mine may have lacked the inner fire, the intensity of the pathos which characterized the original. I may have done somewhat better ten years later when I choreographed it again at the Met with Martha Graham as the Chosen One who brought something fresh and new to the part."

Massine was matter-of-fact throughout this interview. He was an older man by then, but with a clear conception of what he had done and aimed for in the various phases of his career. I had seen him as a dancer and choreographer several times in the late thirties, but, strangely enough, my memory of it is very hazy. My fault or his? Why do I always remember him in *Gaieté Parisienne*? As the marvelous character dancer he was, with an impressive pantomimic range of expression? I suppose the bulk of his work is impressive. As one of the main forces in *Parade*, he turned the balletic clock and helped to move the dance into the twentieth century. And yet it is a strange sensation that keeps me from properly focusing on him, the man and his work. I cannot draw his artistic profile on the walls of my memory. I told myself I must reread his *My Life in Ballet*. Perhaps I will then be able to touch him and, like a blind man, feel the intricacies of his contours. Maybe.

Theater, in general, and ballet, in particular, are impure art forms with many minds clashing in contrast and controversy, igniting and stimulating the flow of ideas. I have often imagined such minds as Cocteau's, Picasso's, Satie's, and Massine's provoking each other, fructifying their thoughts, pushing their imagination to the edge of ever-new ideas. This must have happened when *Parade* was in the making. The title was accepted as the gag idea it was, coming from Picasso. Satie's ragtime music was undoubtedly suggestive and animated Massine's choreographic notions. The circus theme delineated by Cocteau must have inspired Picasso. It mainly was Cocteau—judging from all reports—who never stopped throwing ideas into the ring.

Cocteau was on a world tour in the early forties because of the war, or despite it. One was never quite sure of his motivations and reactions. He was the lie that always spoke the truth, as he felt it. He loved the circus and clowns. He himself was probably one of the great clowns in literature and life. He was all sparkle and wit when I then met him in the home of a friend. It was fascinating to watch him. He did not belie his reputation as a brilliant causeur. There was, in whatever he said, an ironic twist and—what impressed me most—a poetic embellishment. Two British novelists were there, William Golding and Cecil Roberts. They provoked Cocteau to a verbal duel in which his repartees were mostly vehement thrusts, but delivered with lightness and charm, and, above all, he knew how far to go without going too far (as he once defined tact).

It was to be expected that he would be questioned about his versatility. He loathed nothing more than the moment of "standstill," he explained, he constantly needed new challenges in order to feel alive; he disliked repetitions and felt that monotony is the breath of death. His words reminded me of Gertrude Stein's saying, why do something if we know we can do it?

I could sense Cocteau's mental mobility and the playfulness with which he drifted toward an artistic adventure with no obligation to reach a pre-defined goal. What he seemed to enjoy most was the journey, the doing, and it made me better understand his notion that "the course of a river is almost always disapproved by its source." I remembered the fireworks of this conversation and took a few sparks with me for safekeeping. The visual aspect of the scene was just as memorable. In those days I studied expressive movements, gait, and gesture, as well as any possible meaning hidden in the shape of the hand or the configuration of its lines. My book, *The Story of the Human Hand*, partly resulted from this study, for which I mainly used the hands of well-known personalities.

What was so amazing about Cocteau was the physical agility with which his entire body accompanied his words. The gestures of his hands expressed his restlessness and the impatience with his words which seemed to be so much slower than his thoughts, although his speech pattern was rather rapid. His eyes, his lips, and the slight swaying of his trunk played a coordinated symphony of movement while he talked. Whenever I took handprints I drew the contours of the hand with pen or pencil before letting the person sign the print. Cocteau was the only person who felt compelled to add the cuffs to the print. Was it the draftsman in him who could not resist? Or did he feel ashamed to have seen his hands all of a sudden so naked?

Cocteau, charged with Diaghilev's ominous "Ètonne-moi," emerged after five years of relative silence to give the twentieth century its balletic freedom with one of history's greater theater scandals—*Parade*. Seeing *Parade* today one can no longer understand what shocked and enraged its first night audience. From our viewpoint, the scandal of the flagrantly hidden eroticism of the *Faun* is far more acceptable.

We shall hear bravos and boos in the theater as long as theaters exist. It is as old as the East Indian dance drama, where we find the first evidence of applause, of acclamation and refutation. I have often wondered how important a part the audience plays in its double role of sitting in the theater ready to receive and being

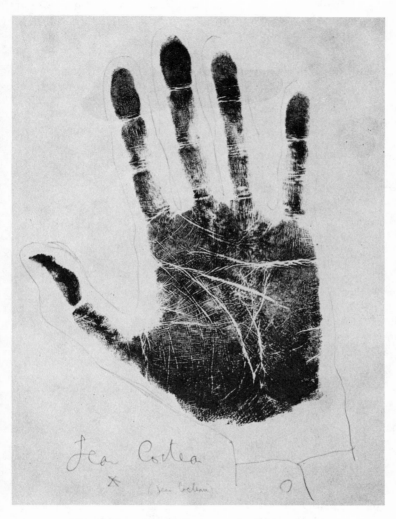

Handprint of Jean Cocteau. Author's collection.

there to give while receiving. The latter is rare. But the question of communal spirit in the auditorium creating a stimulating ambiance for the dancers or players has never been properly investigated. Is not the aura everyone exudes reaching the other person? And does not the sum total of all auras in the theater—a composite of expectations, preconceived feelings, love, indifference, and ha-tred—reach the stage? Feelings are far more potent and contagious than we wish to admit.

Of course, epigrammatic cynics maintain that spectators often go to the theater in order to be seen and not so much to see. Thinking of Cocteau and Massine, of Diaghilev's beloved scandals, and his audiences at the time reminds me of Paul Morand's remarks. This despicable footnote to histrionic history was made on the occasion of the death of Léon Bakst, one of Diaghilev's most admirable helpmates to success.

Bakst was, in fact, a Jew; and it was the great Israelite audiences that established the success of the Russian Ballet, that first great international success, marked by the boldness of the audience's dress, its immodesties, extravagant coiffures, depilated bodies, cosmetics, by that mixture of all modes to the point where one could not always distinguish between the house and the stage.

This footnote deserves a footnote of my own: Although such an antisemitic aside sheds some light on the chapter, "audience," it also shows that certain French right-wing writers have never forgiven themselves for having lost face in the Affaire Dreyfus. Paul Morand, a minor writer, was a major collaborator with the Nazis during World War II.

Certainly, there have always been performances at which the audiences made a social affair of the event. After all, what are gala performances for? And special performances with international stars when the entrance fees are exorbitantly high, guaranteeing exclusivity—but not necessarily great art? On the other hand, there were and still are connoisseurs and lovers of the theater and dance, there are the wide-eyed, enthusiastic youngsters who would queue up for hours, or for a whole night and day, to find entrance when there is standing room only.

Diaghilev may have overemphasized the importance of theater scandals as milestones in the development of the dance. An often told anecdote proves this point. When, in 1916, Hugo von Hofmannsthal's scenario of *Die Josefslegende*, produced by Ballets Russes with Massine in the title role, was loudly acclaimed, the poet turned to Diaghilev saying: "I would have preferred a scandal." Whereupon Diaghilev supposedly said: "My dear Hofmannsthal, it is not easy to achieve a scandal." This reply had wisdom in its facetiousness. Something unfamiliar may easily be rejected by the public as being in bad taste, as revolutionary, decadent, or incoherent. But history may easily prove the audience wrong, advancing the rejection to serve as stepping stone into a new era.

Generalizations, however, are misleading. When, in 1830, Gautier and confrères fought for Victor Hugo and Romanticism, a decisive battle was won. On the other hand, there have been dubious and light-weight scandals. One of them, for instance, resulted from the rivalry between Marie Taglioni and Fanny Elssler, a struggle nurtured by intrigue and money when Elssler dared to dance *La Sylphide*, a role with which Taglioni was identified; on this occasion two fanatical cliques were involved in a boo- and whistle-concert that lasted for hours and often turned to physical violence. A Taglionist sitting with his back to the stage and reading a newspaper was said to have badly been beaten. The newspapers were full of this then sensational incident, and Gautier remarked in his feuilleton with tongue in cheek that he deemed the news exaggerated that "moaning mountains of the dead" were lying piled up at the shores of the Seine.

A far weightier incident, concerning *La guerre des bouffons*, found the adherents of the Italian and French opera pitted against each other in a fight that lasted about two years. The pens of some of the greatest thinkers were as much involved in this controversy as the fists in the theater and on the streets. Theater scandals go back to the earliest performances, and the archetypical event is the one in which Aeschylus was involved and almost killed because his audience was under the impression that he had revealed some secrets of the Eleusinian Mysteries.

We may remind ourselves of Friedrich Schiller's dictum about the theater being a moral institution and of Bertolt Brecht going beyond any educational purpose of the theater and demanding a verdict from the audience, thus turning the theatrical platform into a tribunal. I have seen stunned, bewildered looking audiences when faced with "non-art" art and audiences mesmerized or emotionally whipped up to ecstasies by subcultural experiences.

What lucky people, what a fortunate era, in which the arts can arouse as much fanatical interest as any vital issue in the political arena of a nation! On the other hand, aren't we justified in saying "Woe to an epoch in which no one is scandalized at exhibitions, in theaters and concert halls! Indifference and polite applause drive nails deep into the coffin of the arts." It was Flaubert who said that theater is not an art but a secret. He, undoubtedly, was right, however we wish to interpret it. And the key to this secret has always been the audience.

One day Joyce Trisler said to me: "You made a choreographer of me." It sounded like a student telling or writing me that I have changed her life. Of course, I have done nothing of the sort. All I may have done was to make her see herself. Joyce Trisler always wanted to choreograph. She had always dreamed of heading a company with which she would realize her dreams. She excelled in both as much as in being a wonderful dancer of rare expressive abilities.

I first saw her in Doris Humphrey's *Dawn in New York* and in *The Life of the Bee*. I reviewed both and remember having referred to Trisler as having a "singing body." I could not help thinking that this was the closest verbalization of the poetic line in her dancing. I felt assured in my opinion when I asked Doris Humphrey whether she could recommend someone to me for demonstrations during

Joyce Trisler dancing. Author's collection.

my series of lectures on dance history which, in 1956 and 1957, I held at The New School for Social Research. Doris said: "Ask Joyce, she is a great dancer." I did.

In one of my lectures I wanted to juxtapose a typically dramatic piece with a very lyrical one. I asked Joyce Trisler to do a dynamic section from *Dawn in New York* and to come up with something that was the epitome of lyricism which she should choreograph for that lecture. I remember having said to her that I would like to see her walk on air, caressing it lovingly while groping for the dream of something beautiful. A week later she played for me Charles Ives' *The Unanswered Question* and showed me some basic phrases of which she had thought. She worked on them, and they finally turned into the first version of her most famous piece, *Journey*. It was not merely a wandering through imaginary fog, a lithe solo in which the dancing body—swaying, bending, and groping—tries to clear away invisible obstacles; in her performance, *Journey* evoked that indeterminable feeling of longing in man for something he cannot help envisioning without being able to define it.

In the course of time I saw *Journey* done by a great many excellent dancers, but they were different journeys, their point of departure lacked Joyce's feeling of love that carried her into a dreamlike world of nowhere. Perhaps it was also her "singing body" or the choreographically fulfilled version of that never fulfilled dream locked in herself. But her great gift of expression enabled her to take this piece out of the realm of personal experience into the statement that our life's journey is and remains an endless quest.

If *Journey* creates a luminous feeling of lyricism, then *The Bewitched*, set to music by Harry Partch proved Trisler's humorous—and more often satirical—bent. This bewitching work was produced only twice and forgotten or pushed aside by all annotators of her work. This probably happened because her choreography depended on the willful and weird music played on instruments of Harry Partch's own invention.

Born in Los Angeles in 1934, she received her first training from

Lester Horton. She appeared in many of his ballets and soon in leading parts. There, she discovered the "controlled freedom" to which she often referred; there, she developed her sustained long line for which her subtle body was so well equipped; there, she learned that there was drama in the sweep of her gestural expression. Doris Humphrey brought her to New York. To the freedom in developing ideas through movement which she had acquired under Lester Horton's tutelage she added a heightened self-discipline, a no-nonsense attitude toward the craft locked in her body. She became the leading dancer of the Juilliard Dance Theatre for its five-year existence. It was in this period that Joyce Trisler fully realized the range of her performing abilities, but also the powerful urge to express herself creatively. She continued to dance and choreograph with small groups and—at the end of 1964, after having danced for two years with the Alvin Ailey Company—she appeared for the last time as a professional dancer during the Ailey Company's first European tour.

That year meant a new beginning for her, and the following years were full of many highlights in her career as a choreographer for operas, musicals and plays, with her creative talent finding the outlet she actually desired most. Dance, above all, meant theater to her. Even in her concert dances one can easily detect that the driving motor of her conceits, that the motivation for movement, emerged from a sure feeling for the theatricality of the performer in her. How often did I hear her say: "I just love the theater."

She liked to experiment, to respond to the challenge of the new. Out of a workshop production in 1974 grew her version of *Le Sacre du Printemps.* There is hardly any greater challenge for any choreographer than this Stravinsky score, and it became a turning point in her career. Not only the public and press were stunned by the uniqueness of its dramatic and sensuous quality, Trisler's dancers were also strongly motivated by this success and felt like going on working under her leadership. This was the moment when Danscompany, which she forged into an expressive instrument for her choreographic ideas, came into being. "They are wonderful kids," she wrote me soon afterwards to Zürich, "they wanted a company, and I decided to choreograph for them only."

Early in 1976 I saw her Danscompany for the first time in New York. I was not a bit surprised (to borrow one of Joyce's favorite phrases) to find a brilliant group of young dancers vibrating with energy. It was obvious that Joyce was a relentless taskmaster (at points merciless), but one who, at the same time, could inspire her dancers. I remember some of the classes she taught at Sarah Lawrence College and what a demanding, but also what a guiding and helpful teacher she was. No doubt, she was driven by a longing for perfection which could be contagious. In her work, as in her life, she could sometimes be possessed by a wild spirit which had its rewarding creative aspects.

Over the decades she had done quite a few works that are still in the repertory of the company, and rightly so, since their significance outlasted the seasons for which they were done, from the skillfully structured Vivaldi *Dance for Six*, one of her earlier works, to *Fantasies and Fugues*, set to Bach, one of her last ballets, a challenging juxtaposition and blending of classic and modern idioms. Trisler would never tread the easy way.

It was daring to choose Hindemith's *Four Temperaments*, so well and neo-classically designed by George Balanchine. Whatever Mr. B. created emerged from within the music which he gave its choreographed image. In this respect—and respectfully so—Joyce Trisler was a close relative of his. She deeply plunged into a score in order to find and define its emotional essence before shaping it into a stage-realization. Thus, she was able to envision emotional relationships in four duets colored by the basic human temperaments, a contest that was clearly stated in her own style.

As my favorite of all her later works I would single out *Four Against the Gods*, her "take-off" on the famous command performance of the *Pas de Quatre* in Sir Lumley's Her Majesty's Theatre in 1845 which had been immortalized in the dance world's memory with the help of a just as famous lithograph. In *Four Against the Gods* Trisler transposed the idea of having four stars appear in one and the same work and lifted it from a mere star production to a level of deeper meaning. She chose four female dancers of our time who have revolutionized the dance and given it the twentieth-century expression: Isadora, Ruth, Doris, and Martha.

Had it remained a mere take-off with the choreographer's tongue in cheek visibly moving with subtle irony—as Robert Joffrey did in his *Pas Déesses*—it would have done little more than evoked the pleasant memory of the Jacques Bouvier lithograph. But in choosing the four pioneers for a new free style of expression, Joyce Trisler moved away from the clichéd idea to which the very beginning and end of her piece alluded. The skillful and true-to-technique-development presentation of the *Four* gave the work a salient historic meaning.

In all her works we find a blending of emotionally charged movements with subtle and sensuous suggestiveness, a masterly craftsmanship which never forgets to surprise, but remains human in its expressive language and wit. I have always been impressed by her ability to match the simple to the sophisticated and never to let the action-driven speed run into mere breathless emptiness. She always tried to achieve the essential of what she wanted to say through tightly structured forms and universal meaningfulness. Her death came too suddenly and too soon.

When all is said in praise of her artistry, a rather disconsolate postscriptum has to follow. I loved and admired her. But in the course of the years I could not help sensing a strange streak of self-destruction in her. Her tremendously creative strength was paralleled by a certain restless quality which might exemplify the saying that character defeats genius. From the day of *Journey* I closely followed her becoming. Now I am left with the agonizing memory of a great artist who was deprived of reaching the zenith of her potential greatness, the ultimate gesture of her creative spirit.

1980

Zürich. "Art is something that lies in the slender margin between the real and unreal," Chikamatsu Monzaemon explained. He was a seventeeth-century dramatist who wrote some of the finest pieces for the Kabuki Theater. As a poetic stylist, he became disgusted with the liberties the actors took with his finely chiseled text and turned to working for the puppet theater. There the unreal became the reality of his imagination. I would like to take Chikamatsu's definition of art, to nail this sentence onto the doors of all dance studios, or even better, into the consciousness of all dancer-choreographers.

When will I come to recognize the littleness of greatness and learn to see the greatness of littleness? On the other hand, zero is not less but only more of a zero when blown up. On the other hand (after all, we have two): Everything is a matter of degree and perception. I tell myself I must learn to recognize the littleness of great things, because then I can master the art of seeing and appreciating the greatness of little things.

My mind played football with such irrelevant and contradictory thoughts when I saw Rudolf Nureyev's new staging of *Raymonda* at the Zürich Opera. I have read raves about it in some papers and magazines. So I went to see it. Since then I have learned to mistrust good notices more than ever—including those I myself may have written.

Raymonda has an unwieldy scenario whose basic idea defies all theatrical sensibilities. Its sequential, or rather inconsequential, unfolding has the effect of a sedative. *Raymonda* reminds me of its operatic counterpart, *La Gioconda.* I heard this opera several times, I even tried to read its libretto once, and to this very day I cannot make out what it is all about. Seeing *La Gioconda* I can at least close my eyes and listen to beautiful voices (hopefully they are beautiful). I can't do the same with *Raymonda.* First of all, Glazunov's eclectic music—to call it pedestrian is to compare it with a glorified musical stroll—would soon make me open my eyes again to look for the next emergency exit; secondly, I would miss the dancing. And Nureyev put in some good dances.

The only trouble with them was that the night I saw the ballet neither he nor Eva Evdokimova (in this taxing title role, full of demanding solos and confusing duets) were at their best. I have often wondered what is going on inside an experienced performer when he does not feel like going on, when he can feel in every muscle that this is not his day, when he is tortured by premonitions that something may go wrong. A writer who senses a writing block just doesn't write. He can read the Bible for stimulation, as Virginia Woolf did, or he can read the book for which he has had no time so far or the one he can read and re-read innumerable times, or he can go for a walk. For the performing artist the show must go on. Is it true that, the minute he is on stage, he is very much himself again, the neutral, impersonal, or performing self? Or, do the stage lights—the realization of the unknown mass of people in the uncertain dark out there observing every movement of his—have an electrifying power generating that specific awareness of unawareness which makes the actor-dancer what he is?

However it may work—and it must certainly work differently with different dancers in different situations—on that night the first-act dancing in *Raymonda* had its flaws and was rather spiritless. For some time I tried to figure out whose insecurity made whom more insecure. It is a recommendable game, particularly when phenomenal stars are involved. The moment I came to the conclusion that perhaps the fault may lie in the fact that Nureyev had danced too often and with too many minor and major companies as a guest artist in the last few seasons, both Eva and Rudi regained control over their movements and made any further speculation—in whatever direction it may have gone—unnecessary. There were some beautiful moments in Act II.

Nevertheless, the ballet remained a colossal bore. I was one of the few critics who applauded Nureyev's reworking of *The Nutcracker*, an all-too-naive story which he gave a great many

Freudian touches, culminating in the neat trick of having the sinister Herr Drosselmeyer turn into a handsome prince in Clara's dream adventures. Nureyev had attacked other classics, such as *The Sleeping Beauty* and *Don Quixote*, wiping the dust from their patinated shapes and giving them a more contemporary sheen. I would trust Nureyev with the overhauling of most classical ballets and, for all we know, it may become his forte in his later years. It takes a great deal of insight into the hidden depths of a ballet scenario and, conveniently, fairy tales have many layers of meaning. But it also takes a daring hand to retouch traditional material. A surgeon's movements may sometimes seem to lack compassion. The patient, however, can only be helped if the surgeon's hands know what they are doing.

Raymonda is probably an incurable case or, at least, this is how it looked to me after Nureyev had doctored it quite a bit. I admit, he seems to understand the secret longings of all Raymondas. As he sees them, they must go through the dark channels of desire in order to be freed from their torturous doubts and dreams; they must build up the image of their reality in order to be able to live with it. Raymonda, an immature girl, cannot fully accept the love of her knight, who is returning from one of the crusades. She does not seem to know what love is—at this point of the story. The pagan warrior, Abderahman, her knight's antagonist, fascinates her subliminal being. In her dream she makes him into her rival suitor who later, disguised as a priest, abducts her. (The foreign and forbidden loom tall in her penile imaginings.) In Abderahman's camp, the dancing of the wild warriors further whips up her sensuality, and for some time she seems to be lost to Abderahman. Only a duel between the white and dark rivals can solve her problem. In her dream, she has to experience the bravery of the betrothed, and only Abderahman's death makes her wake up and wake up to her real love.

Psychiatrists may be able to do a lot about her case, choreographers are far more at a loss. On second thought, psychologically her case is so obvious that some analysts may feel as bored handling it as I felt watching it.

The dissenting voice is going out of fashion in a world of conformism, one which likes to be easily satisfied—perhaps because life is so difficult anyway and the arts have had a hard time in maintaining themselves. Improvisation has become a way of expression, and non-art artistry has corroded all standards of the aesthetics. The critic who disagrees with his co-critics may easily be looked at as a man with a quixotic bent, as an intellectual exhibitionist. Whenever I saw a bandwagon pass by, I stopped instinctively and waited for the next empty bus to come. I suppose, in a neatly organized world of many pressures, a world favoring its cliques and consensualists, it often needs courage to say no—and if for no other reason than the one that one looks somehow foolish, or even sheepish, to oneself when looking into the mirror of other reviews.

Well, to come to the point. I saw Antonio Gades, the flamenco dancer, in Zürich first and, a few months later, in New York. He is a good example of what I mean. He was highly praised in Europe and in New York. My arguments fell on deaf ears. Gades appears in a program that runs for an hour and a half without intermission. He begins on a high pitch and stays there, while performing with his group his Balerias, Farrucas, Tangos, Seguiriyas, Zapateados, Fandangos, and ending with a Rumba.

He opens with a theatrically exciting gesture: a play on light and half-dark out of which his dancers step back and forth. This trick is dramatic and fascinating, but when repeated in each number it wears on you and finally numbs you. In the long run of an intermissionless evening you come to expect it to happen and are infuriated when it does.

Gades himself is a flawless technician, and all of his dancers are better than good. But none of them is particularly remarkable or memorable. There's the rub. I could not help feeling that Antonio Gades is not more memorable than any other wonderful technician. He masters steps, carriage, movements, gestures. He uses them on stage as a great artist would use them for class work. He dazzles with his flamenco rhythms. Having an admirable technical proficiency, he relies on it and forgets to give his steps and movements a choreographic image. His lighting effects leave most of his spectators in the dark about his nonexistent creative approach.

I do not wish to say that first-rate classwork, wherever it can be watched, is not enjoyable. But I could have left after half an hour. Also, his dancing would be beautiful and complete in its native setting, say at a Café or nightclub somewhere in Spain. For me, the spectres of Escudero and Antonio hovered over Gades imploring and sparring him to motivate his motifs, to put character into his characters, to relate his dancers to one another, to give *Gestalt* to steps and gestures.

In a Shakespearean mood may I ask, "What's Antonio Gades to me or I to him that I should weep for him?" He is close to film and nightclub performing, and I suppose he will go the way of all José Grecos. And the day a great new Spanish dancer throws all aficionados into their olé enthusiasm, Gades will be claimed by oblivion. I do not want to victimize him (and this is said apologetically). I used him merely as an example with which to show the way from technique to emotion to art, and how difficult these transitions are.

I don't mind when an artist fails. But he must fail as an artist. I am suspicious of an artist who for many years journeys through the world and all its concert halls with the same program, essentially in its same format, and basically with the same numbers in the same sequence and with the same theatrical tricks. Does nothing occur to this performer, not even that nothing occurs to him? Can an artist be an artist and not desire to change while growing or to grow while changing?

An artist must make me feel how he struggled with the gods. When he comes down from the Mount (whatever he may call it) to tell us his tale, I still want to sense the breath and blows of the gods on his creation. I don't want him to tell me how crafty he is. I don't want him to pretend that he believed that he had seen the face of God pass by. I want him to come down from that Mount and perform a small miracle. And I don't mind if it doesn't always quite come off. After all, we are all only human, as the gods also seem to be.

New York. How black! How beautiful!

It is an agonizing experience to belong to any easily identifiable minority. Whether black or Jew, whether Hispanic or Gypsy, the stamp of otherness, the load of prejudice, stupidity, and downright viciousness are roadblocks on their way to self-fulfillment. A never-ceasing curse of human heritage seems to be intolerance.

When I came to the United States at the end of 1939, it was as an exile. In my native land I had belonged to a minority destined to be extinguished. I brought nothing with me, except my thoughts and feelings, my dreams and hopes. I did not make the world responsible for my fate, although I distinctly sensed that all decency had been eclipsed and that the twentieth-century scourge of the human race was permitted to spend its fury in the political game of a most despicable Realpolitik. In cyclic intervals mankind seems to invite itself to an ever more desperate dance of death. Love has always lived an orphaned existence. Any study of history proves that time has moved on, but that man has not noticeably changed. Donning the mantle of progress and civilization is meaningless if the next gust of cataclysmic events can totally divest mankind of its dignity and show it in its cruel nakedness.

My immediate artistic experience with the black people was in a Greenwich Village nightclub. A rather short, strongly built dancer impressed me with her technique, expressiveness, and power of projection. He who has ever seen her leaps will never be able to forget Pearl Primus. Long before this in Europe, as early as 1927, I had seen Josephine Baker in her sumptuous banana costume at the Folies Bergère, but this only told me at an early stage that to be black can be very, very beautiful. Many decades later I also learned that this ebony skin—chiseled by the hand of God, who at that moment must have been a black God—fitted the soul of a great, compassionate human being.

The sinewy Pearl Primus was a revelation to me. Even her nightclub solos were convincing bits and pieces of great artistry. When I first saw her dance in the Café Society Downtown I had not the slightest idea that I would later often see her work and review it. From the very beginning I felt that she would never betray the roots from which the flame of her strength issued. She danced herself in *The Negro Speaks of Rivers*, she danced her race in *African Ceremonial Te Moana*. And in following her career in the forties and fifties, I never doubted the sincerity of what she did and how she did it. She masterly evolved one Negro theme after the other, creating a vast panorama of the black world. Later, I singled her out to speak and demonstrate in my history classes and even preferred to meet with my students at her studio, which was full of African masks.

We can best understand the seriousness of her work when we dare compare it to Katherine Dunham's creations, to which I was also introduced in the forties, works such as her *Tropical Revue* and *Windy City*, to name only two of many. She is a learned lady and, though also an early exponent of the black dance, she is a theater woman before anything else. I still remember having seen her revue *Bamboche!* in 1962, a work full of intense theatricality. She knew how to use her ethnic material in a commercially exciting way, always combining black or Asian folklore with complete stage awareness. Like Pearl Primus she is an anthropologist who knows the roots, trees, and flowers of her race well enough to make us see what it means to be a black. Katherine Dunham has been physically most attractive— which is of great help in life and on stage—but combined with her theater sense this often brought her dangerously close to mere showbusiness.

This can certainly not be said of Trinidad-born dancer Pearl Primus, who came to the States as a very young child, was trained and educated here, and attained a doctorate in anthropology. I felt all along that she went into the depth of things. Starting in 1948, she did research among the native tribes of Africa for a year and a half, only to return there shortly thereafter to make a more limited, but all the more intensive study of the effects of urbanization of African culture. The giant Watusi dancer of the Belgian Congo then renamed her "Omowale," meaning "child returned home."

As with many exiles, this American dancer felt acutely the dichotomy between here and there: "I now feel as if I had two mothers. I am unable to give up either and must try to explain one to the other." The American-born black with his cultural roots in Africa cannot help feeling the heritage of exile. An Afro-styled hairdo alone will not do, it is like trying to carry one's soul in the button hole, an empty gesture of protest which in reality turns against one's very being. A black ethnicity can only be a cultural amalgam between here and there. It is within this "here" that essential differences crystallized, molded by the historic development over centuries. Pearl Primus seemed to have been able to reconcile the realities of her existence on this continent with a heritage lying beyond time and distance. Her success in life was that she was not only a "child returned home," but that she remained an "adult never having left herself."

When she went to Liberia in the fifties her work was toward the perpetuation of African culture in dance, drama, music, the arts and folklore. "At this transitional moment in African history," she said, "its national pride and awareness are awakening concurrent with a rapid absorption of the white man's achievements on many levels. It is therefore vitally important that the traditional arts are kept alive, since in many cases the real reasons for the dances as well as the techniques of the great masters are fast disappearing. There is a great cultural reservoir among the people in the hinterlands." The main purpose for her going to Liberia was to find, encourage, and train the folk artist and provide him with outlets through theatrical experiences. She often referred to the "dignity, beauty, and strength" of this age-old culture which she tried to salvage before it disintegrated.

Like so much in mankind's history, it is scathingly ironic that Pearl Primus went down to Africa to teach the natives their own dances and to revive that lost dignity for which she had to struggle so much where she had grown up, to fight to find what she had lost.

"The thesis for my doctorate at New York University is called 'African Sculpture: Its Function in Society.' This I will dance. It's an experiment in education, and a great challenge to me as an artist. I've long been interested in and a student of African sculpture and have taken the basic dance positions I use from it."

Thinking of how much time has passed since I spoke to her last, hardly anything has changed in her approach to the art and her reliance on her roots, as reflected in what she calls "Earth Theater." Still, when she dances *Fanga*, her solo of welcome, she not only seems to be opening her heart to the world, she also evokes all past memories of the fire that once set her body and mind on its lifelong journey.

However much we may feel we are struggling and reaching out for the fulfillment of our self and however often we may sense that fear of lostness—whatever the circumstances—for the artist in the human being, only the realization of his dream can ultimately count. I have felt this vision to be true in a handful of artists, white, black, or yellow, and also quite often in Alvin Ailey's case. If I had to think fast of a reason for why I like the Alvin Ailey American Dance Theater, my immediate reaction would be that it is the one company creating the strongest kinetic rapport for me. On second thought, it is a well integrated black company, conscious of its racial problems, but even more conscious of the fact that all art is, in some way, propaganda and most convincing when it is not obvious propaganda.

The last time I spoke to Alvin Ailey was in the early summer of 1963, shortly before the civil rights movement gained momentum. He had come up for lunch and an interview I was then writing for *Dance Magazine* on him. As you sometimes recall one little experience out of the past's vagueness, I remember him walking up and down in my room, seething with a badly veiled fury, with the fierceness of a caged animal, beautifully controlled and yet ready to break out any minute. I watched him walking like the panther in Rainer Maria Rilke's poem:

> His gaze, going past those bars, has got so misted,
> with tiredness, it cannot take in more.
> He feels as though a thousand bars existed,
> no world behind him and no world before.

I no longer know what had infuriated him, but I sensed his throbbing emotions and, beyond this dancer and that very moment, the coming of ominous things. And yet, I thought, the beauty of this experience was to have seen his strong muscular body in full vibration. There was dance in it.

Ailey has always preferred a mixed racial group of dancers, though in general—if he does not borrow "white" choreography, such as José Limón's *Missa Brevis* or Joyce Trisler's *Journey* in order to give his repertory a wider scope—his way of choreographic thinking relies on the black ritual and ethnic-folkloric feel spiced and sprinkled with jazz. Indeed, jazz is at the core of the Ailey dancers (no one can top their blues; I fondly remember his *Blues Suite* from his earlier days), they are modern in technique and expression, with a balletic touch here and there. If jazz is in their blood, figuratively speaking, then modern dance is in and on their mind. It is easy to see that without the triumph of the modern dance, the black dancer could never have triumphed the way he did, even though he held on to the technique and dramatic-expressive concepts of the thirties and is still with it, while the white dancer has meanwhile tried in a variety of ways to escape his past, and often himself.

In his younger years Ailey also tested himself as an actor. "As a choreographer and dancer I see in terms of theater. I have never liked to see dancers on stage, but people," he said. "I have always told my dancers: don't look like a dancer, be a vessel for human emotions, try to look like a human being." And then the big dream of almost all choreographers since Diaghilev made Richard Wagner's, Adolphe Appia's and Stéphane Mallarmé's dream come one big step closer to reality: "I feel as if I were born on the stage. I cannot help expressing myself as a dancer, choreographer, or actor. In my work as a choreographer I have always tried to wed dance and drama. I strongly believe that the future of the theater lies in a new kind of lyric theater, in a total integration of dance, drama, and music."

There is a lot of silent drama in whatever he does and he often enough molds his dancers into vessels for human emotions. And he is at his best when he works with music emerging from his black milieu. His choreography is inspired by the folksiest tunes, as his own classic, *Revelations*, first done in 1960, proves. Take, for instance, Mary Lou Williams or Duke Ellington. The music in *Mary Lou's Mass* is a paean to living and love. It has an ecstatic rhythm, a powerful, jazzy lilt which the Ailey dancers translate into exciting movement. There are a few moments in which the music is so overwhelmingly beautiful that the movements can hardly keep step with it, and look overpowered. But, in general, the gospel and jazz spirit finds the dancers in an exalted mood, and Ailey's choreography has the feel of disarming exaltation.

The one section of scripture reading about the beggar Lazarus and the rich man is a miniature masterpiece. Ailey dared to use mime and movements in glorious obviousness, and two of his dancers stand out in my memory: Dudley Williams as Lazarus and John Parks as the rich man. Ailey makes both do everything the book says is wrong. He does it with such sure exaggeration that it is not only right but perfect, dance humor at its best.

However powerful such a work as this may be, it does not supersede *Revelations*, which could similarly be seen as a tightly structured unit of a variety of sections. Yet the difference lies in the even level of singularly poetic power and drama contrasting with joyous lightheartedness, so unique in *Revelations*. It does not have a climactic point, as does the Lazarus story in the *Mass*. *Revelations* is climax as a whole. There is one consolation for Alvin Ailey: he is not alone in being unable to beat himself by topping his seemingly greatest accomplishment.

Perhaps he comes close to it in the solo called *Cry* which he created for the star of his company, Judith Jamison. It is Ailey's *Dying Swan* geste—if one may dare this comparison—however removed it may be in time and mood, purpose and color. Its three parts create a dramatic and lyric ambiance which transcends the obvious pictorial connotations of showing a black woman in different phases of being. It is not militant at all, but so penetratingly human that its cry is unforgettable. It is unforgettable because it is artistically irrefutable. The work was sculptured on Miss Jamison's very distinct looking figure—as Fokine's once was on Pavlova's—and the dancer added to it the expression of her personality which appears onstage imperious and withdrawn, goddesslike and humble. In the first section she seems to be all woman, enduring pain and giving strength and joy. The specific color of her skin becomes clear in the second part, when the challenge of the environmental space around her grows. Anguish finally turns into defiance and defiance into a fighting flame, proud of its power. The strength of this simply staged solo, covering limited space, lies in the drama within the dancing figure created with a surprising economy of movement; it lies in the unpredict-ability of the movement sequences, in their explosive quality due to the self-imposed limitations.

Despite Ailey's intimate feeling for Ellington's music it has not helped him create works of more endurable merit. Of *Three Black Kings*, *The River*, and *Night Creature* only the latter is structurally sound and develops an air of lightness which shows him as the great showman he is. But even when he arouses his audience—which, by the way, is far more white than black—to a frentic applause, I often see in his speed and dramatic push that the showman in him tries to get the better of the artist. There seem to be certain parallels with the Joffrey Ballet in this respect, a ballet company with which Ailey also shares the predilection of reviving older works of the modern dance repertory. Since they were hardly ever created by a black choreographer, it is all the more a most laudable act and one to ascertain that art is art is art regardless of color.

In the sixties, as one also belonging to a minority, I was jolted by the Civil Rights Movement. Looking back in anger on history I have come to the conclusion that revolutions are as unavoidable as earthquakes, floods, or eruptions of volcanoes are within the geological structure of the earth. I could condone revolutions within the sociocultural structures of societies, if they had ever changed not only governments, but the human being. The arts are also in a constant flux and often precede historic revolutions with their (r)evolutionary statements, as in 1916 when Dada heralded the revolutions that ended the madness of World War I, or as the waltz displaced the minuet, anticipating thereby not only Romanticism (which is inherent in the waltz) but also the French Revolution (for in its very beginning the waltz with its gyrating turns symbolized the drive for freedom from the coqueteries of a sham existence). When the black dancer flirted with militant gestures onstage in the days of the Civil Rights Movement, it was a concomitant experience with those in the streets, or at best an echo of the awakening faith in the black community. That political reality and not black art stood in the forefront of the struggle does, of course, in no way lessen the black dancer's sincerity and his belief in a colorless justice of fate.

Donald McKayle's personality and work had fascinated me for many years. His *Games* has become a classic of the modern dance repertory, and his interweaving of hunger and fear into mere playfulness is still a remarkable feat of artistry. Another of his timeless pieces is *Rainbow Round My Shoulders*, which creates haunting, though somewhat cliché-ridden visualizations and moods of despair and hope, of struggle and ultimate defeat. That the characters he uses to exemplify the misery of man are part of a chain gang of black men is almost secondary in importance. It simply is man, black or white, and therefore has the impact of universal plight. McKayle may even have been caught by surprise by the militant stance of his fellow dancers.

Another black dancer, one I had befriended in the house of an American poet, is Gus Solomons Jr., for whose work and person I had a feeling of fondness. He performed with the companies of Merce Cunningham, Pearl Lang, and Donald McKayle before he

A scene from Games *by Donald McKayle. Author's collection.*

ventured out on his own. Solomons never "made" a black dance consciously, it seemed to me, though he was far from denying his heritage. He once said in an interview: "There's very little Negro influence in my work. It's more the influence of architecture, the influence of the kinds of movement I have studied, namely Graham and Cunningham." He had studied architecture and thinks in terms of design more than of content when he starts working on a dance. "I hate anything that deals with separation," he said in reference to the Civil Rights Movement.

Rod Rodgers whose stance has become more self-assured from a racial point of view, is all for making this separation clear and distinct. He is concerned about the specialty of Black American identity and wishes to stress the interpretation of his own experience. He is afraid that it may lose its significance when marketed in the established media. His notion seems to be that in dance a heightened means of self-expression is used and it should be based entirely on the experience of a black life-style. Most of the black dancers would agree with this attitude and approach to their art form—"right or wrong, my blackness!"—and differ only in militant nuances. I would agree that great art can only evolve from one's own experiences and that some great art has resulted from a fighting spirit. In the best schizophrenic manner I must immediately contradict my own statement and aver that the greatest dance works of the black man have not been militant and have made a stronger point in behalf of their cause without shouting that their skin is dark. As far as dance is concerned, we do not have to fear that a blind man would sit in the audience— and hopefully not one who is color-blind.

Certainly there is something special or different to the black dancer. There may be more of an innate rhythm in the black people than in any Caucasian dancer, and one must admit he often has a different way of moving which is native to him. Gus Solomons, Jr. tried to outline these differences from an anatomical viewpoint in a *Dance Scope* interview in 1967:

The physical bone structure that Negroes have inherited is different. There's a difference of proportion of limbs, forearm to upper arm, shin to thigh. The forelimbs are longer in proportion to the upper limbs than in white stock. In Negroes, calves tend to be less full, while the thighs and buttocks are fuller. The lower spine tends to have a curvature which is an inherent thing. It works perfectly well but it presents certain problems when one tries to fit into an established pattern of dance like ballet, which was invented on white European bodies.

True, there may be some physical differences, but they can rather easily be overlooked by the audience as so many integrated companies prove, or this touch of otherness can be used to its best advantage choreographically. The spiritual differences may weigh more heavily, as may the entire complexity of the black cultural experience.

On the other hand, the fact is that there are a good number of black ballet dancers—and a whole company of them, The Dance Theater of Harlem. When Arthur Mitchell (together with Karel Shook) founded this company it was quite logical that it should have relied on the neo-classic ballet style that characterizes George Balanchine's New York City Ballet, with which Mitchell danced for many years. The ground that Balanchine prepared became, in Mitchell's vision, the very ground on which to build an edifice that would serve his dream and its reality.

The company has acquired a firm sense of style. This can be related to the fact that they have a company based on a school. When Balanchine came to this country in 1934 he asked first for a school and only then for a company. Mitchell has taken this lesson to heart and assured the maturity of his dancers and their dancing. They have been nationally praised and internationally recognized (Mitchell might say it is the other way around). But one cannot help noticing that they have superior dance instruction.

Whatever their physical uniqueness may be, Mitchell and his dancers have proven that black classicism is for them possible to achieve and to maintain. At a moment of grave socio-economic conditions in the States, the need may have been felt to take at least a few of the many talented black kids off the street. A first impulse. But then the overriding feeling was to give the black dancer an opportunity to perform and, by the same token, to prove that he is technically and aesthetically able to master the craft and art of the classical ballet.

When I saw their *Agon* and *Four Temperaments* I realized that the Harlem dancers can make of such semi-classical ballets a viable version, one very much their own, as if these ballets had never been composed for white dancers. Around 1978, the first blossoming seemed gone. The company lost quite a few dancers to Hollywood and Broadway (it seems that the magnetic power of bank accounts is oblivious of color discrimination), but Mitchell had not lost the momentum of his dream to the mere excitement of novelty. The director of any dance company must learn how to deal with the unavoidable human problems and how to overcome a crisis. He re-formed his group and simultaneously widened his repertory. The range reaches from Balanchine's *Concerto Barocco* to Geoffrey Holder's *Dougla*, from *Le Corsaire* to Ruth Page's *Frankie and Johnny*, from *Swan Lake* and *Paquita* to Valerie Bettis' version of the Tennessee Williams play *A Streetcar Named Desire*.

What an enviable accomplishment! Mitchell knows very well the needs of the individual dancer and how to feed him with challenges and a vast variety of expression. He has never wished to see "little Mitchells" onstage. In stimulating his dancers constantly by exposing them to diverse choreographers, he hopes to keep them kinesthetically happy and also mentally moving. In doing so he played down his own choreographic ambitions, perhaps realizing that his Balanchine-influenced accomplishments are of less importance than his skill in shaping a company and building up a rewarding repertory for it.

Black dancers have come a long way, from Juba to Bill Robinson, from tap and jazz dancers to Katherine Dunham, from eccentric hoofers to Pearl Primus, from nightclub entertainers to world renowned ballet dancers. Nowadays there are about two dozen or more black dance companies of varying merit. But I see in the Dance Theater of Harlem a unique achievement. The classical ballet with its feudal heritage survived socioculturally our two major revolutions: the French (with only a brief hiatus filled with nonsensical mock-revolutionary ballets), and the Russian (since in Russia the ballet has always been associated with the *people*). Now, in an ethno-social respect the Dance Theater of Harlem has overcome the prejudice that has persisted against classical ballet danced with a black skin. From an artistic viewpoint, the black movement has never had a more eloquent and successful attorney than Arthur Mitchell.

A short while ago the Metropolitan Museum had a magnificent display of costumes from the more important ballets produced during the Diaghilev era, and now the Dance Collection at Lincoln Center has put together an astounding exhibition of pictures, documentations, and memorabilia reminding us of past greatness. The historic importance of the Ballets Russes has never been in doubt, but fifty years after Diaghilev's death and his company's collapse we are more aware of the fact that no company can endure without a school. One walks through this exhibit with remembered surprise and suppressed anger about the transitoriness of so much beauty.

What is exhibited are fleeting reminders, since no one can present near-complete visualization of production after production over twenty years. But the few spotchecks at the danced glory that was the Ballets Russes evoke a feeling of dedication and daring that determined success and, in particular, success through seeming failures: from Diaghilev's conquest of Paris in 1908, first with an exhibition, and Chaliapin as *Boris Godunov*, to Balanchine's *Prodigal Son*, produced on May 21, 1929, a few months before Diaghilev's death. Lincoln Kirstein recalled his impression of this ballet in *The Flesh Is Heir* in 1932: " ... It seemed as if the characters stepped from a stained glass window—only their articulation was never stiff. The gestures flowed smoothly and richly into one another like honey into a jar." The stained glass window referred to was that of Georges Rouault's stunning stage designs.

There is an abundance of photographs of some of the memorable dancers of each phase, but the scenic designs and costume sketches are, in fact, the exciting arrows pointing at the sumptuousness and sensation that characterized the Diaghilev era. Walking through the exhibit you are stopped and stirred with every step you make: 1909 ... Saison Russe ... first program bill of *Prince Igor* with Nicholas Roerich's colorful images ... at the end of the same wall Roerich's backdrop for *Le Sacre*. What a painter!

You'll step back to see the unforgettable Nijinsky gestures from *Faun* and read the rarely quoted reaction of Rodin, who wrote for *Le Matin*, 1912: "This beauty is that of antique frescoes and sculpture: he is the ideal model, whom one longs to draw and sculpt." Baron de Meyer took the photos. You are surrounded by aristocracy of the spirit.

Along the walls and in the center of the hall the memorabilia: many of them exude fascination. Among them, Diaghilev's ledger for the years 1909-1911. The annotation speaks of 180-odd pages. Or you find one of the eight exercise books maintained by Serge Grigoriev, the complete records of performances, journeys, and rehearsals. They are all little treasures, especially some of the letters strewn in. Isadora writing to Gordon Craig in 1920: "The Russian Ballet is hopping madly about in Picasso pictures. Very silly. . . . If that is art I prefer aviation." Or a Bakst letter in Russian, dated 7. October 1921, apparently addressed to a Diaghilev and Bakst admirer wanting to put together an exhibit—perhaps one similar to the one we can now enjoy at Lincoln Center. Bakst says in it: "Alas, I have nothing to exhibit. I have not the right to show *The Sleeping Beauty* designs until after the first performance in Paris, at the Opéra." The would-be exhibitor must have complained to Bakst about Diaghilev's inaccessibility, since Bakst wrote in this letter what ought to have been a word of comfort: "Dear friend, what can one do with Diaghilev—he has been like this all his life; he never answers letters, lets people down, is always in a hurry, always absorbed in urgent business. Everyone is always complaining about him."

Alas, what can one really do about such a man as Diaghilev? Nothing but extol his memory through productions of the ballets he put on and through exhibitions like this one. What an unpleasant fellow! Nevertheless, we must be grateful that, at least, he kept the rendezvous with his own greatness . . . .

Zürich. I met him again in Zürich in his favorite Café Hotel de l'Europe where the entire ambiance is one of vanished times. There is a sumptuous feudal touch to the wall paintings and chandeliers. Everything there is wide-spaced; coffee is served in gold-rimmed cups, and everything else is also in the aristocratic style. I am always struck there by the thought that this was the elegance of a modernized past permitting any kind of dream reaching far back. Balanchine had just come from a stroll along the lake. He loved to look at the church steeples from the bridge where the Limmat river unites with the lake. "I like it here," he said. It reminded him of St. Petersburg and his childhood when the German governesses were taking the privileged children out for a walk. The Swiss dialect spoken here may even have sounded Russian to him from a distance.

There was something childlike about him those days, something constantly hankering back to the era of his formative years. I have always had the impression that a few dreams are written all over his face; one may even be hiding behind his nervous tic. Dance, music, and women—and not always in this sequence—are all he has always lived for, a trinity that almost has a touch of the religious.

It is a wonderful feeling to sit and talk with him. There is a kind of inevitability hanging over our discussion, his genius hiding behind a strange simplicity. Never before this afternoon have I sensed so strongly the human in him. Until then it was quite different. We had met now and then. When taking my leave, I had the ambiguous feeling of having known him intimately for a long time, while being sure of never coming close to him. But that afternoon at the Café Hotel de l'Europe I felt the many bridges between us taking a most definite shape, for moments our visions collided, we saw our dreams smiling at each other. It must have been the ambiance of this city and the odd sensation of having stopped time for a moment to see our dreams fulfilled in the mist of reality.

The Chinese very strongly revere the aged. The Americans have always believed in the Hollywood image of youth and glamour. In this respect, the Europeans have learned a great deal from the Chinese while flirting with the American idolatry.

I met Suzanne Perrottet in Zürich some time ago. Last

September the city and her friends celebrated her ninetieth birthday. She is one of those grand old ladies, a living proof of the fact that age is purely fictitious and that any relationship between the person and his factual years of life is merely coincidental. When I expected the visit of Karl Lorenz, a German professor greatly interested in Emile Jaques-Dalcroze—in fact, he dreams of rebuilding a modern version of Hellerau—I asked Suzanne Perrottet to join us. She was the life of the party, telling us of those days at the turn of the century when she became a Dalcroze student whose method—to experience music through the rhythmic expression of the body and, at the same time, to loosen and heighten all mental and creative forces in man—was then new.

"It was new and revolutionary," Suzanne said. "Dalcroze liked the way I moved, and I advanced to the position of being his assistant. I began to teach my co-students." She soon mastered the rhythmic Dalcroze lingo. The pedagogue in her could easily follow his intentions, but the dancer in her tried to go beyond his system and to explore rhythmic movement as a means of expression of emotional stimuli. In 1905 Dalcroze toured Europe with his students, giving demonstrations in many cities. In Paris, Suzanne remembered, "when we danced for Auguste Rodin, his enthusiasm brought tears to his eyes." (I must permit myself an aside at this point of her story. Rodin was first enamored with Loie Fuller in the early 1890s and then, a few years later, idolized Isadora. When I read the reports that men wept into their beards at seeing Isadora dance, Rodin's beard must have been among them. I have always preferred to take this image as a simile rather than a fact. But there was Suzanne Perrottet, a living witness to those tears.)

Dalcroze and his pupils then toured as far as Poland and Russia which is noted because a Polish girl called Miriam Rambach, later Marie Rambert, later Dame Marie, was soon to join the Dalcroze group. "When we settled down at the institute that was built for us in Dresden-Hellerau," Suzanne said, "Mary Wigman and Marie Rambach were among the students I worked with."

When in 1913 the famous meeting took place between Nijinsky and Rambach—that was the historic moment when Diaghilev took his company to Dalcroze in order to have their rhythmic sensibilities improved—Suzanne Perrottet was no longer there. Marie Rambach had taken her place as assistant to Dalcroze and, being from Poland as Nijinsky was, the two spoke the same language, linguistically and mentally.

Suzanne, having heard of that magician of "rhythmic movements" called Rudolf von Laban, had joined him in Ascona, Switzerland, and his workshop on Monte Verità, the mount of truth. It was during that very summer that Mary Wigman was there too. At the end of the summer course, Wigman had shown Laban her contract as a teacher at the Berlin Dalcroze school. Laban's historic words: "Congratulations. Now you have a job for a lifetime. But you are an artist and belong on the stage," made Wigman tear up the contract, and she became the artist she was.

"She soon left us," Suzanne continued, "and tried to find her own way. I took the other route. I stayed with Laban for many many years. I was with him in Zürich when Dada was born. I was very close to him all the time and bore him a son. André Perrottet-von Laban had made a name for himself as a scenic designer. This gift he inherited from his father. André became best known for his project of a round-theater in which the auditorium could be moved and turned around the stage."

"Coming back to those early years with Laban," Suzanne said, "it was an exciting time. We had a Laban school in a small place near Zürich where young people were instructed in music, movement and the expressionistic dance. We experimented all the time. During certain months Wigman was with us. There was not a day on which Laban would not work on his notations. But then with the first great World War continuing over the years, we suddenly were without students. We made a meager living, with Laban delivering well-attended lectures in Zürich and I playing the piano. Often we did not have enough money for a decent meal. Yoghurt helped us along."

In the twenties Laban left Switzerland and founded his Kammertanz Theater in Hamburg and Laban-Schools for teachers and dancers in several German cities. In 1938 he emigrated to England. Suzanne remained in Switzerland and established her own school at the Seegartenstrasse where she had previously worked with Laban. The road to be taken alone was not always easy. "I had rough days, but also wonderful ones," she explained. "I taught wherever I could, even at beaches on the Lake Zürich. But over the years my school grew, and I am still teaching. Sometimes more than thirty hours a week."

This is quite an accomplishment for a nonagenarian. In the course of our conversation she often got up to demonstrate what she did for Dalcroze and how she experimented with Laban. If there had been a piano in the apartment, she would have played something for us, I am sure—perhaps Schönberg, whom she performed during World War I in Zürich, at a time when his compositions were still anathema to bourgeois ears. To this very day she is curious what the new generation has to offer. "To be alive means to begin each day with great expectation." And Suzanne Perrottet was very much alive at the age of ninety.

New York. He who exposes himself to the public cannot expect to walk unharmed from Jerusalem to Jericho, he runs a risk of undue praise and punishment, of awards showered on him and of all kinds of attacks, from mild censure to vicious distortions and insults. He faces the glories and dangers of someone involved in warfare, with the one exception that there is rarely a Red Cross around willing to come to his succor.

What is the artist to do? Not to take it sitting down, but to go on working on himself. It may be difficult for him to accept the critic's rebuke or advice, but he should think about it and let it sink in if it only makes some sense to him. He should take praise with a big spoonful of salt twice a day only, as if it were a pill against a possible swelling of his vanity glands. But the last thing he should do is to talk back at his critics. True, it may help the artist to avoid getting peptic ulcers, but, with a very few exceptions, it will neither enlighten the critic, nor clean the air, nor further his own artistic development.

I remember the days when the powerful *New York Times* inaugurated Allen Hughes—one of its music critics—as head of the dance department. Allen Hughes was not a dance aficionado and, while trying to act a part in which he was miscast, he was not aware of the many trapdoors on the slippery stage floor on which he had to move. Ted Shawn, the mighty father figure in the modern American dance in comparison to the neophyte "dance" critic, wrote a rebuttal which the *Times* could not help publishing. Shawn felt that his own *Kinetic Molpai* was downgraded by the critic and wanted to set the record straight. However, he started it with a preamble amounting to a general censure of the critic:

I have read the recent dance reviews in *The Times* with growing concern. In my opinion, the sum of them has been depressing, for their overall tone seems to me to be negative, almost destructive. Whether the judgments contained are just or unjust, the dancers or choreographers have no court of appeal. This I find contrary to our American ideals of justice.

Murray Louis published a book, *Inside Dance*, containing a chapter, "On Critics," in which he lumped all critics together and sent them down to Purgatory, then sent most of them onward to eternal damnation. (Only John Martin was excepted, seemingly in an act of gratitude for having put the modern dance and also the Nikolais Dance Theatre on the map.) Murray Louis spat his venom into all four corners and proved that acid, satiric thrusts are not the prerogatives of critics. But this is not the first time that he turned against the critics. "At one point," he tells in *Inside Dance*, "I asked the press not to come, they were welcome—if they did not review. Most of them accepted their tickets on that basis—and proceeded to review anyway." I was among them—mea culpa—and wrote in the *Dance Observer*, January 1964:

Murray Louis in Chimera. Chimera *Photo. Author's collection.*

A *Nightmare, New Facets and Criticism*
A Non-Review

One night, Murray Louis must have been tortured by a nightmare.

Clichés holding on to their threadbare life were swinging from a warped trapeze of cocksure notions into the echo of a hollow phrase; the familiarity of a word in the nude jumped at his throat while nods were smiling and smiles were lying and a typographical error rode on a broomstick. Bold-faced types kicked and leaped in front of his sleep-dead eyes.

Phyllis was wagging her head until a masked man (who had entered with a few pliés) cut off its beautiful blondness while Gladys wiggled by with a charming looking stranger and Bill embraced Bill and Roger was chasing the man who had Phyllis' head under his coat (doing a few more pliés in between) when an energetic looking lady rushed after Roger and began her comments to Vivaldi's music with the words: "Far from the regular pulse beat of Manhattan's dancing steps, in the historic and history-making Hentry Street Playhouse we saw all the *Facets* of Murray Louis and two premieres. What about them? We thought and thought of them for a long time. The *Suite for Divers Performers* is another fun-fundamental, provocative dance with a mock-heroic, pre-classic flavor. Its apparent hilarity, however, dies too soon in its own wit and wantonness" . . . .

The masked man, holding his plié position, interrupted her: "Of the two new works *Interims* is by far the better. Murray Louis is one of our best dancers and most daring choreographers. Here one can see what sculptural transfiguration can do to moving bodies in juxtapositions and rhythmic variations. And what lovely bodies they are, particularly". . . .

The good-looking stranger took the floor: "I have always given Murray Louis and his Maître the critical acclaim due to them. True, their approach to the art is full of rhythmically organized movement with a touch of Viganó, sprinkled with a few depersonalized attitudes. The pictorial effects are supported by light and sound that gives the impression of a total theatre . . . .There are wonderful performers at the Henry Street Playhouse and the works are theatrically inventive. What they are doing is, of course, difficult to describe and, even after closer acquaintanceship with the extraordinary fusion of movement, color, light and electronic sound (or music), these difficulties remain. Nevertheless, I do not understand why Murray Louis should ask a critic". . . .

This was the cue for all to break into a simultaneous moving of lips and tongues whose articulations, however, were drowned in a din of gibberish, the very same effect Murray Louis achieved in the intervals between the Vivaldi sections in his *Suite for Divers Performers*. Caught in the nightmare, printer's ink was running down his cheeks until, with decisive effort, he heard himself shout: "Silence!" and woke up.

One must respect the courage of an artist to say no to an accepted custom which may be little more than one of the lesser evils with which we have to live. To be more exact, when Murray Louis presented a program consisting of three numbers during the weekends of November 30 and December 7, he invited critics to attend but requested them not to review his performances. His request endeavored "to strengthen the relationship between artists and audience directly, rather than through intermediary opinion." . . .

I can well imagine that the first critic was a frustrated artist with the gift of the gab who felt he could do better by verbalizing what he could not create artistically. On second thought, he may have become a critic through a thousand-and-one coincidences of which life is so full. This does not make his task any smaller, nor his problems less problematic. . . .

I want to see him totally involved, emotionally and intellectually, in what he is criticizing. Above all, he must be human before he is a critic, and to demand from a critic to be objective is asking him to deny that he is human. I want him to be armed with all his foibles and prejudices as much as with his deep and honest concern with the art itself.

I want his integrity to be integer, and I want him to be ready to stand by each statement he makes without committing critical or artistic perjury. I want him to speak to the dancer-choreographer as well as to his public, warning the artist that what is the meat of his professional attitude may be another man's poison, and warning the public that if it solely relies on his judgment it is eavesdropping on another person's heartbeat to gauge its own pulse. And, of course, I want the critic to play his own instrument with the same virtuosity as the greatest artist masters his. I want him to evoke the images of the dance with verbal pyrotechnics and to thunder his condemnations with the gentle restraint of one who knows how difficult it is to steal a kindling spark from the Creator's eye.

Murray Louis may have thought of all this when he attempted to rise above the complex machinery of life of which he is a part only. Let us be charitable and not forget that the dancer-choreographer's range of movement is as unlimited as his imagination and gift of expression grant him, while . . . the critic has nothing but a lone typewriter, the onus of judgment and the spectre of the way he formulates it. The artist has a great dream which no one can take away from him. And it should be the critic's responsibilty to see to it that the artist goes on dreaming.

In his ire against the flippancy, arrogance, and the want of sensibility on part of some of the critics, Murray Louis' reaction was understandable. I can hardly be cited for contempt of mankind or for perpetrating the crime of gross generalization when I express my anxiety about the superficiality to which the world becomes geared more and more. One can only be frightened by the incredible masses of books and art works being produced and marketed to satisfy a relatively shallow interest of a steadily growing number of people whose taste has become commercialized and depends on those prompters who whisper their cues in printer's ink.

It is difficult to say whether an artist ought to prefer a malicious critic to a stupid one, or vice versa. Or can a clever and smooth phraseologist be forgiven for making fun of the artist? A blown-up zero does not necessarily add up to an imposing figure. Taking a second look at ourselves may be a rewarding task, leaning back and wondering where we have gone wrong and when we have done right.

I was often told that artists do not bother to read reviews written about them. The most notable example is Rainer Maria Rilke, whom I trust to have said the truth. His cocooned mind retreated to his ivory tower in Muzot, in the mountainous Valais of Switzerland, where he was fed by his fertile fantasy and the rich pocketbooks of his patrons. He rightly claimed that reviewers could not add any nourishment to his mind. In singling him out I wish to point to the obvious fact that a writer is never as dependent on the daily, weekly, or monthly accounts of his creative activities as the performing artist, whose work is of a frightening nowness.

In his critique of critics Murray Louis mentioned one thing that has puzzled me all my life—audience response. He wrote:

I don't think audiences are to be ignored . . . . When they are roused to cheering and ovations, something must have happened. Yet, I have left theaters with audiences tearing the roof down, only to read grudging sourness in the morning press. I suppose that when one shuts his eyes, his tears turn off as well.

Every audience creates its own aura. Enthusiasm can spread like fire whether the cause of it is deserved or undeserved. There have been historically notorious cliques and claques in theaters. One can kill the best comedy with ten persons strategically placed in the auditorium if they laugh about the wrong lines or ostentatiously clear their throats at tender passages. Fans will bring down the house whether Nureyev is in good or bad shape. I have observed press agents shout "bravo" at the top of their voices, kindling enough applause for one more curtain call. I have witnessed standing ovations for the purest crap. After all, it remains the prerogative of the multitude to cheer the naked Emperor. I applaud the critic who is not swayed by the mood of the audience, but properly acknowledges that the audience liked the performance. And how often does the public wildly acclaim a dancer who has done well, while at the same time recognizing how bad the choreography was? You can boo the choreographer at opening night, but you cannot divide the applause any other night.

I sympathized with Murray Louis when he tried to shock the reviewers out of their complacency. I fully understood his spent fury, and I do even more so at this point. I am not sure that I can condone my own non-review, although I jumped at the opportunity to say something about criticism in general, something that was and is vital to me. But did I not circumvent his request when writing about his production by insinuation? Did I not betray the trust he had put in me?

I now see criticism with different eyes than in 1964. Since that time a dozen or more books of mine have been published; my plays have been produced and exposed to critical views. Have I not personally experienced how willful distortion and a lack of sensibility hurt the most? What was my reaction to the statement of the cultural editor of one of the greatest newpapers that he did not believe the premise of my book, *Three Women*, in other words, he did not think that any woman has ever inspired any man to create a work of art (as he said verbatim)? What could my feelings have been but powerless fury? Or when the cultural editor of a famed European magazine enumerated half a dozen omissions in my book, *The Swiss*, when I had treated all of these subjects on many pages which he quoted as missing? The word is: exasperation. With some critics, I understand, callousness can top mere stupidity. As a critic, one cannot help being angered by Murray Louis' action. After all, he intended to curb the critics' activities and, as a matter of fact, jeopardize their raison d'être. As a creative writer I could not more wholeheartedly agree with him.

There are situations in life in which one feels caught in a machine which one helps run—without one's own volition—by running with it. The intricacies of our interdependence are stupendous. Where is the point at which you will tell your general that your conscience silences your gun—and will you muster the courage to put your gun away?

Deborah Jowitt has become one of the more important dance critics today. Her Village Voice has sounded all over town for quite some time now. With her typewriter keys she opened the gates of the *New York Times*. I think a great deal of her as a human being and appreciate her as a writer of integrity. She herself confessed once in a New Year's resolution column that she finds herself too loquacious at times. Sometimes, no doubt, the words seem to run away with her, but her reviews have remained descriptive, informative and convincing. It is her prerogative to be

partisan to the young and wayout dancers whose headquarters are
mainly in the Village.

In January 1962, when Louis Horst, editor of *Dance Observer*,
assigned me to cover *An Afternoon of Dances* I knew very little
about Deborah Jowitt. When I returned from this concert I clearly
recall having had an argument with Louis. I asked him to relieve
me from the duty of writing about this recital. In my eyes it had
not reached the level on which dance productions—successes or
failures—must be taken seriously enough to be recorded. These
were very young dancers, I insisted. Knowingly and unnecessarily
hurting a young artist still struggling with himself and his seemingly
desperate need to create is like whipping him publicly. Louis Horst
remained unmoved. If artists rent the Lexington "Y" and ask the
critics for reviews, they take themselves seriously enough and must
face the consequences, he said; moreover, it is the *Dance
Observer's* obligation to put on record whatever happens in the
field of the modern dance.

I had no longer any choice in this matter. I vaguely remembered
Miss Jowitt as a dancer in other companies, but apparently she has
never impressed me as a dancer of whom one could say she might
make headlines one day. And choreographically she was—at that
point—not yet ready to be judged. As in Murray Louis' case I used
this opportunity for rather general statements which were
apparently uppermost on my mind. To this very day I deem it
important that one's early choreographies are shown to knowledgeable friends, or responsive as well as receptive critics, in their
developmental stages. I know that, for instance, Robert Lowell had
Stanley Kunitz go over his poems before publishing them, that
Friedrich Schiller's relationship to Johann Wolfgang Goethe was
rather similar, and that Joseph Conrad had Ford Madox Ford
check his manuscripts before they went to the printer. I suggested
the dancer seek such initial advice, although I knew that any
suggestion was usually neither properly absorbed nor responded to
by the young artist. After all, the young so often doubt that they
could be wrong; but at least sometimes honest and warm criticism
at the right moment could be used as a security valve.

I still recall the hours when this critique went through several different versions. I utterly dislike to write in what I do not believe. So I wrote another kind of non-review:

"Art is priesthood, not a pastime." These words of Cocteau should be sent to all dancers and would-be choreographers as memento.

I recognize the vital need of the young artist to prove himself and, what is more important, to grow through trial and error. At a certain stage of his growing pains he should have a studio at his disposal where he can perform, to see his work through the eyes of his friends, co-workers and those critics who would gladly give their time and advice on such occasion rather than to have to sit through three hours of a pretentious and, more often than not, amateurish performance that could easily be confused by some people with professionalism (as it hides behind a treacherous varnish), although it is little more than high-schoolish.

The young artist, too, has a responsibilty toward the art as such, toward himself and his future as well as his potential audience. He must have humility. He must learn to have it. He must learn to be simple and to the point. He must realize ... that at times it may be more important to sharpen one's self-criticism than one's wits, and that it is most important to be able to wait until one knows—and not only thinks—one is ready.

In *Afternoon of Dances* Deborah Jowitt and John Wilson were the choreographers and leading dancers. Their program lasted three hours, consisted of seven long numbers and two short intermissions. The supporting dancers were Shareen Blair, Cathy Boyd, Penny Frank, Sally Stackhouse, Gus Solomons, Jr., and Koert Stuyf. There were two pianists, one flutist, and two costume designers. Mr. Wilson sang.

Some of those mentioned were even very gifted.

Miss Jowitt continued to dance and to choreograph, even while she donned the mantle of a critic. I did see her occasionally on stage and, though she improved constantly as a practicing choreographer, her creative work has never made as indelible an impression as her ciriticsm. I know of no precedent of an accredited critic appearing at the same time as a performing and creative artist. (Let us except Jean Georges Noverre who continued to choreograph while writing his *Lettres*. Virgil Thomson was a music critic while he composed and was performed. This dual existence was never without its frictions.) I do not wish to decide how wise it is to judge while being exposed to judgment, or whether it is recommendable for imitation. But that Deborah Jowitt dared to challenge convention and unwritten laws is certainly admirable.

I am sure that she has never really forgiven me for having written this review and the way I did it. While we were flying together to a panel discussion on dance criticism held in Milwaukee many years ago, I tried to explain to her in a most apologetic tone how I failed to convince Louis Horst that this review should not find its way into print; I have always felt that it makes little sense to hurt someone without being able to help. After years, it was the first time that we talked to each other again. Now that we were headed for a discussion on dance criticism I should have asked her what kind of review she might have written about her first choreographies if she had been in my seat. I did not ask her this question since I dislike talking shop with my colleagues.

Even critics who do not wish to lose their humanity or temper sometimes find themselves in a difficult situation. I have often noticed that critics have blind spots. When I once invited Birgit Cullberg (with whose work I felt a certain kinship) and Clive Barnes for a gathering in my home, I was unaware of Mr. Barnes having attacked her ballets mercilessly through the years. When I tried to introduce them to each other I immediately sensed my faux pas and their enmity. Miss Cullberg came to my rescue by shaking hands with him and saying: "He doesn't dislike me as a person, he only hates what I am doing on stage."

To this very day I do not know how one acquires blind spots and whether such a vehement dislike does not often say more about the critic than the criticized artist. If John Martin had not championed the modern dance from its very beginning, but had maligned it with acid words continuously, he would not have prevented its emergence, but may have severely slowed down its development. Blind spots can often drive a critic into a dead-end street. Baudelaire, an astute art critic and as such a staunch defender of all Romanticism—this is how his fondness of Gautier is to be understood—fiercely attacked Courbet and the realistic Barbizon School, but also reproached Ingres for lack of creative imagination; in doing so he did not foresee or recognize the emergence of impressionism developing into the most vital renewal of painting at his time.

I have never been impressed by Glen Tetley, to put it mildly. I realize that many dancers like to work with him since he has a way of advancing the showy and narcissistic trend in them. With so many turns, lifts, and extensions they hope to look good on stage. But in spite of all the commotion happening in Tetley's ballets, there is little direction in them, even though one sees the dancers enter and exit as if persecuted by a dancing devil, and there is little meat to the content. At least, I was never able to detect any basic structure and idea in what he did. It may be all my fault, as it so easily may be with blind spots. I have seen his most often produced and best accredited work, *Pierrot Lunaire*, several times, also on German television. It could never make me change my mind. Of course, I am fully aware of the facts of history. Tetley has made his way, as one says, he headed his own companies for which he was the chief choreographer and he choreographed for many other companies. For a short time, he took the place of the late John Cranko in Stuttgart.

Once, early in Glen Tetley's career as a choreographer, I reviewed him. I may have been too blunt and vehement in my reaction. The only excuse I could bring forth for my irritation and verbal whip lies in the fact that the performance I had to review lasted until close to midnight. It was in May 1962 that I wrote:

I have always thought that Glen Tetley was a good dancer with a brilliant modern and ballet technique. Now that I have seen four of his choreographies, there is no doubt in my mind that he is not a good choreographer.

Carmen de Lavallade, Glen Tetley, and Scott Douglas in Glen Tetley's Pierrot Lunaire. *Author's collection.*

It was the most pretentious and unimaginative evening I experienced in a long time. The inner cry for bigness is a sign of the amateurish. To compose four dances for the same three dancers, but to have twelve live musicians, a conductor and a singer, to commission music from Carlo Surinach and Peter Hartman and to have iron constructions built for two dances by the American Stage Equipment and Iron Works, Inc., is putting the accents on the wrong values, the extraneous before the artistry.

The dancers, Glen Tetley, Linda Hodes and Robert Powell, struggled in vain to save the choreographer. The first piece, *Gleams in the Bone House*, was still acceptable and somewhat promising. *Birds of Sorrows* showed lack of style and composition, *How Many Miles to Babylon* was an ill-fated excursion into humor and went nowhere, and his *Pierrot Lunaire* violated Schönberg. It all proved how infinitesimal the creative spark must have been to ignite so much fire that left one cold.

The orchestra under Robert Cole's direction was excellent and in the work of Schönberg soprano Jan de Gaetani sang beautifully and merited all attention. Peter Harvey, Beni Montresor, Rouben Ter-Aroutunian and William Ritman contributed scenery, costumes and the lighting in abundance of their diversified talents.

Each intermission was twenty minutes long. The first one was still promising, during the second intermission beginning exhaustion caused a long queue at the fountain, the last one was inexcusable. A few minutes before midnight all was over. Friends stayed to cheer and to give the funeral of the creative dance a brilliant appearance.

P.S. The moral of this evening: The more is not necessarily the better. There are born dancers, such as Glen Tetley, but choreographers are chosen by God.

I then disqualified myself and vowed never to write about Glen Tetley again. I have kept my promise.

After observing a choreographer for some time I have often had the feeling I would like to sit down with him, take him by his hand to make him sense the sincerity of my intentions and talk to him. Of course, this situation is not very likely ever to happen. The next best thing to it is an open letter addressed to the artist. In March 1972 I was instinctively impelled to talk in this way to Eliot Feld.

Dear Eliot Feld:

I have wanted to write you for a long time. I felt like doing it after the electrifying premiere of *Harbinger* which, no doubt, was the harbinger of that rare phenomenon, a good choreographer. But then I thought your second ballet will have to prove you, and *At Midnigh* did just that. There was no longer any need for conveying my private joy.

The whole dance world made it easy for you to leave American Ballet Theatre, although I thought it was a bit premature. But everyone wanted you to succeed. Of course, you had to give your own company a name. But to name it American Ballet Company was somewhat close for comfort to American Ballet Theater, and I began to worry about you.

With a Balanchinesque gesture you began to build your Feldian repertory. It was amazing what you could achieve within two short years. Once in a while there was a slight faux pas, like your version of *Rite of Spring*, but one could easily forgive and forget these minor failures, they were a part of your daring attitude to keep your public and followers *au courant* on what was going on in your workshop. The display of the bulk of your work was impressive. I mostly enjoyed and admired what I saw.

However, my worries grew in proportion to your growing ability to create more and more—I am looking for the right word—in terms of the most difficult challenges, as you had to prove time and again that you could do at least as much as anyone of those who can do amazing things. As an example let me refer to your *Intermezzo* with which you did a surprisingly good job in making your own statement while paraphrasing Mr. B's *Liebeslieder Walzer*.

I know, Jerome Robbins also went back to an *Afternoon of a Faun* and to the second act of *Giselle*, but he did not try to top anyone who was still around. He became inspired by a classic and semi-classic work and gave one a very personalized and the other a highly contemporary new face. He may have lifted something, but only to uplift it.

You may think you have done something similar to *A Soldier's Tale*. You have and you haven't. You have by throwing out Ramuz' perhaps by now antiquated story and words and by turning the Devil into a Pimp, the Princess into two Whores. But you have not—when you tried to juxtapose Pimp and Whores on the one side and the Soldier on the other. The story did not come easily to you. Like Stravinsky-Ramuz' and your own Soldier you were caught unawares in your lostness.

There were the times of the 20's, the Ragtime spirit. There was the pitiful figure of a Soldier whom you had to liberace from his fairytale existence. To throw him into reality, you let him slip under your creative legs into that tango-of-death feeling of the 20's and 30's—who doesn't loathe all wars?—and like a pistol shot you had lifted *A Soldier's Tale* from under *The Green Table*. Thematically, spiritually, choreographically.

Apparently there is a war on. A Soldier—perhaps on furlough--gets entangled with two whores. The dance of these three was a *tour de force*, enough proof of your choreographic skill, your light and lightning wit. I would have loved to shout bravo! But then, there was Ramuz' Devil turned into a Pimp and Death's clothes. You danced him beautifully.

However, his key movements, his coming out of the dark from upstage stepping, sharply accented, stepping on the center line towards downstage was Kurt Jooss's Death in a Pimp's clothes. Again my compliments. How skillful a pimp's movements were wedded to the Death's simple stereotype movements of *The Green Table*! And then, there was the typical Joossian image of the diagonal, repeated over and over again. There were your Soldier's long diagonal lunges, there were your fighting soldiers whom you took from Jooss to add to *A Soldier's Tale*, there they were, there they fell and got up again, as Jooss visualized it.When they were dead Jooss had *his* Pimp remove the rings from their fingers. In your version he was supported by the two female vultures who removed all the soldiers' valuables.

There is nothing wrong with Stravinsky, nor with Jooss, nor with Feld. I just wonder why you had to bring Jooss and Stravinsky together in your own name. If it were only a sign of your difficulty to develop story ballets, it wouldn't really matter. But I am now wary of what makes you tick choreographically. And thereby hangs a soldier's tale.

I ask myself aloud: why does he have to test the limits of how far he can go in his sophisticated daring, challenging good creative taste, taking from here and there and juggling it all in bright stagelight with breathtaking skill to loud applause? Forgive one who cannot help shouting: "Eliot, watch out, your hubris!"

In sincere admiration, but with a tinge of sadness,

Walter Sorell

In the last analysis, an open letter instead of the regular form of a review is simply a review in *italics*. It wishes to emphasize displeasure, perhaps to voice anger, concern, and distress.

But why should I feel the slightest anxiety about a highly successful man? Just because of his great potentialities. There are very few gifted choreographers around; you can count one choreographer to a thousand dancers. A couple of years after my open letter to Eliot Feld was published, I felt reassured when

Arlene Croce—whose dance critiques are written in a kind of cool fervor and are mostly to the point—voiced similar objections to Feld's approach to choreography in her column in the *New Yorker*: "Feld's method as a choreographer is a frank attempt to make art out of art by copying existing models in other people's ballets. Sometimes he succeeds in converting a model to his own purposes; often he achieves only a reduction."

Eliot Feld made me think of how the human psyche can play its games with the creative urge. How often have we heard that character defeats genius! Why, then, should not genius play havoc with one's character?

I have never quite understood why the artist and his critic face one another as if they were natural adversaries. They are not. They are in the same boat, figuratively speaking, loving the same art form, defending it to assure its existence and development. They are only performing different duties. Especially in an era such as ours, when all aesthetic sensibilities are constantly under attack, when all values and the very quality of life seem to be in jeopardy, the artist is called upon to shape his experience of being and to spiritualize the reality of existence into whatever artistic image he may envision. The critic may merely report about the artist's creation, he may evaluate its aesthetic validity, adumbrate his own involvement in it, or mark his personal distance from the work, but whatever he does he ought to do it as the protector of the art, the guardian of the artist, and in the name of the greater Creator who knows about all human limitations and can but wonder about the endless ways of how the creative genius of man can express itself.

1981

New York—Zürich.

It is as if the East were the dream image of Western man, an eternal well, his goal for an ever-recurring pilgrimage during which he brushes the spirit of something he apparently and desperately needs in order to replenish and rejuvenate his self from time to time. East and West are seemingly an hermaphroditic totality, two halves that were destined to be separated by the wisdom of some evolution like man and woman. They are the eternal antithesis and yet united as day and night with the emphasis on the one in order to reveal the other in its dramatic contrariness.

Western man, a visionary with myopic eyes, action-driven as he is, has built for himself a world that can easily be shattered, a world shaped by dogmas and principles. Like a knight-errant he feels compelled to stay on a course of surficial search of the new and for more and more of it. With the help of Christianity he accepted an orderly cosmology which, through the last seven centuries, he gradually debunked and destroyed with the genius of his scientific mind leading to technological madness. Modern man finally put himself into the unenviable position of being able to pry the secrets of God, that glorious architect in whose image man was conceived and who in His inscrutable wisdom, left so much open for the fool in man to explore and probe. Modern man achieved the ultimate in creation, imitating his own Creator without realizing that with each progressive step he would undermine his own genius and must of necessity defeat himself in the last stages of his Great Experiment with the god in him and the world outside.

He must do so because in his arrogance he overlooked that with his progressing accomplishments he became more and more alienated from his self, that he exchanged the myth of his humanness for a new ritualistic cult of the machine, yielding to ever more distant goals, surrendering to streamlined little gods. Western man has never learned to accept and absorb intuitively the inseparable polarities of existence, a universal vision of life in which good and evil, right or wrong, the creative and the destructive are only two sides of one and the same. He has been so busy progressing that he never found the time to find the way to his real self, to make his blown-up ego acquainted with the spirit flowering within.

We have never quite understood that it is more important to be religious than to have a religion. Zen Buddhism teaches us:

> There is nothing true anywhere,
> The true is nowhere to be seen;
> If you say you see the true,
> This seeing is not the true one.

Perhaps if we had known this, less evil might have been done in the name of the good.

Of course, we all envision an ideal image of Eastern man who believes in the wholeness of existence, who is not haunted by fear of an afterlife-punishment, who can hear the voice of an intangible spirit and tries to touch a philosophy of life at the root of its very simplicity. Chang Ch'ao once said: "Only those who take leisurely what the people of the world are busy about can be busy about what the people of the world take leisurely."

Undoubtedly, the nature of belief and the outlook on life differ individually and basically with the Indian, Tibetan, Chinese, or Japanese. An Indian yogi, with absolute mastery of his own being, is light-years apart from a Japanese samurai who, as Alan Watts says, has "a sense of social shame quite as acute as our more metaphysical sense of sin." While the Chinese with whom Zen originated believe that "in Buddhism there is no place for using effort," the Japanese is self-conscious, and Zen is for him the way, the way to overcome his self-consciousness, his innate compulsion to compete with himself, a compulsion, as Alan Watts stresses, "which turns every craft and skill into a marathon of self-discipline. Although the attraction of Zen lay in the possibility of liberation from self-consciousness, the Japanese version of Zen fought fire with fire, overcoming the 'self observing the self' by bringing it to an intensity in which it exploded."

When the way of the Japanese Zen is different in its fascination with the self from occidental man, there are nevertheless many tangential affinities as Existentialism and the philosophy of Ludwig Wittgenstein proved, or the school of John Cage and Merce

Cunningham translated into a non-conceptual edifice of artistic expression. This explains why so many Japanese have been attracted by a variety of modern dance forms and especially found Martha Graham's approach a ready-made mould and artistic refuge where their minds felt liberated from conventional thought. This, after all, is one of the guiding motifs of Zen.

Shapes and direction of the grooves of self-discipline within which the Zen artist moves depend on the artist in him. If he is an Asian he must not give up his own way of being in an attempt at pleasing Occidental eyes and ears, in other words at 'making it here.' If he is a Westerner attracted by Zen a mere gesture toward the East—in other words, a rebellion against his own culture, or a flight from the established social order à la Ginsberg and Kerouac—will not quite suffice; he must move from the center of his own culture—shedding his self-consciousness, liberating his mind from its subjective fetters—toward a very personal experience of awakening in a spiritually self-contained existence. Then he may find a happy artistic expression of his self. It is like building a bridge from here to there, with the artist in the center reaching neither to the right nor left, simply looking upward. Not everyone is so fortunate as Isamu Noguchi. He did not have to build this bridge. He was on it when he was born.

In our own time we experience the most subtle and crudest dependence on Eastern influences. We only have to consider our reliance on certain gurus and their messages, on meditation aiming at clearing the debris of our consciousness, emptying our mind and trying to reach shores of replenishing wells. This has become a desperate need for many of us in the declining years of Western civilization, a malaise with which we attempt to cure the malaise caused by our anxieties.

The East has always been the one from which the West borrowed. The Greeks absorbed many things from many lands, but knew how to make them their own. Homer maintained that the cult of Dionysus came to the Greeks from Thrace, some modern scholars trace this cult back to the Babylonians. Whatever, it made a case for danseomania and established the dramatized lie, as Solon called it, which developed into our form of theater. Corinth was the border between East and West, and Asian motifs flowed through its gateways into Greek art. When we follow history, then Romanesque art received its strongest impulse from the icon worshippers whom Emperor Leo III drove out of Byzantium in A.D. 730 and who brought to Italy and the Frankish realm a new vision of beauty, loosening the then architectural austerity. They also introduced to the West the elegant Byzantine ivories.

It is the irony in man's fate that his acts of cruelty and foolishness often open vistas into unexpected marvels. When in the eleventh century the coarse Christian crusaders discovered the Orient with its leisurely, sumptuous life and the poetic silver lining at its edges, their own life-style turned full circle into the age of Tristan and Isolt, the troubadours and Minnesingers. The discoveries began at the height of the Renaissance, and white man was determined to establish commercial bridgeheads in the East, South, and West. The excesses of the baroque, later derogatively referred to as rococo, would be unthinkable without Chinese influence. If not everything was Chinese (Voltaire and Noverre bowed successfully to the fashion of the day), then it was Persian (Montesquieu), or Arabic with its Thousand and One Nights. Turks, Incas, and Iroquoi peopled the stages (Rameau) and belles lettres during the first half of the eighteenth century.

Eastern influence returned, as if with a vengeance, in the nineteenth century and ours. When Japan was forced to open its gates to the outside world in 1853, the influence of its visual art, mainly of its prints, on the European artist was gradually growing, and toward the end of the century unique in its far-reaching impact on many painters from Whistler to Degas to Gauguin. It coincided with the cancan mood of despair during the fin-de-siècle period and with one of the first articulate reactions to the Industrial Revolution: Escape. Escape to the East, to Africa, to remote islands. It was an escape from Western civilization and its spiritual bankruptcy. When Gauguin, on his way to Tahiti, wrote Strindberg that in defending the European civilization he tolerated barbarism, he might have said more politely 'civilized barbarism.'

The Impressionists received, indirectly the strongest impetus from photography, but, more directly, they took metaphysical sustenance from the Japanese prints. There would have been no Aubrey Beardsley and Gustav Klimt or any of those stunning decorative ornaments of the works labeled Art Nouveau or Jugendstil without the discovery of Japanese art. And speaking of the ornamental: if Henri Matisse had not been influenced by the color schemes of Oriental rugs and North African scenery, he would have become another painter. Moreover, if Pablo Picasso had not been invited by Matisse for dinner one night he may not have seen that Congo mask in Matisse's house, the famous point of departure for Cubism, and painting might have gone in another direction. Is there not a mysterious sequence of events in history, a link of unpredictable circumstances determining cause and effect, bringing about far-reaching consequences of startling revelations?

There are historic happenings which the arts cannot help but registering. The turn of the century was such an inescapable confluence of events. It prepared for the coming of a cataclysmic era. The Eastern influence was accidental, the need for escape was, however, very real. The French novelist, Pierre Loti, was only one of many writers at that time to express the people's desire to renounce reality and find relief in exotic adventure and love. The American Lafcadio Hearn sang the praise of Japan and David Belasco staged his play *Madame Butterfly* in 1900. Painful pressures of a menacing progress of civilization found a variety of articulations under the shibboleth of escape. It was a time that cried out for a dancer like Ruth St. Denis whose first successes were in Europe where people had just been captivated by the charm of Japanese and Cambodian Dancers. When they came to cities like Paris or Berlin they found a most receptive audience that would have paid a small fortune to be able to escape to the East and suddenly found their dream of a lost paradise delivered to the doors of their subliminal awareness.

The poetic minds of Hofmannsthal and Rilke broke out into lyric ecstacies in prose over all these dances done in the illusion of incense and the dream atmosphere of sophisticated innocence. Shortly thereafter, Pound and Yeats began to explore the esoteric realm of the Noh play, after Appia and Craig had successfully campaigned for utter suggestiveness on stage. Eastern dancers came regularly from all parts of their world to Europe and America, from India, Ceylon, Java, or Bali. When Antonin Artaud saw the Balinese dancers in 1936, he became inspired to dream of a theater of cruel purgation. But his Theater of Cruelty found its realization only in the sixties and seventies when man's mind was more receptive to Artaud's struggle against our mechanized and conventionalized civilization which he wanted to fight onstage with the raw elements of myth and magic.

When America brought Japan down on her knees militarily at the very end of the Second World War, Japan conquered our minds with Zen Buddhism. It was the most valuable loot to bring home with us in this desperate struggle for survival. Existentialism, The Theater of the Absurd, John Cage with Merce Cunningham followed suite.

We cannot assume that one man alone can turn the tide of events or instigate a revolution. But he can be better attuned to his time than others or sense undercurrent messages with uncanny intuitiveness .It would be nice but naive to imagine that one day in the mid-forties John Cage had come back from Japan with his rucksack full of Zen Buddhism and opened it—as if it were a twentieth-century Pandora's box—to distribute a bit of Zen here and there among the musicians, dancers, and painters. Cage and Cunningham were doing little more than expressing the mood of their time with vociferous, but also exciting, articulation.

That we do not forget: Eugène Ionesco created what was called The Theater of the Absurd in 1950 and, shortly thereafter, Samuel Beckett wrote—out of stark naked reality—a most unreal, metaphysical play, *Waiting for Godot.* The year was 1952, the very same year in which John Cage staged the first Happening at Black Mountain College in North Carolina. That we do not forget: It was the era of existentialist thinking when irrationalism and the image of futility pingponged before our eyes.

This is where John Cage came in, admonishing us to adjust to life's indeterminacy, not to try in vain "to bring order out of chaos nor suggest improvements in creation but simply to wake up to the very life we're living, which is so excellent once one gets one's mind and one's desires out of its way and lets it act of its own accord." Sit and meditate on what illumination arises. Predetermined plans were thrown out of the windows and, with a clandestine look at the sacred book I Ching, randomness was asked to enter.

John Cage wrote an enlightening book called *Silence: Lectures and Writings* which I reviewed for the *Dance Observer* in February 1962. I said in part:

> Something remarkable
>   has happened:
> a book on "Silence" printed in a
> typographical rage   speaks so loud
> (it is a collection of lectures, of words
> that fill the silence) that you cannot
> help hearing it.
>   Sometimes,
> "it is simply a matter of going on
> talking which is neither significant nor
> insignificant, nor good nor bad, but
> simply"
>   happening while you turn the
> pages   leaves (the stuff books are
> made of)   leaving an imprint on
> your mind. In spite of
>   yes
>   in spite of his inde-
> terminacy of performance a world opens
> up   by mere chance   it operates,

functions, is maddening and enlightening
          a world CAGEd (sometimes, John,
I admired you for your daring, wit, for
the wisdom in parenthesis, for the meaningful anecdotes lost at the bottom of a
page as if all the
                    asterisks of the world
would begin to shine like bright stars
penetrating the darkness of chance
          illuminating   transporting.) Do
you really let go of each thought as if
it were void? And then it happens,
          doesn't it? Adding, as it were, to
the order that characterizes life.
     Shall I ask questions?   I   have to
ask so many. I know sound is just
vibration,   but there is time and
distance and measure there is past
present future and the great silence between them and still there are many
questions of method and order within
chaos and chance. And if you toss three
coins six times   sometimes you lost me
(or was I, together with contemporary
music—how fleeting everything contemporary is!—in the dark, surrendering to
and embracing disorder?). But then what
does it matter when I saw how very much
you are yourself, how you make what you
alone must make, on and on, in and beyond
silence.   A healthy lawlessness of a
prophet-pioneer and then on page 93 I
     stopped. I thought I could not go on
any more. But there you said to me: Are
you getting bored? Read another fifty,
sixty, a hundred pages and you will
          dis-
                    cover
"it's not boring at all but very inter-

esting" ... Perhaps you are right, we
should not try "to bring order out of
chaos ... " -- look where it got us, after
all, nowhere except where the darkness is
darker and chaos more chaotic ...
          The telephone rings. Must I answer?
          Tranquility
                    Emotions
     Impatience   let it ring   Still
another eighty pages of irritation and
wisdom   yes   did I say so? I meant it.
There can be greatness in madness as there
is madness in greatness. Surely, there is
intangible reward in "Silence". Try it.
Hold John Cage's book in your hands. Look
up from time to time, go on dreaming your
own measures of chaos for "there is no such
thing as silence. Something is always
happening that makes a sound." But there is
silence, and the words help make silences.
If nothing else you will learn a caressing
wisdom floating with you. Through irritation
you will become calm. A rare experience.
That reminds me of the story John Cage tells
on page

I looked up the entry in the Encyclopaedia Britannica devoted to
Cage, John, and I came away with the feeling that it is not enough
to place Cage into a pigeonhole. If we can't grasp the philosophy
behind his entire being, the determined indeterminacy for which
he has stood all his life—or did he fight for it? I can't envision him
fighting—, his liberating laughter about all the nonsense with
which we try to make sense of our mind's systematic chaos, we
shall never do justice to him. Probably he is right, as much as
anyone can know, and things *are* as life *is*. All we have to do is to
let things, i.e. life, happen to us in a random way. With whatever
art we are faced, we should not grope for meaning behind its
symbols related or unrelated, and we would be so much happier

for just accepting and enjoying what we are experiencing the very moment that is and the very way it is. This seems to lean less on Zen than existentialist thinking, particularly as elucidated by Sartre, whose affirmation of the "in-itself" leads to the notion that this life is what it is and is uniquely the way it is.

I wish he were right that there is a kind of fulfillment in nothingness and that everything leads anyway on the road of chance to its ultimate inconclusion. But is not destiny what we make of chance? In the long run history may have a second thought on John Cage, and, as much as anyone can predict, it may then be caught in a non-intentional process of total indeterminacy. And John Cage's ideas might triumph.

When all this is said, a postscriptum may become necessary. It could be maintained that he and Merce continued what Jean Cocteau had started with *Parade* in 1917. Cage made Cocteau's remark come true that "for centuries one generation has handed down a torch to another over the heads of the public, whose breath has never succeeded in extinguishing it."

Most of what happened to us artistically in the fifties and sixties goes back to Cocteau's concept of reducing everything to "the rehabilitation of the commonplace," to a poetically heightened simplicity and banality. He was out to surprise (Diaghilev to Cocteau in 1912: "Ètonne-moi!") and to enrage the public. He succeeded in making the first and vital step in the process of liberating the theater arts from all nineteenth-century conventions. From then on surprise for the sake of surprise was in as the cliché of the anti-cliché.

Cage went one step further in transferring the reflection of everyday life onto the stage. Art is not there to be enjoyed but to be used, he declared, and we must use it as if art and life were one and the same, which boils down to the dictum of life being life being life being, in its sum total, art. Cocteau made the finality of nothingness possible, Cage—with the help of Asian doctrines— lifted nothingness onto the pedestal of life-art as the virtual entity of 'non-esse' within our existence. Cage issued the passport to all happenings—and, though the period of the "real" happenings that started in 1952 is over, the awesome aspect of all life and art being nothing but a more or less improvised happening still hovers over us.

He often managed to infuriate me wildly—but this is probably part of his raison d'être—when he made his sound effects or music (however you wish to be attuned to his way of expressing himself) rise to a hysterically ear-splitting volume. I felt irritated and provoked—after all, my ears were hurting and I did not want to lose my ability to be exhilerated by the most subtle sounds of Mozart, Bach, or Mahler in my private silence—and in such a mood of pardonable fury I lost my critical temper and, in reviewing a Merce Cunningham recital, I lowered my standard as a critic by saying Merce seems to accomplish more when "uncaged." Today, reconsidering many of Cunningham's works—not to, but:—with music or sound collages by John Cage I may have to plead guilty of a pun below the mental belt.

Over the centuries the East has meant many things to many people, but Asian art has always embraced life and a higher form of spirituality which cannot exist without a touch of grace, and in the way this spirituality is creatively expressed it cannot help transcending mere reality. Even if you wish to "move away from simply private human concerns" and symbols, to speak with Cage, the artist can find means of creating "images powerful enough to deny our nothingness," to speak with Malraux. This is the other side of one and the same coin. An artist is free to express himself in the manner he feels like doing it, and yet he is only a prisoner of his own self. But who tells us what goes into the making of an artist and what kind of an artist at which time? Is he not always an exponent of a mysterious force?

Whether East or West: Not every work of art is a masterpiece, but every masterpiece is a purification of the world in its time; not every artist is sufficiently blessed to overcome himself, but every great artist scores eternal victory over death. Each work of art is only as great as the onlooker's eyes are perceptive. Erick Hawkins expressed about the same when he said: "the dance does not occur until the one who watches sees it as well as the one who dances *dances* it; until the dancer is sitting in the audience as well as standing on the stage." During this century and its many "isms" we have learned to see and hear differently than before. What once passed as primitive has risen to the level of sophistication. Van Gogh and Bach have become idols in our time. African, Aztec, or Sumerian images are no longer the archaeological treasures they were, our senses established a new, a very intimate kinship to them. Our senses have matured.

If Erick Hawkins had not become a dancer, I could envision him as an American revivalist teaching the scriptures of Buddhism, Taoism, or the philosophy of Confucius to the Indians in the Dakotas, in the mountains of Colorado, or in the Mesas in New Mexico. When you ask him (as he asked himself): What is the most beautiful dance, he will answer: "Dance that can paraphrase the ancient Hindu saying: 'Let those who dance here, dance Him.' Dance that knows dance can be, should be, and is a way of saying now."

Some modern dancers can articulate their philosophy of life with their bodies and tongues. Hawkins can. In March 1971 I wrote about one of his recitals at the Anta Theatre:

Before entering Erick Hawkins' world I always feel like taking off my shoes and leaving them in the checkroom with all the street noises and insulting sights of the daily dirt. I feel like reclining in my seat and letting him guide me into his imaginary world where time is of no duration and the West is as close to the East as it ever can be.

Hawkins' work lies outside all confines of theatricality and beyond all traditional concepts of pacing and phrasing. Based on the philosophy of the Tao-Te-King which says, "By non-action everything can be done," Hawkins and his company move with utter tranquility, seeking an expression of purity, the feeling of movement itself . . . Like the lines of a *haiku* poem, Hawkins' movements evoke, instant by instant, a sensation of poetic significance, a sensuous impression, a fleeting thought. . . .

. . . the premiere of the evening was *Of Love* . . . and Erick Hawkins' choreography was a serious lesson for those who do not know the

From openings of the (eye) *by Erick Hawkins. The picture shows Erick Hawkins. Design by Ralph Dorazio. Photo: A. John Geraci. Author's collection.*

difference between sex and eroticism. The piece . . . danced with all nuances of gentlest suggestiveness, created a series of "free flow" movement images of surprising and memorable beauty. I have never thought that naked human bodies can evoke a sensation of so much chastity in an erotic pas de deux.

Of Love sent me back to rereading The Tao-Te-King in which I found a line describing best what I felt marvelling at this work. The Taoist scriptures speak of a sage who, without going out of the door, can know the whole world and "who accomplishes everything without doing it." In Of Love Hawkins accomplished to convey the sensuousness of sensuality, the poetry of physical union. . . .

This elusive spiritual entity, called Eros, is woven into the tapestry of most Buddhist as much as non-Buddhist thoughts, the erotic and spiritual of a subtle and noble oneness, alien to Western man, but sometimes hiding between movements of a dance (as the depth of an image can live between the lines of a poem): in Martha Graham who owes so much to the East, in Erick Hawkins or Nancy Meehan, and in a very personalized manner in Merce Cunningham. It is very much there with many Asian dancers who, over the decades, have tried to acquaint our eyes with their vision of being.

A Westerner who, let us say, has studied any kind of Indian dance and presented herself as an Indian dancer may have studied the craft itself to perfection. As a critic I may appreciate her learned delivery. But I will always be stranded with a great deal of doubt about that one and most important step from her craft to art. How very few, I am sure, have given it breath of their own breath and the ultimate finesse of the dance's deep-bedded meanings. Is not every Western critic donning the mantle of purple pretension when playing judge in the case of Asian dance? Did he grow up in an atmosphere that unveiled vistas of greater understanding? How many hours did he spend with teachers in their studios in India, Java, China, or Japan? How much of the needed insight into folkloric background can anyone imbue by osmosis— and do not

his basic instruments, comparison and analysis, become questionable crutches in these cases?

I have always been aware of the spiritual remoteness from which
I had to view, for instance, such an experience as the Kerala
Kalamandalum Kathakali Company, as it was presented at Hunter
College Assembly Hall (November 1971):

I knew it was all wrong to enter the auditorium of Hunter College with
the street noise still in my ears and the headlines on the proverbially
invisible screen of my tortured mind. There I was trying to forget the
realities of existence and to mesmerize myself into a state of non-Western
patience.

The program note cites an incident of the Hindu epic Ramayana. It
tells of Rama in exile with his wife Sita and his brother when the mighty
demon king of Lanka abducts Sita. Various subplots complicate matters,
but finally, with the help of the future king of the monkeys, Sita is
rescued, the evildoers are punished or killed and Rama returns to
Ayodha to be crowned as the rightful king.

The story matters only if you understand the symbolic meaning of
each gesture. What the Kerala Kalamandalum Kathakali Company
presents is more pantomimic drama than dance, ritualistic movement at
its most subtle and ecstatic expressiveness, vocalization of feelings and
not verbalized thoughts, minute shades of groans and grunts and laughter
which must have weighty meaning on the scale of their sensibilities.
What is mystery and elusiveness to Western eyes seems to be symbolic
realism to Eastern spectators.

Our unfamiliarity with their gesture language makes us at first resent
watching them (as we resent having to listen to people conversing in an
idiom unknown to us). But the incessant, beautifully controlled,
rhythmic beat of their drums, the whine of the narrating singers, the
colorful costumes, the fantastic make-up looking like a mask hypnotize
us into believing that we know what we see. And the inexplicable
happens. We still don't really understand the language they are talking,
but we become completely drawn into a mysterious wonderland in which
we quickly learn to hear what we see and to see what we hear. It is as
simple as all magic is, and that is what theatre is all about.

Leaving Hunter College and walking down Park Avenue I wondered
how any sensible man can live in such real reality. I called Rama to

The subtle, highly stylized language of gestures is an essential part of the pantomimic dance drama, Kathakali, developed in Malabar, India. This picture is taken from the Kerala Kalamandalum. The Asia Society. Photo: Andrew Arnault.

transport me back into his world of real wonder, but all that came was the crosstown bus.

When Uday Shankar came back to New York after more than a decade (November 1962) and I renewed acquaintanceship with his style of dancing, I opened my review deliberately with the statement:

Whenever reviewing dance companies from the Far (and sometimes Nearer) East I cannot help feeling that they first of all remind me of how different their world is from ours and how very much they differ from each other. Watching these companies brings back a state of remembered childhood in which a magic dream world opened up to me when shown picture books of "far away people." Today I realize how much we could gain from accepting some of their traditional philosophy, of their obvious within-ness, of the spiritualization of our living existence.

I remember the appearance of a Korean dance company presenting a program in its native interminableness. The Eastern threshold of endurance is totally different from ours. Their productions can run for hours and days and are seemingly attended either like ceremonies or in a haphazard manner. In contrast to our never ending quest for the novel, the sensational, or the titillating experience, their stories, told against a religious or mythological background, are familiar to Eastern audiences. This theatrical concept spilled over into ancient Greece and was basic to the medieval Mystery and Miracle plays. Only Renaissance man and those who followed him, with stress on the individual, his daring and exploits, created the Western type of theater as we have come to appreciate it.

The above-mentioned Korean group, whose original program was only understood by a few initiated people, returned the following year with the same dances, cut and pruned to be made palatable to our taste. It was then a great success and did not fail to bring into play the very characteristics of the people. This only goes to show the two worlds of theatricality here and there and our dependence on a *Dancer's Digest* version.

Despite the highly traditional content and form of Eastern dancing, we must allow for individual expression, and it is particularly in this respect that the Western critic is most challenged. In her climactic days Shanta Rao was probably a prime example of an Indian dancer whose style was very much her own. In November 1963 I wrote:

The program notes and press releases speak a great deal of how this dancer has saved certain Indian dances, or form of dances, from oblivion. . . . However this may be—and I have no doubts that some of her colleagues may question a certain statement and quibble about this or that—, Shanta Rao's performance settles all disputes. Hers is a very personalized approach to whatever she does, she uses the traditional forms to suit her own sparkling personality. She is not only a beautiful human being, but also a performer of absorbing beauty who draws you into her enravishing circle the minute she enters the stage. It is one of those theatrical experiences, rare enough, in which you cannot help surrendering to the magnetism of the performer and, becoming a willing captive, you find revelation in the mystery to which you yield....

There were many curtain calls for her, and the enthusiastic audience enjoyed the variety of thank-you-gestures in her bows which were enchanting dance vignettes in themselves... We must be grateful to Shanta Rao that she can introduce us to a world so very much removed from our daily existence with such theatrical excitement as one rarely experiences in the more familiar world of our own make-believe.

Actually, what is the secret of our enchantment with Asian dance? Is it only our lack of familiarity with it, its remoteness with a built-in fairy-tale quality? The answer seems embedded in the enigma itself and is only revealed by the revelation of its poetry in each work. Otherwise, I could not explain my overenthusiastic reaction to Kazuko Hirabayashi whose every movement made me feel like I was under her spell when I saw her recital at the Japan House in March 1971:

Spiritually, Kazuko Hirabayashi's choreography has a quiet flow that questions in a con-sordino mood and lingers on. Technically, it is in between modern dance and ballet. Factually, it is one of those rare, beautiful experiences in the world of the dance, a marvel you take home with you, carefully wrapped in your memory and protected against the harshness and ugliness of the real world because you know it is soft and gentle, fragile and tenuous—and you don't want to lose it.

No, I will not easily forget it. Not perhaps because it was flawless. There were phrases and turns and mood expressions which were repeated time and again, but they were not bothersome. In their way of being they were distinct and reminded me of someone beautiful taking another-other look at her own reflection. Miss Hirabayashi likes to build up a movement idea and then hold it for a moment, as if saying: Look, I did it again. And she did.

It is the first time that, seeing a dance recital, a verbal image stayed with me in the corner of my mind all evening long (which seemed so incredibly short): compelling grace. I wondered about the ease of the flowing bodies, and loveliness as propelling force, the lightness of the lifts, the cliché-free transitions. And in wondering I felt like writing a poem. Of course, I did not do it, because Kazuko Hirabayashi did it for me.

Each piece had a very distinct quality and yet the whole evening was a spiritual oneness. Perhaps *The Stone Garden* is the epitome of what the choreographer has to say so far. The light—Jennifer Tipton was inspired, indeed—slowly revealed human garden figures. A girl moved through the garden which became alive. What followed in several sections was an encounter of one girl with nine men. A delicate, and yet assertively strong, flow of movement unfolded. Like a river it came flowing down, passed, and was still coming. I'm no longer sure that I realized while it happened that one section, for instance, had to do with the Four Seasons, or why another one was called Conversation. It mattered little. Something was real as long as it was there, I mean real in a very unreal way, and it meant a variety of things to me. The conversation was fluid all the way through.

In its way, *Suite I*, intrigued me. It was a solo for lance Westergard who reminded me of a male Botticelli angel (I've never been sure of an angel's gender). It is a difficult solo in which he managed to combine cool detachment with a glowing intensity. He is a very special dancer whose limitations were skillfully used as his fortes by the choreographer. The group has quite a few excellent dancers, but Lance Westergard and Yuriko Kimura have responded best to the elusive and poetic style of the choreographer. I have often, and with different companies, observed Miss Kimura and have come to the conclusion that not much can go wrong as long as she is on stage. And nothing did so far.

I do not know whether, one day, Kazuko Hirabayashi will disappoint me. I want to forgive her now in case it should ever happen, and I promise to remember gratefully what she has done for me now.

I have tried to make the secret of such poetic impact clear to my own mind in a variety of ways whenever watching an Asian dancer, but—however eloquent my response may have been—basically I seem to have repeated my inability to fathom it; I only couched it in different words of wonderment:

The aesthetic effect and beauty of such dancing lie beyond any obvious apprehension. It has always been a very special magic world for me in which the slightest movement evokes new images of which a great deal probably eludes me. . . .

However much our kinesthetic rapport and mental grasp are handicapped by our exclusion from any real and detailed understanding of the subtlest touches of her characterization—and it would be foolish to pretend to have a knowledge that cannot be proved—one is nevertheless drawn into a sensuous experience which, in its accumulating effect, is a theatrical magic of otherness.

The difficulties in verbalizing our response to the experience we live through is almost as difficult as the Asian attempt must be to come to terms with the dance of the Westerner. Can form and expressiveness be fused into an artistic entity without betraying one or the other? George Balanchine's *Bugaku* is a telling point in case. He did what every good translator is supposed to do: save the flavor and inner rhythm of the work rather than attempt a true word by word translation. In all its postures and movements *Bugaku* is only suggestive and not imitative of the Zen spirit and Japanese court life. He caught the mystery of it all, though not leaving the idiom of the classical ballet. He listened to Toshiro Mayuzumi's music (what an accomplished master of listening he is!) and translated the vision of a Japanese painting in all its subtlety and delicate eroticism into ethereal and sensual balletic images.

Since a great deal of Martha Graham's art had been nourished by the Asian feeling for the ultimate things in life, it is understandable that her company became a haven for such dancers as Yuriko, Suzushi Hanayagi, and many more. Probably Yuriko adjusted best to our way of being. But when she went out on her own, something decidedly Eastern could get a hold of her as in her solo *And the Wind*, which I thought was "a masterpiece in a minor key," a work in which she proves her power of expression in three different sets of mood. Here, she probably comes closest to displaying an Asian feeling and a mysterious touch in blending her innate lyricism with accents of drama. But when she became involved in the dramatic visualization of a story, with action-driven Western accents, she was less convincing than "in painting a mood, in expressing a lyric statement." Another example would be Hanayagi, who impressed me in 1962—and my judgment seemed justified when I saw her again in 1974—as having discovered her "own style" which is "far less an Oriental and Occidental mixture than a perhaps daring deviation from and modernization of the classical dance of Japan. While still deeply rooted in tradition her form is free and tries to communicate with a deliberate sparseness of movement at a slow pace."

Quite a few Asians seek means of letting their native way of being become one with the expressiveness of the American modern dancer. Miss Chiang Ching, for instance, dreams of "more universal inter-cultural communication." But all her explorations in this direction so far remained flawed if they did not fail altogether. Great difficulties arise—let me blame my personal aesthetic sensibilities for it—when white dancers are incorporated in such companies trying to camouflage themselves as Chinese, dancing against the background of a Chinese story. There is an innate otherness to the gait, posture, and movement of a Chinese or a Japanese person, and any Caucasian emulating or imitating what is basically alien to him or her cuts a bad dancing figure and interjects a jarring note into the choreographic image.

Universal communication is badly needed in the realm of Realpolitik which decides our naked existence. But is it in the arts? How wonderful it is to study a Ming scroll or a Hokusai print of the Fujiyama! When it comes to art, however, then maybe we should give Kipling the benefits of our doubts: "Oh, East is East, and West is West, and never the twain shall meet." We may permit ourselves to be carried away ecstatically by the spirit of the strange. But why not leave it at that and take home with us sufficient inspiration from it to strengthen our own poetic vision? Why strive so hard to accomplish something that even when almost miraculously achieved could never be a total denial of one or the other half of ourselves, neither of East nor of West. Does not the beauty of life lie in being what we are and in being able to yield in joy to the wonders of otherness?

On second thought, the difference between East and West may not be quite as unbridgeable as it seemed to Kipling and certainly not as insurmountable in a variety of ways. When we make a judgment, however validly based on past experiences, at least we should leave the lights on above an emergency exit. As the philosopher F. S. C. Northrop pointed out in his *The Meeting of East and West* we had better view these two worlds as supplementing and reinforcing each other:

They can meet, not because they are saying the same thing, but because they are expressing different yet complementary things, both of which are required for an adequate and true conception of man's self and his universe. Each can move into the new comprehensive world of the future, proud of its past and preserving its self-respect. Each also needs the other.

I don't know whether the choreographer Lin Hwai-Min felt that he needed to reach out for Western dance techniques, ballet and modern with which to present his home-grown concepts—his geographic home was Taiwan; the spiritual home of his Cloud Gate Dance Theatre was thoroughly Chinese. I saw the company perform in Zürich, the heart of Europe. All the more was I struck by the miraculous and seamless fusion of a mainly American technique with substantially Chinese story material. Amazing how the acrobatic skill so innate with Chinese suddenly spoke fluently with a Graham accent! Whatever original story was performed, emerging from myth and folklore, from legend and opera material, it was all done in a technically flawless presentation, basically using traditional elements of the Chinese dance, never forgetting the Chinese flair for the operatic and folkloric components interwoven with ballet steps (or allusions to them) and the psychologically motivated modern dance postures.

Although I do not see any need for such an artistic melting of East and West, Lin-Hwai-Min proved that it can be done with a Chinese smile when the release follows the contraction. He probably succeeded in this melting process because he only told the stories with which he grew up and told them competently with a charming lilt in his personalized modern dance expression. Whatever language he technically spoke, he never let you forget for a moment that you were seeing a Chinese dance group that had discovered the poetic touch of its own mystique.

1982

Vienna. Not far from Nietzsche's thoughts were Laban's endeavors to see man grow beyond his averageness and reach for a lofty state of *festliches Sein*, of a festive existence celebrating being. In his fashion, Laban was a mystic philosopher who believed in the magic of movement through which the individual as such or the individual within a group could gain a heightened awareness. He was preoccupied by the thought that man could achieve universality through harmony of movement.

Who was the man whom we know as Rudolf Laban (with or without the "von")? His name was Rudolf Jean-Baptist Attila Marquis de Laban de Váralja, and when he began to change the course of dance history between 1913 and 1918—those early years of his search for what became the *Ausdruckstanz* giving the strongest impetus to the modern dance everywhere—he still signed his name Laban Váralja. Above all, he was an autodidact whose accomplishments have become history. In his younger years he represented everything that an aristocratic mind could have saved as a nineteenth-century heritage: He was a Schöngeist (aesthete and wit) with a scientific bent; he was a dreamer; he was a charmer who broke many hearts as he inspired to find greatness in life and in themselves. Mary Wigman said of him:

He was my teacher, though never in the sense this word is generally used. He was the moving spirit, the guide who opened the gates to a world I had dreamt of, not yet knowing that it was dance I was seeking for. He was the one who showed me the little path leading into the jungle, which later on I had to clear for myself so it might become my own place to live in, to grow in, and to spread out from.

I fleetingly brushed his genius in Vienna in 1929. When we think of the wisdom and equanimity of the older Laban, we must also accept the impetuosity, yes, the lightheartedness and flippancy of the younger man in him who could never often enough preach the beauty of life or the life of everything beautiful, as he could never get enough of it himself: Mary Wigman expressed it with a gentle innuendo when she said:

Laban always was a great wanderer, who after entering an unknown country and having found what he wanted or what happened to meet his need, would soon leave it for the next one to be explored. But wherever he stayed, even if it were only for a short while, he left his traces.

This, no doubt, referred to work and women. He strongly believed in his own magic as much as in the magic of movement. And he became a master magician.

It may be irrelevant who the forebears of a great mind have been. In most cases it is. In Laban's case, however, it may have some significant bearing on the man he was. His ancestors were Huguenots, driven into exile under the reign of Louis XIV in 1685. Some of them also found refuge near or in Bratislava (then:

Pressburg) in Western Hungary next to the Austrian border. Some of them settled beneath a fortress called Váralja ("on the mountain"). Since the Huguenots blended splendidly with whatever new environment they found, Laban's forefathers distinguished themselves as patriots of their new homeland—his father was a general in the army of the Austro-Hungarian Monarchy—and it was not unusual that they were knighted as "de Váralja" and that his father named him Rudolf in reverence to the reigning house of Habsburg. Obviously, our Marquis would have been destined to become an officer had he not tricked destiny by becoming a dance magician. But originally dance was only a way for him to realize his partly religious, partly Nietzschean vision of the new man in a new society. Nietzsche died in 1900, and it was that very year, on the threshold of the twentieth century, that Laban broke with his military career, his past and heritage. It now seems inevitable that his visual-mindedness should have forced upon him detours via painting and sculpting before having him embrace the human body in motion and space as the very ideal that set his thoughts afire.

He may have been a genius in improvisation, as Mary Wigman said, "inexhaustible in his ideas, imagination, inspiration and experimentation, he could often glide seemingly playful from one creative dance level to another, while on the other hand he turned out to be the most consequent researcher, searcher and theoretician who, fanatically and restlessly, traced the laws of the human body." What a scientific mind he was, never giving in, never losing sight of the goal which he envisioned: to give the dance its logical foundation and its literate means to assure its future as a credible and credited art form!

He can only be compared with one other person in the dance field, with Carlo Blasis who, in the Romantic era, also tried to create a solid scientific basis for all dance movements, steering the old classic school into new Romantic channels. There was no one among the dance theoreticians as erudite and well-read as Blasis who could stun his readers with quotations from Dante, Voltaire,

Boileau, Horace, da Vinci, Metastasio, or Rousseau; he was a
savant who loved to debate the German philosophers from Kant
to Schlegel. Not aiming as ambitiously as Laban at a change of man
in a declining society, Blasis nevertheless shared with him the
belief in an absolute of ideal beauty. A believable attitude toward
universality can be detected in Blasis as in Laban. "I love all arts,"
Blasis wrote and, to bring such universal embrace of the arts closer
to realization, he had, of necessity, to reach out for a broad basis
for his theories, an attitude we can easily detect in Laban, too,
whose ideas are of course closer to our feelings and understanding
than those of Blasis. However, we do Blasis wrong when we do not
see in him a historian of the cultural scene. He was a well-versed
biologist, anatomist, and philosopher beside being the dance
historian and choreographer we know. "Blasis' writings have in no
way thrown Noverre's genial *Letters* from their pedestal, nevertheless his was the most significant attempt in the nineteenth
century to summarize all knowledge about the ballet and to tie it
up with the general aesthetic and psychological conceptions of his
epoch," André Levinson wrote. Certain parallels with Laban are
here quite obvious.

In the fall of 1910 Laban moved with his second wife to Munich,
where he worked as a painter and illustrator and where he
was strongly drawn to dancers and became interested in dance
productions. There and then he had a first-hand opportunity to
study the methods of Dalcroze, Bode, and Mensendieck, among
others. It was in Dalcroze's Hellerau that he met Suzanne
Perrottet.* She left Dalcroze to follow the man and magician
Laban who, at that time, decided to devote his main efforts to the
dance. In a small studio on Munich's Theresienstrasse (Rear
Entrance) he gathered his first disciples. There, he worked with
them on his ideas of rhythmic gymnastics based on the natural

Suzanne Perrottet, who was Laban's companion for many years, is now in her early nineties
and at work on a book of memoirs which will tell the story of her life with Laban.

organic movements of the human body. There, he first tried out his danced improvisations. It was at that time in Munich that he made his first stab at notating movement, after having studied old notations in the Bavarian Staatsbibliothek.

Laban's decisive field of activity shifted, in 1913, to Monte Verità in Ascona, Switzerland, where Mary Wigman entered his *Schule für Kunst* (School for the Arts). The school was devoted to practical workshops, such as cooking, weaving, shoe-making, and tailoring, as well as painting, sculpting, and the applied arts; the curriculum included speech courses, exercises in music, instrumental and singing, and of course the art of movement and dance. This school later sailed under the name of "Labanschule" and, during the war years, remained in Ascona and Zürich, where his group was tangentially involved with the founders of the Dada movement. After the war Laban and his school could be found in several German cities, mainly in Hamburg and Berlin.

Before 1929 I knew of Laban and his activities from a distance and hearsay only. I then lived in my native city, Vienna, where he arranged his famed *Gewerbe Tanzfestzug* (a pageant of handicrafts and trades). It was his fantastic idea to re-introduce and give the Renaissance *carri* a modern, and particularly Viennese, touch. No doubt, in our century it was the first time that such a gigantic undertaking was dared at all. It was watched by about half a million people, who lined up for this spectacle on the feudal Ringstrasse. I was among them and it was then that I had my first taste of Laban bravura. (We can somehow imagine what this *carri* was like if we think of the annual Macy's parade. But Laban's pageant was new then and produced with the lack of today's technical means.)

In his book, *A Life for Dance*, he described his diplomatic feat of gaining the approval of the municipal government and the various representatives of trade and industry, how he impressed them with his aristocratic background and charmed them with his linguistic talent (his native tongue was Hungarian, his second language French, and his third German). With a gesture of an officer he seemingly could evoke the spirit of the old Monarchy—which had never totally died out in Vienna—and cut through the intrigues and political feuds of the various guilds. His pageant was approved and worked out by Laban with some stunning ideas. He could write about it: "When it was all overcome it seemed a fantastic miracle . . . there was no trace of that awful jumble of convictions when they followed one another dancing happily and peacefully, united in the celebration of craftsmanship."

Everywhere there was an allusion to work rhythm, work attire, and work atmosphere. On innumerable vans he had his trade representatives mingled with dancers and music bands. On other floats were installed loudspeakers which had to broadcast, by means of new recordings, music Laban had commissioned for this occasion from such well-known composers as Krenek and Wellesz. One of the masters of the Viennese operetta, Bruno Granich-staedten, had successfully responded to Laban's demand to have the Blue Danube waltz metamorphosed into a march of bells. Understandably, the waltz was the dominant music accompanying each van, even though there were seen a few other dance steps and some marching. The people were so enchanted that they shouted for *da capos* and, as one of the surviving dancers, Cilli Wang, a dance satirist and mime, told me, it was rough on their feet to dance a waltz time and again on the hard pavement of the Ringstrasse.

The success of this pageant contributed to its one weakness which was the breakdown of its technical organization. The many *da capos* kept the vans from moving on as envisioned and they created huge gaps between them. "But despite of everything it was a great success, also for the dance," a Berlin reporter noted. "The people braved the singeing rays of the sun for six to eight hours. The tightly packed crowds did not give up their spots. And often enough they shouted in unison, 'Dance, more dance!'. The good girls followed suit, and so happened the whole debacle." But taken all in all it was something no one had dared before until then and certainly not at such scope. It was brilliantly conceived by Laban, who could proudly boast that it worked beautifully. He felt emotionally overcome when "the hundreds of thousands of people lining the route got into motion and I was fêted in a way which I had never dreamed of. A victorious general might have been used to such things, but a dancing master. . . . "

In a footnote of the same book Laban referred to two names as co-workers: Fritz Klingenbeck and Gertrude Kraus. The latter I could no longer interview; she had emigrated in 1938 to Israel, where she died a few years ago. But to refresh my memories of this event in Vienna I called upon Fritz Klingenbeck, and our discussion brought to light a few fascinating aspects of Klingenbeck's work with Laban and his contribution to Labanotation which remained unknown and unnoticed by the dance world so far.

"In 1925 I went to Hamburg to study with Laban," Klingenbeck said, "and soon afterwards Laban asked me to become his personal *Mitarbeiter* (co-worker). Later on, I often had to step into his shoes—even when they were too big for me—acting as a substitute. I gladly took over classes in notation or practical movement exercises. But he put so much trust in me that one day when he had sustained injury he asked me to choreograph and perform a Czardas in *Die Fledermaus*, a production at the Berlin Schlosspark Theater, without being prepared for it. On another occasion he charged me to take over the part of the fool created for himself in his *The Fool and Death*. With a most serious mien he said to me, 'I need a clever man for this part,' though he must have known that I was not yet quite ready for such a role. Nevertheless, I did it." Mr. Klingenbeck had an embarrassed smile when he added: "In the years between 1926 and 1929 I often heard him say to me: 'I need you!' "

It was the same phrase which Laban used when he asked Klingenbeck to come to Vienna in the spring of 1929 when he staged his pageant there. He may have well needed his assistance for this endeavor which one man alone could hardly oversee. "Laban's ideas were really those of a man of Renaissance calibre, of genial conceptions. But as soon as everything was outlined, he left most of the pageant's execution in my hands. I was only too much aware of the flaws I could not avoid, the sudden gaps between the moving floats. I felt hopeless and therefore less proud than Laban about the whole thing which, despite its brillant ideas, could also have been called a magnificent mess."

The year 1929 was a great one for Laban, and his mind was probably very much preoccupied with a variety of things. He also had to prepare a movement choir celebration on the anniversary of Mannheim's National Theater; the Universal Edition in Vienna brought out the first two issues of *Schrifttanz* which was to be Laban's famous *Kinetographie*; he would reach his fiftieth birthday on December 15 of that year and probably anticipated to be duly celebrated; moreover, he had pardonably fallen in love with the dancer Gisa Geert, a fascinating creature.

What interested me most was Fritz Klingenbeck's collaboration on and contribution to Labanotation, since Albrecht Knust and Kurt Jooss are most often mentioned in this connection. "Let me preface what I have to say in this respect with a few words how it all came to happen. From being his student I quickly advanced to being his Man Friday. In 1928 I wrote down the choreographic score of Laban's *Titan*, a full-length work, which, based on my notation, was successfully staged by Albrecht Knust at the Hamburg Circus Busch. It was the first dance score written in Laban's *Kinetographie*. It undoubtedly was the great breakthrough. When Laban showed me his notations I missed the continuity in the movements of each member of the body. Laban invented innumerable versions of notations and his first vital realization was the need to notate the movements from the bottom to the top. Without quite knowing how it happened I adjusted the body to five lines with the basic idea of seeing the body from behind, with feet closed and, moving the body away from a middle line, I could get the various parts of the body properly composed within two more lines on both sides. I suddenly realized that, in this way, one could write and read the "Who-Where-to-How" with one stroke. I showed my drawing to Laban who looked surprised at me, saying: 'Do you realize that you hit upon the five lines of the musical notes?' I had not been aware of it. All I had tried was to put all parts of the body into a systematic frame that would hold them together. And whatever happened later with it was the result of Laban's genius. Shortly afterwards Laban showed me examples of his finished signs based on the principle I had outlined. I then taught Labanotation at his Berlin Institute, in Gillstrasse 10, a huge villa with a beautiful garden, but my immediate task was to create grammalogues and, as I had mentioned, to notate the whole score of his *Titan* in 1928. I stayed with him for some time, but when asked to assist him in his work, *Vom Tauwind und der neuen Freude* (*About the Dew-Wind and the New Joy*) which he did for the Olympiad in Berlin, 1936, I had to decline since I was married to a Jewess and had too many Jewish friends in Austria. It was also Laban's final job in Nazi-Germany. He was arrested after the first performance because he had a few Jewish students while having been ballet director at the Berlin Staatsoper. The rest is history. As you probably know, he managed to flee to Paris sometime later and from there to England in 1938. We corresponded on occasion to the day of his death."

As can readily be seen, Fritz Klingenbeck would be the last man in this world of many historic wrongs who would not bow to Laban's genius, even though, now looking back on his own life from the vantage point of his mid-seventies, he feels—with all vanity put aside—somewhat bitter that neither Laban nor the records of history give due credit to the one vital and decisive contribution he had made to Labanotation. As if he could correct history at a last moment destiny offered him, he arranged a Laban exhibition in Vienna's Theatermuseum and, later in Graz, in commemoration of Laban's hundredth birthday.

"After fifty years—in which I had changed professionally and filled a number of important positions in Austria's theatres—all of a sudden the undeniably beautiful days of the Laban era stood again in front of my eyes. Had I forgotten them? Only seemingly. Freud would have said repressed. Now I don't know whether it was necessary or worthwhile to put this Laban exhibit together, to bring back to life what had disappeared with the past, so many grand recollections, so much personal pain."

History is as fair or unfair as man is in his time. But there have always been moments in which historic mistakes could be corrected.

Walking through Vienna's nineteenth district and the street called *Labanweg*, the greatness of this man in all its humanness, with all its fascination and warts was upon me. In his often striking humor he liked to refer to himself at the beginning of his career as "Gaukler" which can be a juggling circus acrobat or buffoon. At moments he may have felt like it, but deep within he was a dreamer and mystic whose vision of a great work of art, a combination of dance, music, and poetry started him on his way, as Mary Wigman told me. The way she saw him, "there was always Laban, drum in hand, inventing, experimenting. Laban, the magician, the priest of an unknown religion, the worshiped hero, the lord of a dreamlike and yet ever-so-real kingdom. How easily he could change from the gallant knight into the grinning faun! How kind, how humorous and friendly he could be, and how terrifying with his sarcastic smile . . . ". Neither the ballet dancer nor Isadora Duncan's and Ruth St. Denis's neo-romantic concepts were the material that could be worked into his scheme of thoughts. The modern dancer he had then envisioned was not yet born.

For him, the new dance had to be a necessary and obvious concomitant of the human development in an era of galloping industrialization and commercialization of all values, and he came to the conclusion that "it might be permissible to call Modern Dance the movement expression of industrial man." The historian in Laban also mused about Noverre's attempt to do away with the old stage costumes and rococo paraphernalia in order to create a "new movement expression." When Laban saw in the *ballet d'action* the first harbinger of free movement and the expression of industrial man, I think he went a bit too far in his historic interpretation of Noverre's concepts which, in his eyes, "foretold the spiritual trends of our present time." It is doubtful that Noverre could even sense the rumblings of the French Revolution in 1760 when he advised his dancers and students to study the movements of their contemporaries in the streets and in the market places instead of copying the polite behavior of princes and courtiers.

Laban may have been on safer ground when he saw in the dances of Isadora Duncan a greater awareness in the various efforts in movement and the realization that a combination of effort elements guarantee the enjoyment of any action movements. Her liberating act led to what Laban called "dance lyrics" which, in turn, led to the expression of the raw experiences of her "soul" through movement.

Laban's main concern was the "methodical approach to the universal forms of movement," independent from any particular stylization, to the understanding and practice of "the principle of moving" and its application in movement education. From there it was only one more step to utilize experienced movement as it exerts its stimulation on the activities of the mind. When Isadora liberated the spirit of the body in the ecstasy of her mind, Laban gave the interaction of effort and space and its resulting shapes a scientific foundation. Again and again, his concern was "the beneficial effect of the creative activity of dancing upon the personality" and not the triumph of the creative ego.

Wuppertal. The climactic moments in the development of the American musical—with *Oklahoma!*, *My Fair Lady*, and *West Side Story*—had made me hope time and again that we were on the right path to a great new theater experience, with the word and music, with movement and light finally creating that theatrical oneness of which men of the theater have dreamt ever since wise Solon called Thespis a liar because he had stepped out of the chorus with which he started a dialogue. Until now we have often come close to a total theater, but only close. And the musical theater probably failed us because show business is show business is show business, whereby the show became more and more subservient to business.

The most experimental dance work may now be done in Germany, where, in various ways, dance companies try to create a theater dance which combines the spoken word, music, and movement, as well as all possible stage effects. But here the theater, or rather everything theatrical, is the predominant feature. There is action, but not necessarily dance, even though it may be movement. There are now two or three well known companies working with similar means toward the realization of this new form of *Tanztheater*. The group in Wuppertal and the name of Pina Bausch are identified as the carrier of the entire trend. She was able to create an aura of magnetism, her personality became transformed into a symbol.

Since neo-expressionism has been a trendy label for the style of a group of German painters in the first half of the eighties, we can easily see why Pina Bausch's theater would be tagged as neo-expressionistic because of the time when expressionism became a native German form between 1914 and 1924. It was then described as a highly emotional, highly personal and intuitive re-creation of what one's senses perceive. All likeness and true-to-life images were discarded for the expression of inner necessity, for creating the intensity characterizing the object or theme, if necessary with the help of distortion and exaggeration.

All this is basic for Pina Bausch's dance theater. What she does is not mere self-expression, but self-expression as a symbol for man, for our time. She did not go back to Mary Wigman, she went beyond her. Bausch subscribes to Wigman's dictum: "Art grows out of the basic cause of existence." But she follows her only to the point on the way where she meets Brecht with his *Verfremdung* (alienation) theory, demanding a verdict from the audience. There is no dance work in her repertory that would not have a message. The monotony of minimal art is wedded to Brecht's epic theater concept. The thematic, picturesque repetition of contrasts turns into drama.

She aims at the essence of life's corrupt current; at the dramatic relationship between the sexes; at human interrelationships: here the male, there the female, and at the unbridgeable gap between them; the difficulty of familiar proximity; longing per se; the existentialist pain. Hers is always a dance of experience. There is the geste of endlessness, but also the excitement of conflicts. It is the dance of life translated into danced theater.

No one has to say yes to all this, but no one can doubt that this is one and a different form of theatrical expression, that it is a way to reach a goal which many have tried to reach before—though coming from other directions. It is a way, but no one so far has reached the goal of total theater, a goal which, with every step toward it, moves further away from us.

I don't doubt the validity of Pina Bausch's vision. But we also must not forget how much greatness has often turned into the historic garbage of yesterday and how many unexpected miracles have been resurrected from such garbage. This, too, is danced theater: the message of life.

New York. A packed house in The Kitchen (the facsimile of a stage and improvised seating), with people sitting on the floor, standing where there is no standing room. The expectation is at a high pitch. First, some slight bewilderment. Then, applause growing in intensity. It is a mixed audience, not only the usual crowd of modern dancers and dance enthusiasts. The majority are young.

The fascination with any theatrical experiment done in the twenties or even somewhat earlier has already been going on for some time. First, we experienced the realization of an artistic dream for which we had to wait for seventy years: Kandinsky's *The Yellow Sound.* For Kandinsky and for us it was worth waiting for.

Between 1908 and 1914 there was a surge of creative innovations as rarely before; there were so many "isms" emerging, as if the artists felt a need to rearrange the world—at least their world—in their minds before it was enveloped in its first cataclysmic catastrophe. One of them was Vasily Kandinsky, who was obsessed by the idea of the total theater, mainly painting, music, and dance. In the years between 1910 and 1913 he worked together with the composer Thomas de Hartmann and the dancer-choreographer Alexander Sacharoff on a concept he called *The Yellow Sound.*

They experimented with this idea, which went through several stages, but never found a stage on which it could be performed. The scenario—often revised—was published in the *Blaue Reiter* in 1912, and from the incipient concept in 1909 there is much information, bits of notes about the intentions of these three artists, only some coming close to performance instructions. In other words, when the idea to resurrect Kandinsky's dream of *The Yellow Sound* ripened about a year and a half ago, rather loose ideas had to be re-thought and re-felt by Gunther Schuller, who reconstructed poorly preserved musical notations of Thomas de Hartmann. Then he and Ian Strasfogel made Kandinsky's scenario and basic notions live on a stage for the first time.

The production was a stunning visual experience in many ways. With the modern means at our disposal, the envisioned intentions became a living document of the past and, simultaneously, an exciting performance. Scenery, costumes, and lighting proved how far we have come in the use of technical gadgetry; they not only helped to make Kandinsky's dream come true, indeed, the entire production went far beyond what this painter could have imagined. Everyone working on it could claim to have followed Kandinsky's intentions, while, in fact, they translated and transplanted the spirit of his visualizations into modern stage design at its best.

Similarly, we know Alexander Sacharoff's work only from pictorial and literary sources. He certainly was one of the first pioneers in the modern dance field and, if we may believe Rainer Maria Rilke's overenthusiastic accounts, he must have been a fascinating dancer. This would make him an historically neglected figure. In all fairness, it seems that he was another Kreutzberg who, by a few years, came too early into this world and to the world of dance.

A dancer of whom I have heard, but whom I had never seen before, Hellmut Fricke-Gottschild, a Wigman disciple, appeared as the Man in White in a scene featuring a rather long solo dance within these loose vignettes; this would have been Sacharoff's part. Kandinsky spoke of a "kind of a dance" ending with a pose reminiscent of Rodin's *The Thinker*. Mr. Fricke-Gottschild was quite impressive in giving us the feeling of a period dance behind which we could discover the contemporary viewpoint and accomplishment. No earlier performance, not even the one planned by Oskar Schlemmer in the Bauhaus about the mid-twenties, could have achieved anything close to the stage magic and allusive power which was the artistic fulfillment of this 1982 production.

This brings me back to Schlemmer and the question of why his name comes up time and again in our days. Strangely enough, this painter-designer is somehow becoming a symbol of those many experiments that were going on in the twenties. He staged rather short pieces with dancers in body-concealed costumes and in geometry-alluded forms. His aim seemed to have been to wed technology to the arts, a general concept of the Bauhaus. Schlemmer's name came first to be known in this country when about thirty years ago Alwin Nikolais started his total theater experiment, also with the dancers' bodies more than less concealed. However, to say that Nikolais took off from Schlemmer is like saying that the Wright Brothers copied Leonardo da Vinci. He wanted to fly, and they did.

Schlemmer was not a man of the theater but a painter who created two-dimensional images with which he wanted to merge the functional with the metaphysical. He was more influenced by Kleist's concept of the marionette and the Russian constructivists than by Laban and Wigman who, at the very same time, were also concerned with dance and space. They investigated the kinetic range of the moving dancer in space, while Schlemmer was interested in "the metamorphosis of the human figure and its abstraction," how the dancer can obey "the law of the body as well as the law of space."

Schlemmer's ideas were never really resolved as stage experiences, they remained didactic experiments, today we would say "workshop productions," even though they were successfully shown in several German cities at that time. But those were the days of stage experimentations from Gordon Craig to Jean Cocteau to Rolf de Maré, from Rudolf Laban to a good number of Russian experimenters. They were "in" and the public went all out for them, and if only to boo.

What Debra McCall so skillfully put together gives the impression that these presentations are some studio ideas thrown out for discussion. In a variety of vignettes Schlemmer wanted to investigate the interrelation between the geometry of man and the architecture of space, and in their way all six pieces shown at The Kitchen were interesting excursions into history.

The works that came closest to some kind of theatrical experience were the *Hoop Dance*, which achieved some beautiful images, and the *Pole Dance* which was—in the intricacy in which sticks became an extension of the human figure—the epitome of Schlemmer's concept of an "endless range of expression" in a mechanistic sense and in scenic environment constructed for the dancer. It was the highlight of the evening and gave us a very clear idea of the potentials that Schlemmer called the *Tänzermensch* growing into a *Kunstfigur*, the mechanical human figure.

Not all in Schlemmer was pure didacticism or search for abstract precision. He decried the materialistic age of ours, claiming it has lost "the genuine feeling for play and the miraculous . . . ". To prove his playful gift he created the *Block Play* in which he made fun of the architectural fury of functionalism with glass and steel cubes—and that was exactly what his colleagues at the Bauhaus stood for.

As an afterthought I cannot help wondering that we have become so much interested in the Bauhaus era at a time when architects try to get away from the Bauhaus's mere functionalism and those abstract nightmares with and in which we had to live long enough.

There are geniuses and geniuses and, among them, there are also fake geniuses. As great masterpieces can be forged so meticulously that even the sharpest expert eyes cannot easily recognize them as fakery, so can the artistic nature of a theatrical genius be acclaimed and admired all over the world until time passes him by—time, the great corrector of human flaws and fads.

Undoubtedly, Robert Wilson is considered a genius, or a major talent of the theater, a Regisseur of magnitude. I see in him a perfect paragon of our time, which is so much out of joint that it must escape into the bigness of emptiness, filling the crevices with a pasteboard of shiny phoniness. His is a theater of movement which does not necessarily feature dance, but it somehow moves and mostly manages to move without moving. It is all so simple:

Wilson is a visual magician and out to prove that the world of our vision is so unreal that we can never perceive what we see nor do we actually see what we perceive. To prove this he needs time, time to numb you, to bewitch you. He can't do it within the usual period of playtime. He often needs five hours, and his voodoo concept of the Civil Wars needed many evenings. Fortunately, I saw one of his shorter productions, which lasted somewhat over three hours: *A Letter for Queen Victoria*:

The stage is magically lit. Smoke fills the stage creating wondrous images as it winds its way without any purpose through darkness into the sphere of light cones where it whirls and dances—oh, what a dance of nature!—in surprising shapes of no meaning and yet with the eye-filling power of surrealistic beauty.

Smoke and light fill the stage several times, and I greatly enjoyed the play of smoke clouds in the light, their interlaced designs, their twisted, twirling forms, the way they coiled and spiralled their busy loops into poetic planes with miraculous figures dissolving the moment they take shape. I could have looked at those images of smoke and light for a long time, if the stage action had not interrupted my pleasure with shots, screams, groans, gibberish talk, squeals and other happenings of little consequence. Beverly Emmons is a devilish genius at her light board.

No, there were a few more moments of imaginative beauty, staged tableaux that could have been painted by Magritte, and then a scenic image that Francis Bacon could have thought of—only he would have been more daring in his scurrilous, frighteningly naked satire. Or, there was a café scene. Gray-garbed people sitting, two at a table, in an atmosphere of the late 20s. A vase with one tulip on each table. The people were all made up to look almost alike. The words "Chitter" and "Chatter" were written, geometrically exact, all over the backdrop. And it was an automatic chitter and chatter you heard, probably a satire on society's hollowness. Empty phrases, inarticulate words. A shot. One person at a table died while the partner went on speaking while the dead uncrumpled to live again in order to chitter and chatter. Until more shots were fired—how we love shots nowadays!—and more people died and then went on uttering sounds of no meaning. I liked this scene. It reminded me of what we had done in the European literary cabarets in the late 20s and early 30s before the real shots of a real madman were heard and people went on dancing and millions did the real dying.

How does one end such a scene, fraught with the frightening image of a phony world? With more gunfire and the appearance of a dea ex machina in the shape of a charming old lady holding up her arms with a sweet noncommittal smile. We are told that she is Queen Victoria in the unsung opera of Robert Wilson, whose 88-year-old grandmother, Alma Hamilton, only pretends to be Queen Victoria in what is called *A Letter For Queen Victoria*, only pretending to be an opera or a play or perhaps even a ballet.

Then, is it real make-believe? Yes, but make-believe heightened to the point of total absurdity. Two dancers, placed on each side stage front, turn incessantly in a kind of spinning dervish dance, in incredibly slow-motion, with only their hands quivering at times. The opening scene: four characters read *A Letter For Queen Victoria* and read in canon form. The overlapping sentences turn into gibberish with one or two words clearly pronounced. No doubt, the leitmotif of this opera, not only pretending to be one while being neither a play or ballet for sure.

There is a silly game with sounds and the alphabet in front of microphones. And there is Mr. Wilson in front of the curtain during a scenic change—apparently the show must go on, and on it goes without letup and mercy trying to mesmerize you to believe in Robert Wilson's make-believe world. Now he has his great aria, full of sounds only, hissing, cries, squeals while bunches of lettuce are brought onstage. Or is it cabbage as a symbol? It all could have been Chinese, and perhaps it was. But Mr. Wilson has an earsplitting scream, and he screams until his face is flushed and he is on the verge of busting.

Some stage pictures, with the people coming and going like puppets or falling to the floor without reason, are sculpturally beautiful. There are many vignettes, such as the Civil War scene with aviators, masked and with something bigger in mind than fighting an enemy, but no one really knew what the fighting and dying and getting up again and shouting something into the ether was all about. But whatever it was, it went on too long. Everything was keyed to repetition and monotony, brightened visually here and there. Is it profound redundancy? The dialogue is playful nonsense, enjoying sound melodies of "okay hat haps," tiring wordplays, suddenly interrupted by clearly pronounced sentences such as: "It doesn't seem right." "I just don't want to get lonely," "We may never know what took place here," "You sit on a bench and wait for me," while the two dancers turn and turn.

Robert Wilson wrote this non-opera which could be a play (but isn't) or a ballet without much dancing. Perhaps a ballet of doomsday. He wrote all the screams, squeals, nonsense sounds and fragmentary sentences and directed his concoction. If he invented all the tableaux— some of which were visually stunning—then he has a wonderful flair for theatrical gimmicks. He can hypnotize, bore with precision, surprise, puzzle, irritate and annoy you. They have called him a theatrical genius in Paris, London and New York. I think he is a skillful theatrical operator who tells his audience to enjoy unhesitatingly the Emperor without his clothes as long as they believe Robert Wilson that the Emperor is wrapped in velvet and purple colors.

On the other hand, it could easily be that Mr. Wilson is as confused as our time, but pretends to have a cure for our aesthetic and artistic ills. His magic prescription is actually simple: Mix some of the proved Dada like Schwitters with a huge portion of surrealism, preferably from Magritte, and shake it well with the repetitive vigor of Gertrude Stein while filtering everything through the grotesque absurdities of the age of anxiety which, now in our age of confusion, can be obtained as a remainder at much reduced prices.

To be quite sure he is understood, his plays or operas or ballets or whatever are of mammoth length. In comparison to his other works, *A Letter For Queen Victoria*, I was assured, is of epigrammatic brevity, lasting only three long hours. Length being unavoidable where monotony and repetition are used as dramatic tools has never been anything but proof of an artist's insecurity. An empty canvas that is big is, of course, more convincing than a small one. Robert Wilson may, without being aware of it, use the theater for his therapeutic needs. Then, it certainly is well used.

A *Letter for Queen Victoria* is a torturous, visually exciting, aurally devastating experience. I don't know why it is called by that title. It makes as little sense as the entire nonopera. It should—with greater justification—be called: *Robert Wilson's Primal Screaming*. I was happy that from time to time it all went up in smoke.

Dr. Samuel Johnson had his James Boswell, Johann Wolfgang Goethe his Johann Peter Eckermann. Because of them we gained great insight into Johnson's and Goethe's minds. Robert Wilson had his Stefan Brecht, who published a book on Wilson which is four hundred pages long in small, often minute print. It is full of detailed footnotes and interviews which create the impression of an exact replica of reality with Wilson's stammer and his many "uhs" and "ahs" in the text, repetitions of words, sentences, and thoughts. As brief example, Brecht interviewing Wilson on Freud:

BRECHT: In your own mind, there must have been some kind of a guiding thing, some objective at some point—what did you want? What did you head for? About Freud,—or, as a total effect on people?
WILSON: I think I said for the—the guiding thing about Freud—I didn't know quite so much at the time, as just something I-I sensed—it, it was something I would have liked, you know—I could get into something—just sort of not to do it uh when then—later when I was actually working on the piece I was very clear and I could say you know what that was—and I had gone through that process—that I knew that I wanted to say—I-I felt, I never talked like this—that there were very definite times in his life and I and I don't like to say so much what they were but they were like general times in his life I felt that somehow they conveyed that one layer—was like a time in Freud's life, and I didn't care

what people saw—I realized—but I felt that that information also was was large enough that it could tell a very raw thing—outside of just Freud's life—it was—Also then, I felt that was another thread and I even told it like it weren't Freud and the different times in the play and then they're together at the end of the table and the whole—one little scene—setting up that picture there was very specifically then that moment that I wanted to, like, underline about Freud—this is a very important point and about Freud and so, that —that scene is like most literal—it's like the only real—to me it was in the whole piece—that thread—

This was spoken in 1970, a year after Wilson's production of *The Life and Times of Sigmund Freud* and seven years before he sent Einstein to his beach.

The book is called *The Theatre of Visions: Robert Wilson*. It is the first in a series of nine books planned about "the original theatre of the City of New York from the mid-60s to the mid-70s," as an umbrella title, referring in detail to Foreman, Schechner, Chaikin, Gregory, to the 1970s hermetic theater, to theater as collective improvisation, to black theater, to Merce Cunningham, Yvonne Rainer, Meredith Monk, Douglas Dunn; with notes on Grotowski, André Serban and Ping Chong. It would be a mammoth task.

Stefan Brecht's book on Wilson was not published in the States or in England. Strangely enough, the publisher is the Suhrkamp Verlag in Frankfurt am Main, one of the important publishers in Germany, who also brought out Bertolt Brecht's collected works. Since the author's name is Stefan Brecht, and happens to be the son of Bertolt Brecht and Helene Weigel, things do not seem to be too strange, after all. As a tidbit from this vociferously inarticulate histrionic gesture blown up to gigantic proportions (quite à la Wilson) I selected at random:

Wilson's theatre is set up not only to induce the spectator's experience of the individuality of the performers, to sustain it in each case, and to give the spectators a generalized disposition toward it, but to prevent backsliding, the normalisation of the experience: not by prolonging that experience indefinitely, but by leading the spectator smoothly from one experience of an individuality to another, by a systematic repression of references to normal reality,—whether that of the theatre-situation, or one represented by a play or its characters—and by promoting a shift in the spectators' attention from the individuals as individuals to the images of their appearances and actions (as individuals), viz. to images structured by the motions of figures acted out by the performers.

The author thinks that "Wilson's pieces up to *Letter* were initiations." A few pages later he tries to explain in depth:

Whereas in the pre-*Letter* spectacles, movement lacked the forms (such as expressiveness and indication of purpose) conveying personality and ego, speech in *Letter*, if only formally, just like regular theatre exhibited these forms—denotation, assertion and denial, expression, purpose, address and response; so that whereas in those spectacles movement, individualized but without the psychic denotations of mind and will, integrated the moving performers into insubstantial images, speech in *Letter*, retaining the attributive character of being the speech of *someone*, of a substantial ("real") person or ego either 1) could not achieve any integration, namely if the absence of effectively and consistently attributable specific meanings prevented the construction of stage-characters,—or else 2) did achieve one, but not into insubstantial image, namely if a spectator construed a character from the specific meanings conveyed.

This ecstatic non sequitur and convoluted Ping Pong game with words, this celebration of appearances and pretenses reminded me of the night I saw *A Letter for Queen Victoria*. Quod erat demonstrandum!

Zürich. The editors of *Dance Scope* asked me to write something on education for them which I speedily did, as if our lives depended on it—as, in reality, our lives do.

It is not difficult for a studious person to become well-educated. But what matters is the application of knowledge and the way we keep its storehouse in working order. With the help of education, goals can be reached which, however, will no longer be recognizable as such the very moment they are seemingly arrived at. They appear and disappear like Fata Morganas to the hopeful eye of the wanderer (and wonderer) in search of a spiritual haven.

The often quoted slogan of knowledge making us free is only ambiguously true.

As a longer aside: Marx recognized the need of the worker to acquire knowledge in order to get the better of the bourgeois holding him in economic and spiritual bondage. And ever since the latter part of the last century the socialistic movements have carried the banner with the words: Knowledge is power! well into our own time. This undoubtedly significant dictum goes back to Francis Bacon who, in 1597, published his *Essayes* first in Latin. A year later they were issued in English by the same publisher. The eleventh section of this work was called *De Haeresibus* and contained the phrase: *Nam et ipsa scientia potestas est*, meaning that "science itself is power" which in the anglicized version *Of Heresies* was translated as "knowledge itself is power." This only goes to prove how subtle a translator's work is and how much of all knowledge has always been tied to the wonders of semantics and the retouching hand of a mindful translator falling into idiomatic traps.

From the very beginning of all time the notion of knowledge has vexed man. Already the writers of the Bible had trouble with putting knowledge in its right place and defining it knowledgeably. "A wise man is strong; yea, a man of knowledge increaseth strength," according to the Proverbs (24:5) which, however, are contradicted by Ecclesiastes (1:18): "He that increaseth knowledge increaseth sorrow." Indeed, the Socratic irony of *scio nihil scire* indicates that to know is as limitless as it is tenuous. "Only when we know little do we know anything; doubt grows with knowledge," Goethe elucidated. At the very end, if the man of erudition does not become enlightened enough to wed knowledge to wisdom, he may succeed superficially and even be "doctorated" *honoris causa* several times without being able to "utter wisdom from the central deep,/And, listening to the inner flow of things,/Speak to the age out of Eternity," as James Russell Lowell poetized. He was seconded in a more succinct way by Alfred Tennyson, who wrote in *Locksley Hall:* "Knowledge comes, but wisdom lingers."

It is much easier to inflate the appearance of your cleverness than to hide the emptiness of your mind which only proves how far some knowledge can go.

The greatest joy in life is to begin because it is an innocent joy. The further we advance in whatever it may be, the harder it becomes to be happy with what we know and do. Only when we have really learned to master something—or rather believe we have—can we again begin enjoying it. Then the only danger is that all challenge is gone and that we are trapped by boredom and the routine of the familiar. Gertrude Stein once rightly said: why do something when we know we can do it?

Education as a means of acquiring knowledge is a badly beaten cliché. To most people it means the accumulation of information about certain subjects, in classrooms, under the supervision of instructors, a procedure finally leading to the procurement of a paper which at best legalizes the fact that this procedure had taken place.

Acquired knowledge is no guarantee against mediocrity. It should only be a crutch in helping us to promote our own thoughts. Of course, in acquiring knowledge we cannot avoid living on borrowed ideas from time to time, but we must learn to force our own rhythm upon any borrowed wing of wisdom. Lessing believed that he may have read too much for his own good. But it seems better to rely on a solid frame of reference before taking off on a flight of one's own imagination, especially if we are not quite certain of the strength and elasticity of our wings.

It is said that we can learn from books or from experiences. Experiences are adventures in living of which one may read in books. Experiencing books remains a second-hand adventure.

The competitiveness of our social system is the most cruel

taskmaster. The school is as unfair as life. Our speed-mad time gives us little chance to catch up with ourselves in order to find our real self. I cannot reiterate enough: Since our school systems omit the teaching of two of the most vital subjects, namely, "A Philosophy of Living" and "The Appreciation of the Real Life Values," we are left without spiritual guidance and a non-material goal when thrown into the jungle of existence. Of what avail is the knowledge of higher mathematics if we do not master the simple algebra of living, if we fumble because we lack a viewpoint, if we stumble because we have no vision?

As strange as it may sound, the process of becoming human is a question of spiritual exercise, it is something that can be learned. But no elevator leads up to the highest stop, to the point of being human. Everyone must use his own staircase. Going up in the elevator we would deprive ourselves of the possible experience waiting for us at each turn of the staircase; we might never be surprised by those little joys which can engender tremendous strength, or we may never learn how to overcome Angst at any next turn. While walking up we may find it important to stop from time to time in order to look inward a little. We must also turn around to wonder. It will enable us to read between the lines (an ability no school teaches us) and to see the things between the things (where appearances will fall apart to show the truth behind the many truths). While walking up we must try to carry our dreams to the edge of reality in order to test them and to bring them as close to fulfillment as possible.

You are a born teacher as someone is a born artist, or you are no teacher at all. The great teacher can even teach what he does not master (philosophy, for instance, trying to investigate and circumscribe our involvement in being, can only be probed and never mastered). The ideal teacher can convey his ideas as a choreographer—whose dancing years are over—imparts the images of his mind to the dancers. The true teacher gives by sharing, he shares by inspiring, but he also doubts while being certain, wondering at his wisdom, awed by what he does not know, amazed at being himself. If teaching is only a job, it becomes a spiritual crime that pays, often rewarded by tenure.

Good teaching does not force the students to store knowledge for the purpose of making them think alike, but asks them to use what they perceive to challenge their own thoughts and those of others. Mental corruption begins with our mind and vision adjusting to established norms and rules without questioning them. As a matter of fact, a great teacher creates the need and desire in his pupils to turn against him.

One of the great difficulties in life is to make someone love something he does not yet know. This is the most important task a teacher faces. He may find out that he can more easily reach the student's mind by entering through his heart, mind and emotions being inseparable. How can I set someone's mind afire without striking a spark of his feelings?

The fact that no one can learn from the mistakes of others may tempt us to make more mistakes of our own than necessary.

The educated mind is held together by its compartmentalized division into Daliesque drawers labelled somewhat like: To be opened daily—To be forgotten quickly—To be looked into one day—Useless to worry about—Garbage container for burdensome thoughts—Special compart- ment for repressions—Urgent matters to be handled with care— Reserved for abandonment—Good for the ego—Useless for any purpose—etc.

Great men's errors are more significant and helpful than all the accomplishments and truths of little men.

"To be true to oneself" is one of the best polished clichés. It only becomes meaningful if you have learned to grow and change while letting no one notice that you have remained true to yourself.

I can endure failure more easily than success. Failure introduces me to myself. Either I feel miserable for having been trapped by myself or furious for being misunderstood. Success makes me dizzy with joy and despair: joy about having had mere luck, despair for perhaps not being able to trick fate again.

One of my students, when she decided to become a dancer, wrote me that I changed her life. Of course, I did nothing of the sort. She had always wanted to be a dancer, but only became aware of it when she took my classes. I never felt like an opinion-maker, at best like a mind-maker. A true teacher's work is comparable to that of a plastic surgeon who has done wonders in beautifying his patient's face without, however, having changed the expression of her personality.

When Ruth St. Denis was well into her eightieth year she made plans for the next twenty years. She taught me how to keep time attuned to my needs and how to intimidate death by ignoring him. Mary Wigman taught me human and artistic integrity. José Limón taught me the dignity with which to express myself. George Balanchine taught me to doubt each word with which I thought I could express myself.

It is often said that the dancer is not intellectually inclined since his mind is absorbed by how his body moves. I have rather found the contrary to be true, particularly among the modern dancers. The great dancer is very much aware of the fact that his body can move best when his vision reaches beyond his mirror image and when his mind is as mobile as his muscles are.

Compulsive fanaticism may be basic to the accomplishments of a great artist who, however, may accomplish the great with seeming ease, never being aware of being compulsive or fanatic. He simply cannot help working on himself and the thing he envisions day and night.

We do not know, we can only surmise what goes into the making of an artist, what compels us to be creative. What intuitive power lies behind each creative spark, from where does the inspiration come to ignite it? After the completion of a work of art one cannot help wondering how it happened and that it had happened at all. Most artists take the source of inspiration for granted. And rightly so, because the inexplicable lies in the Gestalt of the created work.

Life is like a violin solo which we play in public while practicing on our instrument. Therefore, we cannot live long enough to learn from our mistakes. This should make the preciousness of time more clear to us. And how we treat it! If we had to account for what we do to time, for how we rob and rape her day in day out, we would have to be sentenced to life imprisonment for it. And many of us have to atone for it all our lives without being aware of it. Like Bernard Berenson I also would often like to stand at a street corner with my hat in my hand and beg all passers-by only for one of their many wasted minutes. Certainly, time is the while, the space and season in and with which we grow.

Education is an important part of this allround and lifelong process and, since we are the shapers of our own mental face, it is we who decide on the scope of knowledge to be absorbed and on the manner in which we relate knowing to living, in which we turn information into enlightened knowledge. If the truism of less being more has some meaning, then it must also apply to the acquisition of knowledge. It is probably of little avail if we cram facts, names, and data down our ganglia without being able to envision the world which gave them life and made them live. By the same token, shortcuts to be somewhere fast for no purpose are just as meaningless. Our speed-mad age is tempting us at all corners to deprive ourselves of the pleasure of sowing before we harvest.

"Perhaps there is only one cardinal sin: impatience," Franz Kafka said. "Because of impatience we were driven out of Paradise; because of impatience we cannot return." In our time fruit is being hastened to ripen, animals are being fed drugs to get fatter faster for a devouring consumer society. For some time now there has been a slogan for college teachers: Publish or perish! Of course, it is easier to publish at the risk of having little to say than to perish. Impatience with what we have achieved has made us record-mad. Things ripen toward us, if we have only learned the fundamental poetry of living and the intuitive wisdom to wait for the moment waiting for us.

1983

The year began with a bang that had a sound of deep sadness about it.

Some people say that an era has come to an end with George Balanchine's death. However that may be, there is a timelessness about what he stood for, what he did, what he left for us to wonder at and to think about. He had already helped, quite some time ago, to charter a new way of balletic dancing that was as much of the past as it was of tomorrow. He knew only too well that to be a man of today, one had to have been a man of yesterday's future.

With the years I have come to understand Balanchine better and better. I felt like coming closer to his way of being, which was so different, diffident and self-assured at the same time, to his way of hiding his genius by pretending that he did not create but assemble movement, that, at best, he was an inventor of movement as much as Stravinsky spoke of himself as an "inventor of music." I have never doubted that Balanchine could afford this modest geste, since deep within he was so sure of his artistic worth and creative power. With the years—and particularly in the last years of his life—I felt very much at home with him. On his part it may have been sympathy with my writings, with my love for the poetry in movement, or for feminine beauty—and perhaps also the realization that I valiantly supported Pat Neary in her struggle to make the Europeans—and particularly those at the Opernhaus Zürich—see Balanchine's unique place in balletic history. He may have liked to talk, but it was difficult for him to open up. In rare moments a deeper insight into his mind revealed a clever vision of the things that mattered to him. Sometimes there was a touch of sadness about him which only his eyes betrayed.

Painting by Edwin Denby. Provincetown, ca. 1948. Oil on paper, 8½ × 11″. Courtesy Rudolph Burckhardt.

Whenever thinking of Balanchine's work, the gentle face and mind of Edwin Denby, the critic who may have understood him best, is close by. To hear Denby speak about Balanchine was always a revelation in itself.

I liked Denby a great deal and, when I heard he felt he had to steal away from us and take all his knowledge and enthusiasm with him, I thought that one of the great fixtures in the American dance world was gone. Gone forever.

He was a legend in his lifetime which, I am sure, will live on. He wrote little, but what he said was very much to the point, succinct, clear. I was always under the impression that his was a kindred soul, with his love for the dance, with his poetry and painting. Edwin was such a warm person, lovable in his boyish shyness. There was a touching aura of lyricism around him. Something noble. So was his choice to seek death before his dying nature could make a mockery of his humane humanness.

There was something magnanimous about both Balanchine and Denby. They were so far removed from the pettiness of the many, from the odd quirks of daily being.

Denby's paintings have made me think of that strange, mad, and wonderful feeling that may drive you to easel and brush. Since I myself have started to paint I have been exalted and puzzled by the phenomenon of the creative urge in man to prove himself in more than one way. Such versatile geniuses of Renaissance calibre as Leonardo or Michelangelo no longer exist, but the numbers of writers and dancers who also paint is surprising. Of the musicians, Stravinsky made a few poignant drawings and Arnold Schönberg was quite emphatic about his painting talents. D. H. Lawrence was a passionate painter, Hermann Hesse a minor master of the watercolor, and Henry Miller coined the phrase of "to paint is to love again." Victor Hugo, August Strindberg and Jean Cocteau— to mention only a few—were great masters of the brush and pen.

No one can have enough talent, but, on a certain level, we can easily have too many talents. There are born dilettantes as there are born geniuses. A minor dancer or poet does not become less minor for being also a mediocre painter. Sometimes to lack perfection of craftsmanship may add a certain charm or fascination to the totality of a genius, as the case of Goethe proves. Also, a particular environment, or the ambiance of such periods as the Renaissance and our own, may be conducive to multiple creativity.

Particularly in an age of specialization as ours, certain artists express a strong desire to toy with "other" thoughts, to escape into

A drawing of Picasso by Igor Stravinsky. Author's collection.

an alien landscape, to express themselves differently here and there, now and then. The reasons for not utilizing dormant talents may often be the fear of competing with others in the wide arena of the arts, or after a few initial attempts, the disillusionment with their own abilities, briefly, not quite living up to their own expectations when, in fact, they should only think of their own enjoyment, of relief and the recharge of their inner vision and strength. After all, we should take what we do very seriously—but never our own self. And any unconscious flight or conscious excursion into a different landscape should be little else than one more marvel to be marvelled about.

That dancers are close to music is a truism and that, in its heightened suggestiveness, dance is closest to poetry is also well enough known, even though the dancer, while moving, is hardly aware of it. He may vaguely realize that his movements have something to do with geometrical or architectural designs, or that in his statuesque moments he is close to sculpture. But, essentially, the dancer paints visual images which, in the flow of movement, dissolve while being. He creates a linear as well as a three-dimensional image on stage. At the cradle of ballet, Balthasar de Beaujoyeulx thought of ballet as a geometric configuration. Jean Georges Noverre was very conscious of what the choreographers then called *tableaux* and, before leaving France for Stuttgart, he was determined—if we may believe his diary notes—to visit many museums in order to acquaint himself better with the painters' envisioned imageries and visually arranged details.

The words "action painting" could be best applied to the dancer-choreographer's movement realizations onstage. From Beaujoyeulx to Alwin Nikolais, the dancer-choreographer has used many forms and disguises, but he has always created a three-dimensional visualization with the help of human bodies. He may use all kinds of theatrical accoutrements, such as costumes, lighting, and scenic décors to enhance his painted image. But, basically, it will always be the dancing body and all the bodies of an ensemble which create a pictorial composition from moment to moment, from movement to movement.

It is an interesting phenomenon that the artist doesn't see things as they are, but as he is. To be able to be oneself to the largest degree, regardless of how one may be judged or in which field of activity one is generally recognized, the artist can fully realize his potentialities and move in whatever creative direction he feels driven. The greater the access to his own self and its depths and the freer he is from the repressive mechanism controlling impulse and imagery, the greater will be the possibility that he will express himself through paintings, drawings, and sculpture. If he does so, it only proves that he is in complete possession of his own personal experiences and memories and particularly of those concerning body and rhythm, shapes and colors, and that, in trying to escape a systematized existence, he finds a new dimension for his creative spirit to express these memories and experiences.

The creative mind has all the freedom it can think of, but working habits and a variety of anxieties impose limitations upon it. On the other hand, to enjoy fully another artistic medium, the artist ought to edit his own nature. That so many artists, in their secondary choice of creation, enjoy the smallest sparks, even if they do not always glow in shining flames, is their privilege; and it is our pleasure to come closer to their very private way of being. Though such works of art may be far from perfect, they are a sign of their genius.

Surprisingly, dancers are more articulate than their repute as "into-the-mirror-looking-narcissists" would make us believe, particularly the modern dancers who liberated themselves from the stigma of the nineteenth-century-ballet and its ballerina, captive of her own image. The three pioneers at the beginning of the expressionistic dance translated their very personal poetry of life into the reality of their art and were most eloquent spokeswomen for their ideas. Isadora Duncan had the lilt of Walt Whitman's verses when she wrote:

"I see America dancing, and her dance will be clean! I see America dancing, free, generous, compassionate, tender, brave, standing with one foot poised on the highest point of the Rockies, her two hands stretched out from the Atlantic to the Pacific, her fine head tossed to the sky, her forehead shining with a crown of a million stars."

Ruth St. Denis was obsessed with words, and the easy flow of her pen produced many pages of intoxicating prose and some fine poems which voiced the lyricism of her feelings:

> In terrible aloneness
> I have passed
> From dancer to the prophetess.
> The language of my prophecies
> Is still the dance,
> As in my former days,
> But now the words
> Are differently arranged . . .
> Not by earthly music
> Is my body moved and trembled,
> But by the Ever Presence.

For Mary Wigman, too, language was a way of giving expression to her inmost feelings. No other dancer found such telling and touching explanatory words for inspiration, motif, and the process of creating a dance work as she did in *The Language of Dance*. Some of her letters reveal many lucky phrasings of deep insight into the ultimate things of life, and in her poems nature has always played a dominant role:

> Blooming bells and gold beset,
> primus, crocus, violet
> have been out for quite a while.
> Spring has lured them with its smile!
> Pussy willows in their furry fling,
> saxifrages curled with frills,
> gentian blooming blue on stony hills—
> by God,
>   this must be spring.

Anna Pavlova in her dance, The Butterfly, *contrasted with one of her statuettes in which she celebrated herself as a dancer. From the book* Anna Pavlova *by V. Dandré.*

It is fascinating to observe that—in contrast to these three pioneers of a new dance movement—Anna Pavlova's escape into a secondary creative expression turned out some playful little sculptures, narcissistic images, no doubt, as this great ballerina saw herself moving. The perfectionist in her often made her seek advice of how to improve her sculptural skill, but time and again she was told that her statuettes would lose their instinctive sensitiveness if she attained perfection. Victor Dandré—who was probably closest to her—was of the opinion that these little works conveyed the very idea of Pavlova through the lightness of the figures and the grace of their movements.

Many dancer-choreographers of our time have written or

painted in one way or another: Ted Shawn, Serge Lifar, Doris Humphrey, Martha Graham, Helen Tamiris, Pearl Primus, Angna Enters, and the West Indian dancer-painter, Geoffrey Holder. This list could be continued ad infinitum.

Perhaps our Freudian age can be blamed for having helped the artists toward a greater self-awareness and need to articulate their feelings in a variety of ways. It may explain the long list of dancer-choreographers who made excursions into the field of writing and painting. Vaslav Nijinsky takes a special place among these dancers. His *Diary* has the prophetic language of William Blake. It was written in hours of agony, by the twilight of his mind which sought to fight the meanness of the commonplace while embracing mysticism wholeheartedly. Nijinsky could have hardly read the German mystic Meister Eckhart: "God only expects one thing from you; that you go beyond yourself and allow God to be God inside you," when he signed his *Diary* God and Nijinsky. And just as totally innocent in their loud outcry of the tortured soul are Nijinsky's drawings and paintings, which Herbert Read described as works of pure surrealism denying the principles of logic and reality, the automatic expression of the poet-dancer's unconsciousness.

Writers on the dance may also find their way to painting. I have often stressed the point that I would like to see born poets write on the dance. I can now add: if they have seen enough dancing, they may want to paint, as Edwin Denby did. Théophile Gautier, the first great dance critic, was originally a painter. Victor Hugo, who also painted, talked him into writing. His reviews on the dance are of greater importance—from an historic viewpoint—than those on the fares in playhouses because he felt more strongly akin to the visual imagery of the dance than to the dramatized scene. His critiques paint his attitudes toward a work of dance or the dancer herself, mainly the latter, with verbal colors ("She flies like a spirit in the midst of transparent clouds of white muslin . . . "). Moreover, he once said: "If I ever had the honor of being director of the Opera, I would have the ballets composed by painters."

Drawing by Vaslav Nijinsky. Author's collection.

The painting Dancing Trees *by Walter Sorell.*

I have learned to see the dance with different eyes since I have started to paint. I can see movement like color designs, I can see the texture of a gesture. I can see all shades and nuances in the context of what exists between the bodies and the flow of their rhythm. I have learned to see more clearly the totality of an image the way it takes on Gestalt before my eyes and dissolves into another image. I have learned more about the beauty of becoming and the secret of being, and I have learned even more about the difficulty of creating being as the secret it is.

1984

Breakdance has great meaning. It lifted gang warfare into an *agon* in which acrobatic skill triumphed over brutality. It is street theater at its best. It is to be hoped that commercialism will not sidetrack it from the sidewalks of New York.

The graffiti, however, are a different story. They started in the New York subways fifteen years ago and descended upon urbanites all over the world with relentless inurbanity. Graffiti became the black plague of our time. In the beginning one wanted to suppress it but failed. No psychological explanations, no laws helped. Some still want to check it but fail. Meanwhile it has been hallowed as great art, and with the help of maniacs and gallery owners this new fad halos their cash registers. Of course, it is no longer writing; it has become graffiti painting. The dance world can pride itself on having been the first to elevate a group of spray-painters to scenic designers. Twyla Tharp thus honored herself and the Joffrey Ballet on the occasion of *Deuce Coupe* in 1972.

Now we know. Crude street-style artistry is the creative expression of our days.

Martha Graham is back at the age of ninety, collecting the highest honors in France and standing ovations during each performance of her three-week season at the State Theater in New York, where her career began in The Little Theatre on 41st Street in 1926. At that time she could not afford a big orchestra, just Louis Horst at the piano. And what an accomplished accompanist he was!

Most of her dance works, and certainly such older works as *Primitive Mysteries* or *Seraphic Dailogue* cried out for a smaller stage and the simplicity of her fighting days. There was a nostalgic feeling about almost everything that was done, and whatever was re-done from former years missed the intensity and bite that once was there. Many of the new dancers of her company convey a feeling of balletic lightness here and there which speaks against the innate power evoked by the Graham technique. Sometimes, as in her new piece, *Phaedra's Dream*, she can lose herself in empty stage effects and dazzling imagery leading nowhere. Thematically, the sexuality in this work becomes blown-up to the point of unpleasantness.

In 1930 Martha was the Chosen One in Stravinsky's *The Rite of Spring* with Massine's choreography at the Old Met. It was one of her first popular successes. She brought a new quality of rawness to it. Her latest choreographic version of *Le Sacre du Printemps* does not have that terrifying feeling of a dramatic ritual. She always had the weakness of getting too much involved in the use of drapery, and this seemed to have made her *Rite of Spring* lose touch with the reality of primitiveness. It is not enough to ensnare the Chosen One in a thick white rope, but to liberate her from it again, a procedure of no purpose nor dramatic meaning. Only some of the dancing between the Shaman and the Chosen One caught the feeling of her former greatness. But Shaman's impressive cape (beautifully designed by Halston, yet too lavishly for such a death-quivering scene) and the accumulation of colorful drapery drawn into the action enfeebles the terror basic to the story. But knowing Graham and the artist in her, she will, in her stunning way of saying things as only she can see them, come up next time with a lyrically dramatic or dramatically lyrical work of a startling nature.

She was still rehearsing *The Rite of Spring* on January twelfth when dancers, choreographers, and musicians were paying tribute to Louis Horst on what would have been the day of his one-hundredth birthday, twenty years after his death.

I remember the glow on Louis' face when, in the fall of 1963, he showed the editors of the *Dance Observer* a card he had just received from Martha who, for the first time, scored a triumphant success with her company in England (her first tour, in the fifties, was a colossal failure). It was a thank-you-note saying that all this would not have been possible for her without his help. This alluded to the past, not the recent years. It was Louis Horst who, as an accompanist at Denishawn in 1916, began to tutor the then twenty-two-year-old new company member. In an interview which she gave to the *New York Times* a few days before the opening night at the State Theater, Martha Graham stressed the fact of how much he had done for her in the years of her beginning ("He had the most to do with shaping my early life."), of how he spoiled her and taught her about philosophy (Nietzsche, Schiller, Wagner) and, above all, about music ("I learned all about music from Louis and, if I got off the beat, he said to me, 'I'll rip your ears off!' "). She had fun being with him, they traveled together to the Southwest ("His sympathy and understanding, but primarily his faith, gave me a landscape to move in. Without it, I should certainly have been lost."). He called her "my first and best pupil" and truly loved her while they worked together, from her first recital in 1926 until 1948 (when she slipped into a short-lived marriage with Erick Hawkins) and then continued to love her, even though in a Pygmalion-like fashion. In his eyes she was his creation, and in a way she admitted it time and again.

One must question wisdom and taste of this grand lady of the American modern dance and ask what prompted her at the age of ninety to divulge intimate secrets about her love life with Louis Horst. Standing at the gates of the beyond, did she want to clear the record and straighten things out for the benefit of history and the dance archives? Understandably, she wanted to dispel all doubts: "Horst never helped me do a dance." Certainly. He only was her third, objective eye. And then: she did not love him, she was "only fond of him." And on she went: "He became my lover, yes, but it was like loving a child, because I was a child." At the age of twenty-two, and ten years later, when she appeared on Broadway in 1926, and he wrote the music for some of her works? Yes, we must not forget she said that they never shared an apartment, nor the same kind of love for each other. The lady doth protest too much, methinks.

When Louis had died in 1964, it was his last will to have his ashes scattered over New York. Since his friend and executor, Ralph Taylor, could not get a permit for doing it, they decided on doing the next best thing and cavalcaded down to the Hudson to scatter his ashes there. Everyone close to him was present, only

Martha Graham excused herself, explaining that she was suffering from a cold.

Twenty years later at Juilliard his music was played, *El Penitente* was performed, many now famous dancers, choreographers, teachers, and musicians paid tribute to this protean personality who had given them their first lessons as he did for Martha who excused herself and sent a message:

It is a great honor to be part of this dedication to Louis Horst.

I feel so deeply that without him I could not have achieved anything of what I have done. He played my first dancing lesson with Ruth St. Denis that first summer at Denishawn and from that moment on he worked with me and encouraged me in the furthering of my career.

Louis was a strict man, a very intelligent man and a very lovable man with a passionate devotion to the art of the dance, and it gives me great pleasure to send this message through Martha Hill to this assembly to express the honour I feel for him.

Only something that Louis would understand full well, a rehearsal, could prevent me from speaking to you in person. That the rehearsal should be for *The Rite of Spring* has a special meaning now. For I can still remember the studio on 59th Street where Louis played the rehearsals for the first *Rite* that I appeared in. He was with me then and he is in my memory now.

I remember a very warm night in June during the early sixties. I was standing with Louis in front of the theater on Second Avenue and 12th Street. We were early and watched the people coming in. Louis was shaking hands with every second person and being kissed more often than not ("It's a kissing profession," he murmured at one point). When it was time for us to go in, and he still acknowledged greetings with a nod or gesture of his hand, I remarked: "You seem to know almost everyone here." "Yeah," he replied, "we are a big family." Then putting on his impish smile, he added: "A big unhappy family." I wasn't sure whether it was one of his caustic remarks which he loved to wear in the buttonhole of his mind, or whether he really meant it. There was no time to find out. The performance had begun.

We all are afraid of the moment when both hands of the clock indicate that today is already tomorrow. To cover our fear we celebrate this moment as wantonly and noisily as we can when one calendar year happens to give way to the next. In order to justify our fear and jubilation we adhere to the customary foolishness of telescoping meditative thoughts and resolutions into this non-existent split second between now and then.

I have asked myself the question (which everyone should ask himself from time to time): Is not my whole life a list of errata attached to the last page of the book of Creation? Would I want to live my life differently if I could? Yes, of course. Would I like to be a different person? Decidedly not.

Whenever I have taken a look at myself I've tried to penetrate the reflection in the mirror, to see myself in the perspective of all years past and of all the possible hours and days to come. I've been reminded of Holbein's depiction of the fool, the way this fool looks at himself in a mirror with quizzical self-scrutiny. In it is a hearty inner laugh about oneself, the most liberating gesture I can think of. Erasmus came to my mind not only because I know his image from the way in which Holbein saw him, but also because I visualize Erasmus as one of the first witty sages, one who became more and more profound and human the more satirical and humorous he became.

Every decade was a discovery of hidden secrets for me, of new dreams and recurring disappointments. At times I was afraid of myself more than of anyone else; then again I lived in a state of nightmarish anxieties. I still fear those inescapable realities which are a concomitant nuisance of existence. I have come to the obvious conclusion that I understand less and less the more I experience and learn. But in the process of it I have regained the most important virtue of the child: the ability to wonder. Alfred North Whitehead once said that to wonder is the beginning of all philosophy. I think to wonder is the beginning of living life consciously, of accepting what we think we understand, the seriousness of the moment, the flippancy of events, the constant flow of things; also, of squaring the natural limitations of an artist with the infinite range of the art's possibilities.

José Limón: Sketch. Author's collection.

Every day we face midnight and the uncertainty of a tomorrow. In these frightful seconds when I see in the dark the hands united on my clock light up, I flee into private prayers and try to account for some last lost thoughts. The most difficult thing in life seems to be getting along with oneself. We enter the world like actors, already made-up for our role, even though the play is not yet written. We prepare ourselves for the next scenes not knowing whether the costumes will fit us, not knowing the lines we will be called upon to say, not knowing our properties. Like magicians without wands we gesture and motion, we plead with our partners, and like improvisators we search behind our masks for the right extemporized word.

I believe in man because I can come close to him, even if he speaks another tongue, since he can weep my tears and laugh my laugh. I can meet him with open arms in the hope that he will understand my gesture and intention. But I am afraid of mankind, doubt it and despair about it because, as a part of the masses, man loses God's face. The crack of a whip, the cajoling voice of a demagogue, can make him put on the mask of the mob.

And I myself? Will I hang on to life with that desperate glee in my eyes as if I finally wanted to follow up on so many decade-old New Year's resolutions? To unmask all fallacies while enjoying them, to disapprove of my mistakes, but to defend to the death my right to be wrong; and never to admit that anything can harm me, on the contrary, to make good use of any adverse experiences.

With each embrace of the two hands on my clock I am aware of having made another step closer to the infinite finality. Does age surprise us, as Goethe said? Or do we have to burn ourselves alive time and again in order to be reborn, as Cocteau thought? How much did we think and write about life, when, in reality, we meant death? To be old is admirable. To grow old is intolerable. But is the process of aging not an act of growing familiarity with death? It seems as if it all would happen gradually, when, in fact, it occurs in sudden leaps. Suddenly the light is being dimmed, and you grope for any sunray as though it were the last. Suddenly your outlook has changed, and you learn to see with different eyes. Suddenly you face the suddenness like meeting an old friend who you knew would wait for you.

I like to imagine that by then the earth will have become an electronic village in an artificial cosmologic assemblage. With true authority I will then feel charged to speak about God and the world, finally from my new standpoint, I will also be able to do full justice to the dance on earth.

Index